American Electoral Politics:

Strategies for Renewal

American Electoral Politics:

Strategies for Renewal

Alan L. Clem
University of South Dakota

D. Van Nostrand Company
New York Cincinnati Toronto London Melbourne

Cover art: *The Voting Booths* by Ben Shahn. Copyright © 1981
Estate of Ben Shahn. Photo by Malcolm Varon, New York City.

D. Van Nostrand Company Regional Offices:

New York   Cincinnati

D. Van Nostrand Company International Offices:

London   Toronto   Melbourne

Copyright © 1981 by Litton Educational Publishing, Inc.

Library of Congress Catalog Card Number: 80-51880
ISBN: 0-442-24475-4

Published by D. Van Nostrand Company
135 West 50th Street, New York, N.Y. 10020

10 9 8 7 6 5 4 3 2 1

Preface

American Electoral Politics: Strategies for Renewal gives the undergraduate student a concise yet comprehensive view of the American party and election systems, as well as a framework for critical analysis of the existing party system.

The text is designed for courses in Political Parties, Electoral Processes, and Political Behavior. It can also be used as a supplement for courses in Political Sociology, Politics and Communication, Problems in Democracy, and Introduction to American Government. The text emphasizes citizen attitudes and behavior, campaigning, party organization and leadership, nominating systems, party conventions, and the presidential election system, with particular attention given to signs of dysfunction and malperformance.

We live in a complex political system that comes in fifty-odd shapes and sizes and that changes with sometimes bewildering speed as state legislatures, party conventions, Congress, and the courts tinker with the valves, wires, gears, and fittings of our election machinery. This system needs to be kept in good repair in order to beget political leadership for this large and successful democracy. The text proposes reforms that would affect every level of political activity, from the method of electing the president of the United States to the method of choosing members of county executive committees of the political party. The proposals aim to simplify and democratize the political system without destroying valid idiosyncracies and the limited party responsibility that presently exists, and to standardize political organizations and electoral processes while maintaining local initiative. If there are two extreme positions on the scale of political reform—on the one hand, democratic-oriented reform maximizing decisions by the largest number of citizens, and on the other hand, elite-oriented reform maximizing decisions by the smallest number of leaders—then the text opts for a middle-of-the-road reform model.

Chapter 1 discusses the functions of parties and the electoral process in American government, tracing the evolution of the party system and pointing out some of the deficiencies in the present system. The student is reminded that most political systems have worked even less satisfactorily than ours. Chapter 2 concerns the political attitudes and behavior of American citizens.

In Chapter 3, the degree to which parties and partisan activity affect policy-making is investigated. Chapter 4 concerns campaign organization and election regulation and administration, stressing changes made in the 1970s regarding campaign finance. Chapters 5 through 10, each centering on a particular aspect of American electoral politics, (1) identify problems and signs of dysfunction in the present system, (2) describe and analyze patterns and tendencies in American political experience, and (3) propose specific structural changes. The final chapter summarizes the text and reflects on the likelihood and potential effectiveness of political reform in the United States.

Research exercises, included at the end of the text, are designed to encourage students to further explore topics covered in the text.

I owe a large debt to conversations with politicians, record-keepers, journalists, and academicians. For two decades, undergraduate students at the University of South Dakota, especially those in the political parties course, have contributed to my awareness and interest. Among those students whose ideas and enthusiasm have enriched me are Donna Ball, Will Brost, Bruce Gross, Sandra Hirsch, Julie Jenkins, Jon Knutson, Thomas Keilman, Charles Nail, Dwight Neuharth, Nancy Palmer, and Monte Walz. Judith R. Joseph, senior publisher at D. Van Nostrand, demonstrated interest in this book from very early stages, and her support has been invaluable. For their perceptive and useful suggestions for improving the book's organization and style, I thank Raymond H. Gusteson, Ohio University; Paul A. Smith, State University of New York at Binghamton; James Piereson, University of Pennsylvania; Benjamin T. Hourani, Eastern Michigan University; Roy E. Thoman, West Texas State University; Larry Schwab, John Carroll University; Morris J. Levitt, Howard University; Dale Vinyard, Wayne State University, and Stephen P. Brown, State University of New York at Stony Brook. Maggie Schwarz, associate editor at D. Van Nostrand, has been a most conscientious and helpful editor of the manuscript. Donna Ball solved a number of analytical problems, conducted bibliographical searches, served as a sounding board with respect to some worrisome details, and typed part of the manuscript.

This book is dedicated to my children, Andy, Chris, Connie, John, and Dan, whose generation inherits a proud and enduring, though still imperfect political system.

I am, of course, responsible for the facts and interpretations that make up the book. I hope that readers who disagree with some of the specific proposals will understand that these proposals have been included primarily for the purpose of provoking thought about how our political system might be improved.

Alan L. Clem
Vermillion, South Dakota

Contents

American Electoral Politics:

Strategies for Renewal

Chapter 1

Democracy, Elections, and Political Parties

What confounds American politics is not a deficiency in our constitutional system. Nor is it a lack of intelligence, common sense, good will, or patriotism on the part of our citizens. Rather, what is wrong is the fact that too many of the rules of our political games are unnecessarily confusing, undemocratic, and inconsistent—in a word, dysfunctional. To state the point simply (and with apologies to the telephone company), the system is the problem.

Several signs of political dysfunction have been noted by politicians, journalists, and scholars, namely: (1) the low level of citizen interest in political party affairs, (2) the powerlessness and insignificance of party leaders, (3) the ambivalent policies of Democratic and Republican leaders, (4) the difficulty of fixing a particular party with responsibility for policy, (5) the undue complexity of party rules and decision-making procedures, especially with reference to presidential choice, and (6) the inequitable or unsystematic apportionment of seats in various party councils.

Of course, these vagaries and anomalies in our party system are strongly affected by the philosophical and constitutional environments. First, there are the twin pillars of our system, federalism and separation of powers, which encourage diverse viewpoints and dispersion of authority. Second, there is the widespread respect for civil liberty, which encourages dissent and disputation. Third, there remains, as a residue of the Founding Fathers' reluctance to trust the masses with too much direct authority, the Electoral College through which Americans elect their chief executive. Fourth, and partly as a consequence of the three earlier points, our electoral machinery is very complex. We are told by the Federal Election Commission's *Journal of Election Administration* that "election systems are amazingly complex pieces of public machinery. No two states are alike; and local practices often vary even within a state. It is not surprising, therefore, that every conceivable election problem crops up somewhere."[1] Robert Sherrill stresses the confusion in our system of nominating presidential candidates:

> The proliferation of democracy both in the caucus states and in the primary states has been accompanied by a high degree of confusion. Not only

1. Federal Election Commission, *Journal of Election Administration,* Fourth Quarter, 1977.

does each of the fifty states have its own rules for putting candidates on the ballot and selecting delegates to the national convention, but the two parties have different rules nationally, and different rules in each state as well. In some states, for example, Republicans operate by the winner-take-all principle; the Democrats have outlawed that method, and they now divvy up the delegates in proportion to each candidate's share of the votes. Most of the primaries—both Republican and Democratic—result in the election of delegates committed to voting for a particular candidate at the national convention. Some delegates who run in the primaries, however, are not bound by the results; the primaries are known as beauty contests; their results are only advisory because the delegates are not bound by the voter's preference.[2]

And not to be overlooked as possible causes for weakness in our political party system are four widespread beliefs: (1) that the power and size of government should be limited, (2) that large bureaucracies are slow, inefficient, and seldom if ever act in response to popular demands, (3) that the practical (and probable) is to be preferred to the theoretical (and only possible) in affairs of state, and (4) that there are many things in life more meaningful than political activity, and thus in our democratic society a citizen can enjoy the luxury of choosing not to participate.

CRITICAL VIEWS OF THE SYSTEM

A sampling of informed commentary on the American political system will provide a helpful backdrop for the concerns to be addressed in this book.

The exordium of modern political reform commentary was *Toward a More Responsible Two-Party System,* a report issued in 1950 by a committee of political scientists headed by E. E. Schattschneider. Considerable "think tank" scholarship has been produced in the last decade. From the Brookings Institution have come *Voting for President: The Electoral College and the American Political System* (Wallace S. Sayre and Judith H. Parris, 1970), *Financing Presidential Campaigns* (Delmer Dunn, 1972), *The Convention Problem: Issues in Reform of Presidential Nominating Procedures* (Judith H. Parris, 1972), *Dynamics of the Party System* (James L. Sundquist, 1973), *Convention Decisions and Voting Records* (second edition, Richard C. Bain and Judith H. Parris, 1973), *Perspectives on Presidential Selection* (Donald R. Matthews, ed., 1973), *Third Parties in Presidential Elections* (Daniel A.

---

2. Robert Sherrill, *Governing America: An Introduction* (New York: Harcourt Brace Jovanovich, 1978), p. 232.

Mazmanian, 1974), and *The Party's Choice* (William R. Keech and Donald R. Matthews, 1977). From the Twentieth Century Fund's Task Force on Electoral College Reform has come a plan for improving presidential selection machinery. From the American Assembly have come reports on *Choosing the President* (1973) and *Presidential Nominations and the Media* (1978). From the American Enterprise Institute have come Martin Diamond's *Testimony in Support of the Electoral College* (1977), Jeane Jordan Kirkpatrick's *Dismantling the Parties: Reflections on Party Reform and Party Decomposition* (1978), and Austin Ranney's *The Federalization of Presidential Primaries* (1978) and his *Participation in American Presidential Nominations, 1976* (1977).

Views of the condition of American political parties have been persistently negative. Arthur Schlesinger, Jr. penned a powerful statement: "Something has gone badly wrong with the American party system. All gauges register trouble." He pointed to declining voter turnout, growth of ticket-splitting, increasing numbers of independents, and the displacement of party effort by television and personalist movements as "characteristics of a party system in an advanced state of decay."[3]

A postelection essay in *Time* magazine in 1978 said that "the parties have virtually collapsed as a force in American politics."[4]

Parties, according to Everett Carll Ladd, do manage "to stand in the way of electoral chaos," but today "they are a diminished presence." He envisions in America's future "an increasingly partyless politics that fragments and disorients, and which thereby mocks our effort at mature self-government."[5] The title of David Broder's book, *The Party's Over,*[6] expresses the dwindling significance of the party. Another comment, taken from a comparison of American and European party systems, echoes these concerns about the meaninglessness of our parties today:

> By European standards, the American parties are hardly entitled to the name. The American parties lack the dicipline in both legislative and electoral matters that Europeans expect.[7]

3. Arthur Schlesinger, Jr., "The Crisis of the Party System: What Has Gone Wrong?," *Current*, July/August 1979, p. 39.
4. Lance Morrow, "The Decline of the Parties," *Time*, November 20, 1978, p. 42.
5. Everett Carll Ladd, Jr., *Where Have All the Voters Gone?*, (New York: W. W. Norton, 1978), p. 77.
6. David Broder, *The Party's Over*, (New York: Harper and Row, 1971).
7. Clifford P. Hackett, "Learning from the U. S. Congress: Are There Any Lessons for the New European Parliament?", *European Community*, November–December, 1978, p. 31.

We are told by William Keefe in the first sentence of the preface to his textbook that the American party system "is in trouble" and occupies "an unhappy position."[8]

The Need for Change

Kevin Phillip's *The Emerging Republican Majority*, Richard Scammon and Ben Wattenberg's *The Real Majority*, Walter DeVries and Lance Tarrance's *The Ticket-Splitter*, and William Rusher's *The Making of the New Majority Party* have agreed, at least, that American parties and American voters are changing. Recently the theme of political literature has shifted from the idea of change to the idea of crisis, as evidenced by Broder's *The Party's Over*, Ladd's *Where Have All The Voters Gone*, and Ruth Scott and Ronald Hrebenar's *Parties in Crisis*. In 1975, Austin Ranney, a professor-practitioner who played a central role in Democratic party reform leading up to the 1972 national convention, published a series of essays under the title *Curing the Mischiefs of Faction: Party Reform in America*. Substantial portions of the popular college-level textbooks (those by Bone, Fenton, Gelb and Palley, Greenstein, Keefe, Saloma and Sontag, and Sorauf) concern themselves with party and electoral reforms that the authors feel are necessary if the system is to function properly.

To categorize and explain these reform proposals is beyond the scope of this introductory chapter, but mention of a few of them will convey an idea of the kinds of structural changes that have been recommended. John Fenton identified ways in which a party could exert more control over its members in Congress.[9] Burns advocated three reforms: (1) public financing of campaigns through parties rather than having the money go directly to individual candidates, (2) midterm conventions at which issues could be discussed and the party's platform renewed, and (3) reversing the trend toward more presidential primaries, which were thought to be "expensive, exhausting, confusing, and unresponsive."[10] Schlesinger dismissed most of the suggested structural reforms, seeing great dangers in giving party professionals a fixed proportion of seats in national conventions, in giving campaign funds to party organizations rather than to candidates, and in guarding party organizations from the depredations of the media and citizen activists.[11] He called instead for parties that

---

8. William J. Keefe, *Parties, Politics, and Public Policy in America,* third edition, (New York: Holt, Rinehart and Winston, 1980), p. iii.
9. John Fenton, *People and Parties in Politics,* (Glenview, Ill.: Scott, Foresman, 1966), p. 17.
10. *PS,* Fall 1976, pp. 494–495.
11. Schlesinger, *op. cit.,* p. 43.

could develop ideas to meet contemporary problems, notably inflation and energy, and that could elect competent presidents "who will thereafter act to revitalize their parties in the presidential interest."[12]

With so many faults and shortcomings perceived in the political system, and so many solutions offered from so many quarters that seldom have much influence over policy-makers, it is perhaps not surprising that so little constructive change has been made or even attempted. Comments in *Congressional Quarterly* relating to proposals to change the national convention delegate selection process illustrate some of the immense difficulties encountered:

> Attempts to establish a federal solution to the hodge-podge of delegate selection events have gone nowhere. Over 250 bills have been introduced in Congress since 1911 to federalize the presidential nominating system. The most popular approach in recent years has been to establish a national primary or a series of regional primaries. But none of the proposals has come close to passage and only three bills have even reached the floor—the last in 1952.[13]

Political reform tends to be widely perceived as an acute problem for perhaps 2 months, and as a trivial item on the agenda of democracy for the remaining 46 months of the presidential quadrennium. *Congressional Quarterly* quoted US Representative Douglas Applegate, Democrat of Ohio, a promoter of a national primary: "Unfortunately there is not enough time to change the method before the election and too much time after it."[14]

The cyclic pattern of change and adjustment that characterized the maturation of our political system has understandably bothered those who have sought to perfect the mechanisms of American democracy. Jeane Jordan Kirkpatrick put it this way: "It is a basic article of faith in the American creed that for every ill there is a remedy; by now experience with party reform should have taught that, at least where political institutions are concerned, for every remedy there is probably an ill."[15] She was particularly dubious about past reform efforts: "Of all of these reasons for the continuing decline in the parties' ability to perform their traditional functions, I have stressed reform. Whether undertaken by the parties, the Congress, or the courts, reform, along

12. *Ibid.*, p. 45.
13. "Presidential Primaries Reach Record Level," *Congressional Quarterly Weekly Report,* August 4, 1979, p. 1610.
14. *Ibid.*
15. Jeane Jordan Kirkpatrick, *Dismantling the Parties: Reflections on Party Reform and Party Decomposition,* (Washington: American Enterprise Institute for Public Policy Research, 1978), p. 31.

with its intended and unintended consequences, is, I believe, the most important cause of this decline."[16]

The unintended consequences of political reforms have confounded many activists. Austin Ranney used Ralph Waldo Emerson's aphorism about the sower and his seeds to illustrate the hazards of trusting human reason in tinkering with the political system: "The sower may mistake and sow his peas crookedly; the peas make no mistake but come up and show his line."[17] Or, as Bert Lance is reported to have said, "If it ain't broke, don't fix it."

ELECTIONS AND REPRESENTATIVE GOVERNMENT

Adherence to the principles of the Declaration of Independence and the Constitution of the United States requires that we govern ourselves democratically. For democracy to exist, there must be elections that are open to the masses, free of any kind of authoritarian control, frequent, reasonably competitive, and significant in terms of indicating what officials will do if elected to office. Such elections require permanent party organizations to provide the framework for electoral competition—organizations to encourage and nominate candidates, to focus popular feelings on current political controversies, and to provide a nucleus to carry out the campaign effort. The parties require an ideological, philosophical, or self-interested foundation to help establish popular identification and to be an object of loyalty for its members. From these considerations, a simple catechism for democracy emerges:

No government without democracy.
No democracy without elections.
No elections without parties.
No parties without enduring bases for rational differences of opinion among groups of citizens.

To grasp the realities and the limitations of democratic government in the United States in the last quarter of the twentieth century requires an understanding of the functions that political parties perform and of the election system within which the party machinery operates.

The essential political functions of concern to this study are decision-making by elected officials about current policy controversies and by voters about rival candidates for public office. In the first case, we can observe

---

16. *Ibid.,* p. 20.
17. Austin Ranney, *Curing the Mischiefs of Faction: Party Reform in America,* (Berkeley: University of California Press, 1975), p. 210.

legislators, executives, and judges making decisions everyday, decisions that vary in breadth of applicability, public interest, and their tendency to set elements of society against one another. In the second, our observations are necessarily less frequent; we can see, on an early November Tuesday in even-numbered years, millions of citizens entering voting booths across the land to cast votes that will help decide who will be their president, governor, senator, congressman, or state legislator. Many feel that these processes are sufficient to establish the presence of democratic government. Others, however, feel that the voting process is insufficiently frequent or critical to permit the conclusion that the people do indeed rule. And of these doubting Thomases, a good many are thankful that the people do not rule.

It would be difficult to prove that the hand of the majority guides the everyday decisions of government. To detect the preferences of the public in decisions respecting US relations with Israel and Egypt, disarmament negotiations with the Soviet Union, the development of Missouri river power resources, or the firing of a local high school superintendent would demand vast imagination or complex equations based upon large amounts of obscure data. This kind of uncertainty regarding the connection between people and policy is the breeding ground for disputation and argument. The great argument as to whether meaningful democracy exists in America resolves itself, inevitably, into the question of whether the act of voting is critical to the decisions government officials make.

A thought-provoking critique of representative democracy, related to concerns about the connections between citizen and government, has been developed by Sullivan and O'Connor.[18] They identified four conditions that they believed necessary to demonstrate strong linkage between those who govern and those who are governed:

1. that voters perceive the issue positions or preferences of rival candidates for office;
2. that voters cast their ballots for or against candidates on the basis of these perceived and publicized issue positions;
3. that rival candidates differ in their positions in major public issues, and that they publicize these differences; and
4. that winning candidates, when they assume office, vote in their legislative chambers in accordance with the positions they have publicized.

Needless to say, the authors find much in American political processes indicating that these conditions are not consistently met.

18. John L. Sullivan and Robert E. O'Connor, "Electoral Choice and Popular Control of Public Policy: The Case of the 1966 House Elections," *American Political Science Review,* December 1972, pp. 1256–1265.

Public opinion polls and assessments by experienced politicians, journalists, and scholars agree that there is declining popular support for the political system. The symptoms of party and electoral malaise in the United States
include a lowered sense of political efficacy, and a corresponding higher sense
of political alienation. These conditions are the general manifestation of popular feelings that voting doesn't count for much, because (1) a single vote is
after all but one vote among millions, (2) a vote helps elect a representative
who is likely to be ineffective or irresponsible or both, (3) our representative
and administrative institutions are overloaded with persons whose main aim is
to stay in office rather than to raise difficult problems or to solve controversial
ones, and (4) America's position and role in the world are increasingly and
adversely affected by conditions beyond our boundaries and therefore difficult
to control (such as the supply and price of oil, the balance of payments, and
conflicting goals of nations and groups of nations).

The symptoms can be said to result from three kinds of faults. First, there
are the faults in our political system, including institutions that are unrepresentative or unresponsive, the lack of imagination and courage on the part of officeholders, and the weak position of our political parties. Second, there are the
shortcomings in human nature, represented by the venalities of Watergate and
congressional ethics (Nixon, Hays, Mills, Flood, Diggs, Talmadge, et al). Third,
there are the world conditions beyond our control, such as OPEC decisions about
oil production and pricing and the violent, nondemocratic tendencies in many
countries. This book focuses on the political faults, and makes the argument
that structural reforms in the political and electoral systems are the first order of
business in the effort to raise levels of popular support and participation. This is
so because structural reforms are relatively simple to determine and carry out,
they are appropriate to the alleviation of the symptoms noted, and they are
likely to be effective in reaching the desired results of higher levels of popular
support, participation, and effectiveness. The electoral process can be simplified
or at least clarified and systematized across the nation. The selection of party
leaders and the processes of party organizations can be opened up and democra-
tized. The control of party organs can be localized, thus enhancing the significance of single votes, and the power of specific party officials can be increased.
And the unnatural and unnecessary advantages of tenure and incumbency in
American legislatures, especially Congress, can be reduced. These statements
summarize the essence of the structural reforms that will be suggested later.

THE FUNDAMENTAL LINK BETWEEN PEOPLE AND POLICY

The American political system can be viewed as comprising two distinct
groups. On the one hand are those who make policy decisions. They tend to

concentrate in Washington and the fifty state capitals, though some may be found in financial and communications centers such as New York, Chicago, and Los Angeles and in smaller regional centers. On the other hand are the people, the undifferentiated masses in whose name democracy has been established. Democracy, as a generic term, assumes that the people are somehow significant elements in government. Direct democracy assumes that all the citizens have an equal, immediate, and effective voice in policy decisions. We imagine this kind of democracy to exist in town meetings (if enough citizens attend the meeting) and in local or statewide referenda where the people generally vote on the acceptance of new laws, new programs, or bond issues for public improvements. The people make policy directly, and there is no need for intermediate representative institutions. Representative democracy assumes only that the public determines who shall have the authority to make decisions in the name of the people, as in the election of members of Congress, state legislatures, and city councils. This form of government does not assume that a legislative body will necessarily make policy decisions that agree with the preferences of the majority of citizens, but that the decisions it makes are in their best interest and that the people can replace representatives with whom they are not satisfied.

It is the political party that, by nominating candidates for public office and publicizing their positions on the issues of the day, is supposed to establish effective links between the voters and the government.[19] As such, parties grew naturally with the development of representative assemblies. Jeane Jordan Kirkpatrick, in her study of party reform and decomposition, emphasized that political parties matured in an informal, unplanned way:

> Because this process of unanticipated growth has occurred in every country that had democratized its decision-making process, it is clear that the emergence of political parties is closely related to the establishment of a legal right to opposition, the extension of the electorate, and the popular election of rulers.
> ... though they have an important influence on constitutions, democratic parties have everywhere been extraconstitutional bodies standing midway between the government on one hand and, on the other, the myriad of individuals and groups which compose the society.[20]

Although the focus of this book is on parties and elections, there needs to be some early, if brief, reference to the policy-making institutions, for it is after all the control of Congress and state legislatures that is the primary

19. In Giovanni Sartori's words: "Parties are the central intermediate and intermediary structures between society and government." Sartori, *Parties and Party Systems: A Framework for Analysis,* (Cambridge: Cambridge University Press, 1976), p. ix.
20. Kirkpatrick, *op. cit.,* p. 18. Copyright © 1978, The American Enterprise Institute for Public Policy Research.

objective of political activity. Further, the effectiveness of the entire political system is based as much on the effectiveness of the representative, policy-making institutions as it is on the effectiveness of the party and electoral systems.

Parties link citizens to government by nominating candidates, by formal-izing legislative leadership and responsibility, and by writing platforms that attempt to identify the problems of the day and then to find solutions to those problems. Citizens have preferences and needs, things they want to have and things they ought to have. Consider, as one example of such demands, alter-native proposals to protect the family against the financial costs of illness. The Democratic party might propose a comprehensive health insurance program that would underwrite the bulk of the costs of any conceivable sort of illness. Republicans, on the other hand, might propose that the government protect the individual against catastrophic health costs. Such were, in general, the 1979 proposals of various congressional and administrative leaders. Congress might then debate the merits of the two proposals, agree on various com-promises and adjustments, and finally pass a law. Its actions would be made partisan and responsible by the fact that the sponsors of the two alternative proposals are of opposite parties and that most members of Congress vote in ac-cordance with the majority of their respective party colleagues in the Congress.

How often is real policy-making similar to the hypothetical process just described? Not often enough, certainly. There are too many occasions of dysfunction. The members of Congress are either Democrats or Republicans, to be sure, but several conditions stand in the way of any direct connection between the citizens' votes and the legislature's decisions. First, in most cases the member would have been nominated for his office by a party primary election; even if health insurance had been discussed by one or both of the candidates in the campaign, few citizens would have been aware of their respective positions. Second, the choice of party leadership in a legislative body is seldom based on current or specific policy considerations. Third, party platforms probably would not be specific on a policy question as com-plex as health insurance, or the platforms of the parties would not be notably different from one another, or the platforms would not be followed in the drafting of the bill.

Our model of representative democracy assumes that the electoral process connects the voters' political preferences with policy decisions. But is the connection exclusive? It is clearly not exclusive if other elements become significantly involved. Congress, and state legislative bodies generally, can be conceived of as institutions that make decisions in response to pressures from several possible sources, namely: (1) members of an elite set of idea merchants, found especially in such eastern liberal establishments as the media, universities, research foundations, and corporations, who focus sophisticated expertise on public problems, (2) interest groups such as organized labor and big business, or professional associations such as physicians or teachers, or alliances of such interest groups, (3) party leaders outside the legislative assemblies, (4) political influential people in specific constituencies, (5) political executives such as presidents, governors, or agency heads, (6) internal leaders of legislative assemblies, such as floor leaders, committee chairmen, and ideological or regional spokesmen, and (7) the mass public, as its preferences are perceived or guessed at by politicians through assessments of public opinion. It is striking that only the third group represents the kind of voter-legislator connection envisioned by the pure theory of party government. If such external party controls are not a very significant factor in explaining the decision-making process in Congress or state legislatures, then something is wrong with representative democracy in America.[21]

HOW PARTIES FUNCTION AS LINKAGE ELEMENTS

Parties consist of three kinds of people—the individual members, the officers at the various levels of organization (county, state, national), and governmental officials who are elected or appointed to their positions largely on the basis of their party affiliation. In the United States today, most of these individuals are Democrats or Republicans. The influence of other parties is greatly diminished by two considerations: they seldom win office and they seldom command the loyalty of a significant number of citizens for a significant period of time. But one political segment other than the Democrats and Republicans is potentially important. There are millions of Americans who are not members of any political party; many of these "independents" are quite interested in politics and vote regularly and discriminatingly,[22] while

21. Two lines of empirical inquiry would illuminate the degree to which purely party considerations impinge on legislative decisions. First, one could estimate the percentage of all laws passed by a legislative body that originated in each of the categories listed above. Second, one could study one particular law and estimate the percentage of pressure exerted on it by each of the categories. Either way, we would have a better understanding of the importance of purely party pressures on policy relative to the importance of the other sources of legislative pressure.

22. Walter DeVries and Lance Tarrance made a distinction between independents in the traditional sense of marginally active citizens who vote occasionally but do not feel attached to any political party, and the contemporary ticket-splitter, who is politically sophisticated and usually splits his or her ballot between Republican and Democratic candidates, depending on perceptions of differences in issue stands or personality characteristics of the competitors. DeVries and Tarrance, *The Ticket-Splitter,* (Grand Rapids, Mich.: Eerdmans, 1972).

others are only marginally or irregularly involved in politics, and some participate not at all because they lack knowledge about or interest in the political
struggles that go on ceaselessly around them.

Political parties are expected to perform several specific linkage functions
in a democracy. The extent to which each of these functions operates in any
given nation will vary somewhat; indeed, these variations are what give each
system its individual culture and personality.

The Governmental Function. This first function involves organizing the government. The winning presidential candidate must appoint hundreds of top-level
federal executives; traditionally the bulk of such appointees have been members of the president's political party, some active, others more nominal in
their partisan allegiance. In American legislative chambers, members of the
majority party elect presiding officers, secure a majority on each standing
committee, and generally control the legislative agenda. The fact that we
have administrations and legislatures that are dominated by either one or the
other of the two major parties adds something to the coherence, responsibility,
stability, and discipline of government. However, we should note that our
federal system with its three levels of activity (federal, state, local) and our
system of separation of powers (among the legislative, executive, and judicial
branches) detracts considerably from the clear-cut model of responsible parties.
For such a model to exist in this country, it would be necessary for one party
to control each branch of government at each level. Further, the pattern of
nonpartisan politics in local government (and in the Nebraska unicameral legislature) clearly removes such areas from the possibility of decision-making in
the traditional two-party context.

The Policy Function. The second function of the party system is to encourage
the presentation, discussion, and resolution of current policy problems. Parties
offer a permanent vehicle for supporting or opposing specific policy recommendations, a vehicle that can work from one year to another and from one state
to another. In some circumstances, parties can reconcile policy differences
that may exist between groups of citizens, building towards a consensus. At
other times, parties can act as polarizing agents, tending to separate individuals
and groups into increasingly hostile camps. The drafting of party platforms
at national and state party conventions is perhaps the most dramatic and
visible aspect of a political party's involvement in the policy process. To some
extent, these platform negotiations are highlighted in the news media, with
the result that party activities help to educate and sensitize the general public
as to current problems.

To the extent that party decisions on policy questions cause Democrats
or Republicans across the land to think systematically about a given question,

this policy function can help remove some of the baneful effects of federalism and separation of powers.

The Candidate Function. The third function is that of encouraging qualified citizens to run for office. Political parties provide potential candidates with a permanent political home, a base that can provide continuing psychic aid and tangible campaign assistance. A candidate of either major party can count on money, personnel, and public support from his party.

The Citizenship Function. The fourth function is perhaps the most crucial, since it involves mobilizing the mass of citizens, which is so important to a democratic society. Political parties provide the ordinary citizen with a visible and permanent organization. These organizations have continuing activities and responsibilities both nationally and locally. Democrats and Republicans can expect the party to provide a reservoir of like-minded persons with whom to work in attempting to secure the election of certain candidates or the passage of particular legislation. Whether an individual is a Democrat or a Republican, there are officials and public officeholders of the same party with whom he can share his interests and objectives. Parties, in short, encourage constant two-way communication between citizens and government officials.

Lists of party functions such as the above can be lengthened, shortened, and rearranged with ease. The essential party functions are neither legally defined nor patented, and hence different observers have categorized party activities and responsibilities in different ways. Frank Sorauf, in his widely read and respected textbook, says that three approaches have been used to describe what parties do. The first approach deals with the party as an institution with "commonly held ideas, values, or stands on issues." The second approach studies the party as a social structure, with attention given to party organization and hierarchy, the impact of party on government, and the groups of people who make up the party's electorate. The third approach views the party as a "congeries of activities," and is interested in electoral campaign activity, educational or propaganda activity, and governing activity.[23]

23. Frank Sorauf, *Party Politics in America,* third edition (Boston: Little, Brown, 1976), p. 1. For another list of party functions, see Joyce Gelb and Marian Lief Palley, *Tradition and Change in American Party Politics* (New York: Crowell, 1975), p. 3. Ruth Scott and Ronald Hrebenar present a similar list and go a step further in an attempt to unravel the inventory of party activities by asking four pertinent questions: (1) "To what extent are parties performing these functions?" (2) "What agents or circumstances are challenging the parties' monopoly of these functions?" (3) "Will the political parties be destroyed by these challenges or will they adopt new functions?" (4) "If the parties' functions are completely absorbed by other political actors, what will be the consequences for American politics?" Scott and Hrebenar, *Parties in Crisis* (New York: Wiley, 1979) pp. 1–4, especially p. 2.

HOW AMERICAN PARTIES DIFFER
FROM EUROPEAN MODELS

The presence of these functions in various national systems can be measured, and doing so may help to clarify the functions themselves. The examples to be used are the United States, the United Kingdom, and France; the accompanying table (1-1) summarizes the comparisons.

The United Kingdom's unitary system of government, wherein the regional units have far weaker constitutional status than do the states within our federal system, and its essentially two-party political framework makes its party system most effective in terms of the governmental function. France's multiparty system, in which it is difficult for a single party to gain control of government and for observers to fix party responsibility for governmental decisions, causes it to be ranked lowest of the three nations on this dimension.

As for the policy function, the United Kingdom places first in this also, because its two major parties, Labour and Conservative, have rather clear policy differences that are quickly converted into official governmental policy when there is a change in party control of the House of Commons. A Labour government means Labour policy, in a very direct and straightforward way. French parties are ideological, which means among other things that policy preferences are even more sharply different than they are between the major British parties. However, party coalitions are the rule in multiparty systems, and thus the consequences of changes in party coalition control tend to be less extreme because there is considerable compromising among coalition parties on policy questions. The large amount of policy ambiguity in American politics accounts for our nation's low ranking on this functional dimension. Our party platforms look too much like Tweedledum and Tweedledee, and our legislative mechanisms allow for the play of many forces, in addition to purely party forces, in policy deliberations.

With respect to the candidate function, the United Kingdom and France are rated together, well above the United States because their parties are more

Table 1-1. Relative Functional Effectiveness of Parties in Three Nations.

Function	More Effective		Less Effective
Governmental	UK	USA	France
Policy	UK	France	USA
Candidate	UK and France		USA
Citizenship	France	UK	USA

clearly responsible for encouraging candidates to run and for funding, planning, and conducting their campaigns for office. In the United States, candidates typically raise the bulk of their expenses themselves and often run their campaigns without much cooperation from or integration with the party's efforts.

The citizenship function is perhaps best performed in France. There the parties have a much wider popular base than is the case in the United States, where many politically active citizens are only scantily involved in party matters and where comparatively few citizens contribute money or time to political parties.[24]

Now consider the relative ranking of the four functions in the United States alone. Our party system probably performs the governmental function most effectively, in spite of the decentralizing effects of federalism and the separation of powers. The citizenship and candidate functions are next in line, with the policy function occupying the last position, because of the wide diversity within each party of ideological or issue positions and the lack of strong cohesion on policy questions in American legislative bodies.[25]

In contrast with their Eurpoean counterparts, American parties are not doctrinaire, or, to put it another way, they are not very different from one another. Party discipline is weak. In the United Kingdom or France, for example, party membership is more tightly regulated than it is in America, and party leaders have more reason to expect loyalty and cooperation from their many members than do American party leaders from their smaller membership cadres. Among European parties there are sharp differences regarding policy positions and ideological orientations. Their parties contribute to clear and permanent divisions in respect to fundamental national objectives. In Europe, to a much greater extent than here, there is a high degree of socio-economic class consciousness on the part of the citizenry, and this sense of class translates into national political discourse of a sort that unsettles the typical consensus-oriented politician or citizen in the United States.

In American politics, there is a strong strain of pragmatism, of concern for what is possible, of consensual decision-making, and hence there is less opportunity for divisions that would split society deeply and permanently. Both the Democratic and Republican parties contain healthy liberal and conservative wings, though most Democrats are more liberal than most Re-

---

24. Sorauf puts it this way: "Consider the American adults who insist 'I'm a strong Republican,' and 'I've been a Democrat all my life.' It is unlikely that they ever worked within the party organization of their choice, much less made a financial contribution to it . . . . We do not hesitate to credit their word, for it is in the nature of the American parties and politics to consider people Democrats and Republicans merely because they say they are." Sorauf, *op. cit.*, p. 7.
25. Party cohesion in legislative voting will be discussed in Chapter 3.

publicans, and most Republicans are more conservative than most Democrats. Ideological differences are more pronounced between Democratic and Republican officeholders and party leaders than between the rank-and-file membership of the two national parties. As a consequence, members of both parties can go along with a good deal of the policy objectives and machinations of any administration, irrespective of which party controls the White House.

American parties are frequently criticized for being ambiguous and uncertain and, finally, irresponsible. But this ambiguity is seen at the same time as a major reason for the impressive stability and longevity of the American political system, conditions which seem to be at least partly based on flexible expectations and reactions of citizens.

In short, the party functions are more clearly and persistently performed by European than by American parties. European parties are more efficient and meaningful; whether they contribute more to effective and popular government than do their wishy-washy, poorly disciplined American cousins is another question. Those who feel that American government is more "satisfactory" in terms of efficiency, popularity, and responsiveness would have to base their arguments more on the American constitutional system and the American political culture than on its party system.

PARTY EVOLUTION AND CHANGE IN AMERICA

Whatever else might be said about them, American parties are not static. Our parties change. It is their flexibility with respect to ideas and issues that enables American parties to survive so many crises and defeats. Parties are really shifting coalitions of basic support groups, whose compositon alters almost imperceptibly in response to changes in images of major candidates and nuances of current policy proposals. James Sundquist's model of party change in America illustrates the mechanics for past as well as potential change in the nation's party system.[26] From the time of Andrew Jackson at least, American politics has involved two national parties, and since the 1850s these parties have been the Democratic and the Republican. Occasionally since the Civil War, a third party has risen briefly, based on special regional or economic class interests. In the wake of these transient political movements, changes in the composition of the two major parties have sometimes occurred. Sundquist explains these dynamics, and potential changes as well, in terms of "cross-cutting issues" that disrupt the former pattern of party cleavage and

26. James L. Sundquist, *Dynamics of the Party System* (Washington: Brookings Institution, 1973), especially Chapters 5, 7, and 10.

result in movements of vast numbers of voters from one party to the other. Since the Civil War, when the slavery issue made the Republican party a national party and at the same time divided the Democratic party into hostile northern and southern wings, the Democratic and Republican parties have survived the monetary crisis of the 1890s and the social upheaval of the 1930s, though each party emerged with differences in size and compositon of membership. The realignment of the 1890s resulted in a system in which the Republicans were dominant for a generation, except for the World War I era when Woodrow Wilson won two presidential elections. The realignment of the 1930s produced an overriding Democratic majority in the nation that has persisted until today, excepting the Eisenhower and Nixon presidencies, which occurred as a result of Democratic defections and independent support (and, in Nixon's case, from George Wallace's candidacy in 1968).

American political institutions and partisan loyalties are durable, but they are capable of rapid change when sufficient stress builds up. If the system seems unresponsive to today's needs, it is because in a truly democratic system it is necessary, after all, to move the minds of more than half of the people. Needs, then, if they are to be addressed through policy changes, must be translated and dramatized so that they are felt by strategically placed majorities.

SUMMARY

The essential characteristics of the American political system, as they have been surveyed in this chapter, may be summed up in six generalizations. First, Americans are not highly politicized, that is, they do not see every problem they confront as one to be solved by political action on their part or anyone else's. Second, Americans are not very class conscious. Third, consensus as the basis for political decision-making is greatly preferred by most Americans to polarization, contention, and violence. Fourth, political power is widely dispersed. Fifth, Democrats and Republicans are not very consistent or predictable in their ideological and policy attachments, when compared with European party leaders and citizens. And sixth, it is difficult to fix responsibility for governmental decisions in America.

Chapter 2
The Citizen in
the Political System

The Right to Vote

Citizen Beliefs

Party Identification and Ideology

Citizen Participation

Eight American Perspectives

Summary

Many different kinds of governments call themselves democratic. Since many variants of democracy can be imagined—among them, populist, pluralist, elitist, representative, direct—the term has become quite ambiguous and tells us little about the quality of a political system. The critical question is the degree to which citizens participate effectively and equally in making the significant decisions that determine who the political leaders will be and what policies will be pursued by the government.

In America, the level of political participation is highly variable. Voter turnout is consistently high in certain states, and consistently low in others. Turnout differs for federal, state, municipal, and school district elections. Certain socioeconomic classes, age groups, and ideological groups participate in ways and degrees that are different from the standard pattern. There is variation over the years, with marked increases or decreases from one election to the next, and in a given year there is likely to be significantly more participation in certain races. General elections in November attract far more voters than do the spring and summer primaries.

Voting is not, of course, the only kind of political participation, though it is one of the easiest kinds to observe and measure. Citizens may also take part in politics by discussing issues and candidates with family members, friends, and associates at work, by contributing money or time to a particular campaign, by contacting governmental officials about a matter of concern to them, by running for election, or by serving in public office.[1] Some citizens participate frequently, others little or not at all. This chapter will describe and attempt to explain the diversity of political participation in America, focusing its attention on the legal environment of voting, the political attitudes of citizens and their effect on behavior, the kinds of people most likely to support the candidates of a given party, and the factors that influence the voting decisions of individual citizens.

1. The political participation hierarchy was originally developed in Lester Milbrath, *Political Participation* (Chicago: Rand McNally & Company, 1965).

THE RIGHT TO VOTE

When Americans began their experiment in political independence, the right to vote was largely limited to adult male property owners, as it was in England at that time. The nineteenth century saw a tremendous increase in the proportion of citizens eligible to vote. In England, this expansion of the franchise occurred by means of three reform acts—those of 1832, 1867, and 1882.

In the United States, the right to vote was not spelled out in the Constitution. The right to vote for members of the US House of Representatives was given in the Constitution to persons in each state who were, under the laws of their own state, eligible to vote for the most numerous branch of the state's legislative assembly (Article I, section 2). But since that time, the history of the franchise in America has been one of expansion, as reasons for keeping the ballot from various groups were eliminated by the states or the federal government.

By the end of the Civil War, property qualifications had disappeared at the state level, except that many states continued to restrict the franchise for bond referenda to property owners. With the Civil War there began a long, three-pronged attack on racial discrimination at the polls, by means of constitutional amendments, federal statutes, and court decisions; this long struggle was not completed until the 1960s. Women's suffrage did not come at the federal level (though it had been pioneered in a few new western states before 1900) until the Nineteenth Amendment was adopted in 1920; the women's suffrage movement had only recently achieved success in Great Britain under the stress of World War I. The Twenty-third Amendment (1961) extended the right to vote for president to residents of the District of Columbia (another proposed amendment would further extend District of Columbia voting rights to voting for a member of the House of Representatives). The Twenty-fourth Amendment (1964) removed the payment of a poll tax as a requisite for voting in both primary and general elections for federal office, and this right was expanded to include state elections by the Supreme Court in Harper *v*. Virginia,[2] a decision that was based on the Equal Protection Clause of the Fourteenth Amendment. The Twenty-sixth Amendment (1971), building on a 1970 congressional statute, in effect extended the right to vote in federal and state elections to 18-year-olds; previously, most states had used 21 as the voting age, though Georgia, Kentucky, Alaska, and Hawaii had lower age requirements.

Most states have retained some restrictions on complete adult suffrage. Prisoners, persons convicted of crimes (even though they have served their

2. Harper *v*. Virginia, 383 US 663 (1966).

sentences), the mentally incompetent, and the illiterate are frequently excluded from access to the voting booth. The latter category has been affected by federal regulations requiring bilingual ballots in jurisdictions where sizable numbers use a language other than English. Citizenship, of course, is a fundamental qualification; aliens do not vote.

Voter Registration

States, through county or municipal officials, maintain registration systems by which citizens exercise their residence qualification to vote. There is considerable variety from state to state. Some have strict party registration systems that govern access to the primary election. There are permanent registration systems—once registered, a person need not reregister if he or she votes regularly —and periodic registration systems. There are different requirements for the length of residence required to be eligible to vote in certain kinds of elections (notably, bond elections). The federal residence standard for presidential elections is 30 days. The general reason given for registration is the need to keep voter lists up-to-date and accurate in order to prevent various kinds of political fraud or dishonesty; in effect, agents of one party check the other parties. This notion is exemplified in a statement of party objectives of the British Conservative party: "To watch the revision of the constituency register of electors in the interests of the party and to take steps to ensure that all supporters who are qualified are in a position to record their votes."[3]

Certain kinds of citizens are more likely than others to be registered. For the most part, the groups that register in relatively high proportions compared to other citizens—the whites, the college educated, the midwestern, the older, the well-to-do—are the same groups in which Republican party identification is comparatively strong (see Table 2-1). But there are two notable exceptions to this tendency—Jewish Americans and labor-union members are relatively high in registration rates. Logically enough, there is a close association between rates of registration and rates of voting turnout.

The franchise establishes the eligible electorate. It is worthwhile, at this preliminary stage of the discussion, to describe the shape of the electorate in the nation as a whole and in the individual states. The median voting age for the nation is in the 35-to-44 age cohort. The voting age population became considerably younger in the 1970s as the addition of young voters reaching age 18 offset deaths in the oldest category. Whereas in 1960, 33.6 percent of the above-18

3. The quoted statement is the fifth objective of the party listed in "The Conservative Party Organization," undated, mimeograph, concerning the background, purposes, and administration of British Conservative party, kindly provided to me by Terry Anderson of the South Dakota Legislative Research Council, fall 1979.

Table 2-1. Registration Rates among Various American Groups*

Category	High Registration Group	Low Registration Group
Race	White (69%)	Nonwhite (63%)
Education	College (76%)	Grade school (66%)
Region	Midwest (75%)	South (64%)
Age	Over 30 (76%)	Under 30 (50%)
Family income	Over $15,000 (74%)	Under $15,000 (62%)
Party	Republican (80%)	Independent (59%)
	Democrat (74%)	
Religion	Jewish (82%)	Catholic (69%)
Union status	Member (74%)	Nonmember (67%)

*(national rate, 69%)

Source: Field Enterprises survey reported in Today, *November 9, 1979, p. 16.*

Table 2-2. The Size of Age Cohorts in the US Population, 1960 and 1977

Age Cohort	Percent of 1960 Electorate	Percent of 1977 Electorate	Percentile Change
18-24	13.9	18.7	+4.8
25-34	19.7	21.7	+2.0
35-44	20.9	15.4	−5.5
45-54	17.7	15.3	−2.4
55-64	13.5	13.4	−0.1
65 and over	14.3	15.4	+1.1

Source: For 1960 data, 1969 Statistical Abstract of the United States, pp. 8-9; for 1977 data, 1978 Statistical Abstract of the United States, pp. 8-9. Data for 1960 includes persons under age 21, even though they were not eligible to vote in most states until the Twenty-sixth Amendment was adopted in 1971; had this cohort been omitted in the 1960 data, the percentile increase for the 18-24 cohort would be about twice as large.

Table 2-3. Shifts in Electoral College Votes, by Section, 1960 to 1980

Section	Votes in 1960	Votes in 1980	Change
Northeast	133	125	− 8
South	166	166	0
Midwest	153	145	− 8
West	85	102	+17
Totals	537*	538	+ 1*

*Statehood for Alaska and Hawaii caused a temporary increase in the size of the House of Representatives from 435 to 437 and a permanent increase in the size of the Senate from 96 to 100. The addition of three electoral votes for the District of Columbia after 1960 thus produced a net increase of one electoral vote from 1960 to 1980.
Source: US Census Bureau.

population was under age 35, by 1977 that percentage had jumped to 40.4 (see Table 2-2). In terms of sectional strenth, the center of gravity of the nation's population (and its electoral votes) was at the same time moving west, according to the Census Bureau. While the South's population growth stayed close to the national rate, the West increased at the expense of the Northeast and Midwest (see Table 2-3).

Individual states reflect interesting and significant patterns that differentiate them from national norms in such critical characteristics as urbanization, age, racial composition, and occupation. Table 2-4 highlights these comparisons and gives a rough but useful profile of each state's electorate.

Table 2-4. State Comparisons on Four Population Characteristics

State	Urban	Young	Black	Blue Collar
Alabama	−	0	+	+
Alaska	−	+	−	0
Arizona	0	+	−	0
Arkansas	−	−	+	0
California	+	+	0	0
Colorado	0	+	−	−
Connecticut	0	0	0	0

Table 2-4. State Comparisons on Four Population Characteristics (continued)

State	Urban	Young	Black	Blue Collar
Delaware	0	+	0	0
District of Columbia	+	+	+	−
Florida	+	−	+	0
Georgia	0	+	+	0
Hawaii	+	+	−	0
Idaho	−	0	−	0
Illinois	+	0	0	0
Indiana	0	0	0	+
Iowa	−	−	−	0
Kansas	0	−	−	0
Kentucky	−	0	0	+
Louisiana	0	+	+	0
Maine	−	−	−	+
Maryland	0	+	+	0
Massachusetts	+	−	−	0
Michigan	0	0	0	+
Minnesota	0	0	−	0
Mississippi	−	0	+	+
Missouri	0	−	0	0
Montana	−	0	−	−
Nebraska	0	−	−	−
Nevada	+	+	0	−
New Hampshire	−	0	−	+
New Jersey	+	−	0	0
New Mexico	0	+	−	0
New York	+	−	0	0
North Carolina	−	+	+	+

Table 2-4. State Comparisons on Four Population Characteristics (continued)

State	Urban	Young	Black	Blue Collar
North Dakota	−	0	−	−
Ohio	0	0	0	+
Oklahoma	0	−	0	0
Oregon	0	−	−	0
Pennsylvania	0	−	0	+
Rhode Island	+	−	−	+
South Carolina	−	+	+	+
South Dakota	−	−	−	−
Tennessee	−	0	+	+
Texas	0	+	0	0
Utah	+	+	−	0
Vermont	−	0	−	0
Virginia	0	+	+	0
Washington	0	0	−	0
West Virginia	−	−	−	+
Wisconsin	0	0	−	0
Wyoming	0	0	−	0

*(+ = considerably higher than national norms; 0 = close to national norms; − = considerably lower than national norms)

Urban categories:	+, 80 percent and over;
	0, 60 to 79 percent;
	−, less than 60 percent.
Young categories:	+, median voting age 44 and over;
	0, median voting age, 42–43;
	−, median voting age under 42.
Black categories:	+, 15 percent or more black;
	0, 5 to 14 percent black;
	−, less than 5 percent black.
Blue collar categories:	+, 40 percent or more blue collar;
	0, 30 to 39 percent blue collar;
	−, less than 30 percent blue collar.

Source: Adapted from Republican National Committee data published in the National Journal's Election '80 Handbook, *October 20, 1979, p. 1772.*

CITIZEN BELIEFS

Observers often assess democracy on the basis of overt activities per-formed by citizens—how many vote, how many discuss politics regularly, how many contribute money to campaigns, and so forth. In the same way, the patriotism of a nation could be assessed on the basis of tangible citizen re-sponses to the war effort in the event of a military confrontation—how many citizens volunteer for military service, how many accept the rationing of critical goods, how many give blood, wrap bandages, serve at USO centers, etc.

But these overt actions are only the "outward and visible signs" of inner, private, often deeply felt attitudes and beliefs that individuals have about the relationships that ought to exist among the individual, society, and govern-ment. So it is important to know about the attitudes that might affect the political behavior of Americans.

How do Americans feel about their governmental system? Do they trust the honesty, fairness, good sense, and intelligence of officials? Do they want government to have a greater or lesser degree of control over society generally and themselves and their neighbors specifically? Do they believe that common citizens have enough or too much influence on governmental decisions? Do they believe in democracy, that is, that widespread participation is necessary in our political system?

Opinion Polls

For more than a generation, social scientists have been looking for scientific answers to these questions through reputable surveys of public opinion. A reputable public opinion survey may be briefly described as one in which a sufficient number of persons are interviewed; the persons to be interviewed, chosen randomly, can be expected to understand the questions; the questions are unbiased and unambiguous; and the interviewing itself is conducted in a wholly neutral manner. The attempt to measure popular attitudes toward political issues and candidates has led to the development of a burgeoning public opinion industry in contemporary America. The work of Paul Lazarsfeld at Columbia University, of the Gallup, Roper, and Harris organizations, and of the Survey Research Center at the University of Michigan under Angus Campbell, Donald Stokes, Philip Converse, and Warren Miller have been im-portant foundations of this industry. Pollsters in academic, journalistic, and marketing areas have developed sampling and questioning methodologies that have improved our ability to measure and understand the state of the nation's collective mind. The result is that no longer do the people have to rely on politicians and editorial pundits to tell them what the public is thinking or what it wants. Today one can be reasonably certain of what the opinion of the public is. But for all that, it is worth considering that the campaigners and journalists, from their deeper knowledge of political processes and their wider perspectives on social problems, may be in a better position to judge what the people *need*, if not what they want. It should be remembered that campaign rhetoric and editorial essays do play a powerful role in shaping public opinion.

The foundation of the American political attitude is the degree to which the people trust their government. Levels of trust, of sense of political efficacy, and of alienation are important in measuring the soundness of any political system; trust, efficacy, and alienation scores are like temperature levels on a thermometer that show a patient's temperature and help a physician assess his condition. Such attitudinal scores vary from nation to nation and from time to time. Though the "attitudometer" continues to show levels that are tolerable in a healthy political system, it would be well for Americans to keep an eye on the meter readings.

Americans have viewed their government with "a healthy mixture of trust and skepticism."[4] Twenty years ago, there was general agreement that the government was being run for the benefit of all rather than for the benefit of the few, and that public officials cared what people thought. But just as many Americans thought that there was a lot of dishonesty in government as thought that there was hardly any, and more Americans "hardly ever" trusted their government to do the right thing than "always" trusted it to do so. And far more of the American public was prone to believe that the government wasted a lot of tax money than thought there was "not much" waste.[5]

The level of trust in the political system declined under the stresses of Vietnam, Watergate, and disclosures or allegations of wrongdoing by several prominent members of Congress. The percentage of Americans who believed they could always trust the government in Washington to do what is right declined from 14 percent in 1964 to 6 percent in 1970 and 3 percent in 1974; in the same years, the percentages of Americans believing they could trust the government only some of the time, or not at all, rose from 22 to 44 to 64.[6]

In late 1978, a national poll conducted by the Roper organization reported that 5 percent of a national sample felt that the governmental system was work-

4. Norman Nie, Sidney Verba, and John Petrocik, *The Changing American Voter* (Cambridge, Mass.: Harvard University Press, 1976), p. 35.
5. *Ibid.*, p. 36.
6. Arthur H. Miller, "Political Issues and Trust in Government, 1964–1970," *American Political Science Review*, LXVIII, September 1974, p. 953, and Miller, Jeffrey Brudney, and Peter Joftis, "Presidential Crises and Political Support: The Impact of Watergate on Attitudes toward Institutions," a paper delivered at the annual meeting of the Midwest Political Science Association, Chicago, Ill., May 1975, p. 9. For a summary table, see William Keefe, *op. cit.*, p. 177 (Table 24).

ing extremely well and that another 53 percent believed it was working fairly well.[7] On the other hand, 28 percent thought the system was working not very well and 11 percent responded that the system was working not well at all (the remainder of 3 percent of the sample were in the "don't know" category). The same survey reported somewhat lower scores for Congress, the central agency of the governmental system: 5 percent said Congress was accomplishing a good deal in solving national problems, 35 percent said it was accomplishing a fair amount, 38 percent not very much, and 22 percent very little—hardly a passing grade! As for the reasons the system wasn't working better, the largest number of Americans (42 percent of the sample) felt there was too much influence on government by special interest groups and lobbies. Other reasons cited for poor governmental performance were: too many people vote without thinking (19 percent), the Democratic and Republican parties don't give us a workable two-party system any more (14 percent), not enough people vote (14 percent), the candidates who run for office aren't a good choice to vote for (13 percent), and there is something the matter with our system of government itself (9 percent).

Another national poll taken a few months earlier identified several kinds of systematic changes favored by the public.[8] Fifty-seven percent of the sample favored the idea of a national referendum on any issue for which 3 percent of the voters sign petitions requesting such a referendum, an indication that the public feels its institutions, notably Congress, are not adequately representing the public. Over 70 percent felt the Electoral College system for electing the president and vice-president should be replaced by a direct popular vote system. By about 2 to 1, Americans favored public financing of congressional elections, outlawing private contributions from other sources. By the same margin, Americans wanted a limitation of twelve years of service in the US Senate (two terms of six years each) and House (lengthening the term from two to four years but limiting members to three terms).[9] One final point may summarize this review of American attitudes. Respondents were asked which of four statements best described our political system, with this response pattern:

basically sound/essentially good—13 percent
basically sound/needs some improvement—59 percent
not too sound/needs many improvements—21 percent
basically unsound—7 percent.

7. Roper organization survey conducted for the Public Broadcasting Service, October 1978, summarized by Everett C. Ladd, Jr., in *Public Opinion*, June/July 1979, p. 27.
8. Roper organization survey of February 1977, reported in *Public Opinion*, June/July 1979, p. 29.
9. American Institute of Public Opinion (Gallup) surveys of January 1977 to February 1979, reported in *Public Opinion*, June/July 1979, pp. 28–29.

Table 2-5. Changes in Citizens' Views of Government

Charge/criticism	1958	1964	1968	1974	1978
Government is run for a few big interests.	18	31	44	73	74
Government cannot be regularly trusted to do what is right.	25	22	37	63	70
Government is run by people who don't know what they are doing.	nd	28	39	48	56
Government wastes a lot of tax dollars.	46	48	61	76	79

*(data are percentages of adult Americans supporting the charge or criticism)
Source: Surveys by the Center for Political Studies of the Institute for Social Research, University of Michigan, election studies, 1958-1978, reported in Public Opinion, *October/ November 1979, p. 29.*

Two 1978 studies by the Center for Political Studies of the Institute for Social Research at the University of Michigan (headed by Warren Miller) and the Cambridge Research Corporation (headed by Patrick Caddell) found that two-thirds of the American public felt it could trust the government only some of the time or hardly ever.[10] This frustration is on the rise, as Table 2-5 shows; on every dimension, popular attitudes about American government are becoming more negative.

The problems that worry us change from year to year. Their nature and the role that Americans believe the government should play in their solution are important in assessing the performance of government and the degree of support Americans feel for their political system. Table 2-6 summarizes the issues that have most troubled Americans over the past generation. Vietnam accounted for most of the concern about foreign affairs in the 1970 survey. Government malperformance reached higher levels than reported in Table 2-6 in 1974 and again in 1976, the Watergate era. Social problems—law and order, civil rights, affirmative action efforts, busing—peaked around 1970. Dramatic increases in concern about the economy and energy policy were shown for the late 1970s.

The idea of democracy has broad support in America, as might be expected in a nation so clearly founded on the principles of limited government, civil liberties, and political equality, but at the practical level support for democracy is often low. The Gallup Poll reported in 1940 that 97 percent of Americans

10. *Public Opinion,* October/November 1979, p. 8.

Table 2-6. Public Views as to the Most Important Problem Facing this Country

Year	The Economy	Foreign Affairs	Social Problems	Governmental Malperformance	Energy	Other and Don't Know
1955	10	49	2	0	0	45
1960	18	59	9	1	0	26
1965	8	53	37	0	0	17
1970	10	36	56	0	0	18
1975	80	5	15	7	7	21
1979	62	5	6	3	33	10

*(data are percents; some respondents named more than one problem.)

Source: Surveys by the Gallup Organization, Inc., 1955-1979, reported in the National Journal's Election '80 Handbook, *October 20, 1979, p. 1730.*

believed in freedom of speech, but contrarily that only 22 percent of those same Americans believed in freedom of speech to the extent of allowing fascists and communists to hold meetings and express their views in their community.[11] Some groups were more consistent than others in their support for democratic ideals; such support increased with level of education and with political knowledge and power. Among community leaders, newspaper publishers and bar association presidents were somewhat more supportive of democracy than were mayors, business leaders, or union leaders.[12]

The public's view of the role and effectiveness of political parties has been mixed. Although most Americans have a commitment to one or another of the two major parties,[13] their attitudes about political issues are inconsistent[14] and change over time.[15] Most thought that parties do more to confuse than to clarify the issues, that parties more often than not create conflicts where none really existed, and that the best rule in voting is to pick the candidate regardless of his party label. But, on the contrary tack, most Americans thought it was a good thing to have party labels on the ballot and that citizens who work for

11. Greenstein, *op. cit.,* p. 7.
12. Summarized from *ibid.,* pp. 21–22.
13. Nie, Verba, and Petrocik, *op. cit.,* p. 28.
14. *Ibid.,* p. 23.
15. *Ibid.,* pp. 247–267.

political parties during an election campaign are doing the nation a great service.[16]

Frank Sorauf has summarized America's rather ambivalent views of our party system. He has noted that indicators of "hostility toward partisan politics have multiplied," and that political parties were ranked by college students far lower than such institutions as universities, the family, business, Congress, courts, police, high schools, and organized religion. Further, summarizing Jack Dennis' study of attitudes of Wisconsin respondents toward their party system, Sorauf has noted that although 61 percent agreed that democracy works best where competition between parties is strong, 53 percent felt that the political system would work better if conflicts between the parties could be eliminated altogether. Sorauf concluded that partisan politics in the United States "may enjoy a somewhat ambiguous support within the American electorate but only at a high level of generality and platitude."[17]

PARTY IDENTIFICATION AND IDEOLOGY

Another reflection of the changing attitudes of Americans toward the two national parties is seen in the oft-reported decline in party loyalty since 1952. As Table 2-7 shows, fewer Americans in 1976 reported strong identification with either party, and more Americans were adopting an independent position.

There is a close association between the party identification of Americans and their ideological, or liberal/conservative, orientation. Most Democrats place themselves on the liberal side of the ideological spectrum, and most Republicans locate themselves toward the conservative. But the correlation between party and ideology is by no means perfect; not only are some Democrats conservative and some Republicans liberal, but some conservative Democrats are more conservative than any Republican (see Table 2-8).

Observers such as Kevin Phillips and William Rusher believe America has turned toward a more conservative political orientation over the past few

16. Based on Jack Dennis, "Support for the Party System by the Mass Public," *American Political Science Review*, LX, September 1966, p. 605, as adapted in Keefe, *op. cit.*, p. 7. Another scholar believes that citizens will see that the welfare state, having reached a certain size, will continue to grow in spite of growing popular disenchantment with it; ". . . the size of government cannot be easily controlled by normal democratic processes, and confidence in electoral politics will decline." Ralph K. Winter, Jr., "The Welfare State and the Decline of Electoral Politics," *Regulation*, March/April 1978, p. 11.

17. Sorauf, *op. cit.*, pp. 24-25.

Table 2-7. National Trends in Party Identification, 1952–1976.

Party Identification	1952	1956	1960	1964	1968	1972	1976	Percentile Change, '52–'76
Strong Democrat	22	21	21	26	20	15	15	–7
Weak Democrat	25	23	25	25	25	25	25	0
Independent, leaning Democrat	10	7	8	9	10	11	12	+2
Independent, middle-of-road	5	9	8	8	11	13	14	+9
Independent, leaning Republican	7	8	7	6	9	11	10	+3
Weak Republican	14	14	13	13	14	13	14	0
Strong Republican	13	15	14	11	10	10	9	–4

*(data in percents)
Source: Survey Research Center, University of Michigan, data published in the National Journal's Election '80 Handbook, *October 20, 1979, p. 1731.*

Table 2-8. Ideological and Partisan Identification in the US (hypothetical data)

Party Identification	Liberal	Middle-of-the-road	Conservative	Total
Democratic	12	21	7	40
Independent	4	21	12	37
Republican	4	7	12	23
Total	20	49	31	100

Note: The marginals for ideological and partisan groups are taken from recent national public opinion surveys.

years.[18] In any case, this has not produced any marked improvement in the strength of the Republican party, which was hurt by the Watergate affair. The situation is not at all clear. In some policy areas, popular attitudes indeed seem to have become more conservative, but in others they have not. An AP/NBC News poll in late 1979 on the issues of the 1970s concluded that Americans had become more conservative in areas such as defense spending, school busing and the death penalty, but more liberal on women's rights, premarital sex, and gun control. The Associated Press summary concluded that events of the 1970s made the conservative and liberal labels even less useful than they were before.[19]

CITIZEN PARTICIPATION

The many interrelated belief patterns summarized above determine to a large degree the individual citizen's choice of whether and how to participate in the political system.

Just how extensive is such participation in the United States? To begin with, while it is not as high as that exhibited in some other countries, including the few that artificially attempt to raise participation levels by means of fines and other sanctions against nonvoting, it is relatively high compared with the democratic world as a whole and quite high when compared with the totalitarian world and with those places where political organization is relatively primitive or undeveloped. About 60 percent of the American electorate votes in presidential elections, but slightly less than half turn out in off-presidential years. Presidential-year voting ranged between 59 and 63 percent from 1952 to 1968, but dropped below 55 percent in 1976, by whch time the 18-year-old-vote amendment had been added to the Constitution. Voting for US representatives since 1950 has varied between 49 and 59 percent in presidential election years and between 35 and 46 percent in off-presidential election years.[20]

Regional Differences

There is considerable variation in turnout by region. Using the 1976 presidential election as a case study, one finds turnout far above the national norm in the six New England states, the Great Lakes and Northern Plains states,

18. Phillips, *The Emerging Republican Majority, op. cit.,* and Rusher, *The Making of the New Majority Party, op. cit.*
19. "Opinions Fluctuate During a Decade," Decade supplement to Sioux Falls (S.D.) *Argus-Leader,* December 30, 1979.
20. *1979 US Statistical Abstract.*

and the Northern Rocky Mountain and two Pacific Northwest states. Low turnout areas, all having relatively high nonwhite population ratios, are those of the South Atlantic seaboard, the Southeast, and the Southwest. The two most populous states, California and New York, were slightly below the national average in 1976.

Voting participation in presidential primaries is considerably lower than it is in the general election. Data from the 1976 primaries show that the turnout rate did not reach 50 percent in any state; the range was between a high of 44.2 percent in Oregon and a low of 11.5 percent in Rhode Island, with a national average of only 28 percent. Western and midwestern states tend to have relatively high presidential primary turnout rates, but the pattern is somewhat mixed—in the over-40-percent-turnout rate category are Oregon, West Virginia, and Wisconsin; in the 30–39 percent category are Arkansas, California, Florida, Georgia, Indiana, Montana, Nebraska, New Hampshire, and South Dakota; in the 20–29 percent category are Alabama, Idaho, Illinois, Maryland, Massachusetts, Michigan, Nevada, North Carolina, Ohio, Pennsylvania, Texas, and Vermont; and in the 10–19 percent category are Kentucky, New Jersey, Rhode Island, and Tennessee.[21] Among the factors that might influence presidential primary turnout in a given state are the number and identity of candidates running in that state, the amount and quality of electioneering, the timing of the primary (early, middle, or late in the long-drawn-out primary season), the type of primary, and the state's laws and traditions regulating or affecting access to the primary ballot.

Kinds of Participation

A discussion of levels of political participation must take account of the fact that participation takes many forms besides voting. Fewer than half of the public has high interest in election campaigns or reads about public affairs regularly.[22] About a third of adult Americans try to persuade others on how to vote; roughly one in six has written to a public official expressing an opinion or has worn a campaign button or placed a bumper sticker on his automobile; about one in ten has contributed money to a political party or candidate; about one in twenty has worked for a party or candidate during a campaign; and fewer than one in one hundred has run for or held public office.[23] Lester Milbrath has labeled the various degrees of political activity as gladiatorial,

21. National Journal's *Election '80 Handbook,* October 20, 1979, pp. 1733–1735.
22. Greenstein, *op. cit.,* p. 11.
23. *Ibid.,* and Keefe, *op. cit.,* p. 105.

transitional, and spectator activities; many Americans—the apathetics, perhaps 25 percent of the adult population—are not actively involved at all.[24]

Political participation is relatively extensive among those with college educations, professional and managerial occupations, farm operators, and trade-union members, while blacks, unskilled workers, and those with no more than grade school educations are less likely to have high levels of participation.[25]

Another aspect of political behavior is the degree to which members of politically relevant groups support candidates of the two major parties. Table 2-9 summarizes information about voting patterns in the 1978 congressional races. Democratic candidates in that year received strongest support among blacks, liberals, Jews, the lowest income group, and the youngest voters. Group support for Republican candidates was much more evenly spread; relatively speaking, Republicans did better among whites, conservatives, Protestants, the highest income group, and the oldest voters, but in no case was the Republican edge as marked as the Democratic margins.

One should note, however, that party identification is far from being a perfect indicator of vote choice. Year after year, large numbers of Democrats and Republicans vote for candidates of the opposing party; Table 2-10 illustrates this relationship with reference to the elections of 1948 (Truman-Dewey) and 1952 (Eisenhower-Stevenson).

Investigation of presidential voting results in the most recent elections shows how party strength varies from state to state. The most Democratic states have been Massachusetts, Rhode Island, New York, Pennsylvania, West Virginia, Maryland, Minnesota, Arkansas, Texas, and Hawaii, and the District of Columbia—in those states, the Republican presidential ticket won only in 1972, Nixon's landslide year. The next most Democratic in terms of presidential victories 1960–1976 were Connecticut, Delaware, North Carolina, Missouri, Louisiana, Mississippi, Alabama, and Georgia; in the last four, the Republicans won in 1964 (the Goldwater year) and 1972. The remaining states gave majorities to the Republican ticket in at least three of the five races. By this method of measurement, Arizona appears to be the most Republican

24. The complete Milbrathian hierarchy of political involvement lists the following activities in descending order: holding public or party office, being a candidate for office, soliciting political funds, attending a caucus or a strategy meeting, becoming an active member in a political party, contributing time in a political campaign, attending a political meeting or rally, making a monetary contribution to a party or candidate, contacting a public official or a political leader, wearing a button or putting a sticker on the car, attempting to talk another person into voting a certain way, initiating a political discussion, voting, and exposing oneself to political stimuli. Lester Milbrath, *op. cit.* p. 18.
25. Greenstein, *op. cit.*, p. 19, and Keefe, *op. cit.*, p. 107.

Table 2-9.   Group Voting Support for Party Candidates for US House of Representatives, 1978 General Election

Group		Voting for Democratic Candidates	Voting for Republican Candidates
Race:	Black	83	17
	Spanish	61	39
	White/other	54	46
Party:	Democratic	82	18
	Republican	14	86
	Independent	53	47
Ideology:	Liberal	77	23
	Moderate	61	39
	Conservative	39	61
Religion:	Protestant	48	52
	Catholic	66	34
	Jewish	79	21
Income:	under $10,000	64	36
	$10,000–15,000	59	41
	$15,000–25,000	57	43
	Over $25,000	46	54
Age:	18–29 years	62	38
	30–44	57	43
	45–59	56	44
	Over 60 years	53	47

*(data are percents)

Source: CBS News/New York Times survey, November 7, 1978. The sample included 8,933 respondents, interviewed as they left the polls. Published in Public Opinion, *November/December 1978, p. 21.*

Table 2-10. Party Identification and Voting for President, 1948 and 1952

Voted for:	Strong Democrats	Weak Democrats	Independents & Nonpartisans	Strong Republicans	Weak Republicans
1948					
Truman (Dem)	96	91	55	19	4
Dewey (Rep)	4	9	45	81	96
Total	100	100	100	100	100
Did not vote	30	45	46	34	15
1952					
Stevenson (Dem)	84	62	34	6	1
Eisenhower (Rep)	16	38	66	94	99
Total	100	100	100	100	100
Did not vote	25	31	33	23	8

*(data are percents)

Source: Adapted from Figure 3 in Fred Greenstein, The American Party System and the American People, *second edition (Englewood Cliffs, N.J.: Prentice-Hall, 1970), p. 41, based on Angus Campbell et al,* Elections and the Political Order *(New York: Wiley, 1966), pp. 66, 70.*

state, having gone to the Republican ticket all five times. Another measure of party strength is based on the average percentage of the popular vote for president. In the same sequence of five presidential elections, 1960–1976, Massachusetts, Rhode Island, Arkansas, Minnesota, Louisiana, and Hawaii rank as the most Democratic states, while Nebraska, Utah, Idaho, Wyoming, Kansas, and Arizona rank as the most Republican. The mean Republican presidential percentage for Nebraska was 60, compared to the national median of 49, Massachusetts' 37, and the District of Columbia's 18.[26]

26. Calculated by Donna Ball from data in the National Journal's *Election '80 Handbook,* foldout sheet after p. 1748.

How the Voter Decides

Now we are ready to address the critical question of how various factors exert independent influence on the citizen's voting decision. The final act, of course, is the decision to vote for or against a specific candidate. Our inquiry will proceed along two lines. First, what are the individual citizen's options with respect to the several contests on the ballot at a given election; here, our concern is with straight-ticket and split-ticket voting. Most findings indicate that ticket-splitting is a growing phenomenon in the United States. DeVries and Tarrance, the writers who did the most to dramatize the rise of ticket-splitting in the early 1970s, were careful to distinguish contemporary cross-party voting from the older view that saw the "independent" voter as a person having comparatively little involvement with or knowledge about the political process.[27]

A look at voting patterns in the 1972 races in a hypothetical state will serve to illustrate the curious ways in which a vote can be divided. George McGovern and Richard Nixon at the top of the ballot provided an ideological as well as a partisan choice; this was not so clearly the case with the 1976 presidential candidates, Gerald Ford and Jimmy Carter. In the state's gubernatorial race in 1972, let us say that the Democrats nominated a centrist, business-oriented elder statesman with experience in the state legislature and that the Republicans nominated a controversial, tough, populist law enforcement officer making his first bid for statewide office. In the senatorial race, we will posit that the Democrats nominated a fiery, antiestablishment, conservation-oriented veteran congressman who had represented one of the state's seven congressional districts for a decade and that the Republicans nominated a personable Presbyterian clergyman who was a newcomer to politics. The combinations and permutations of party choice with but three contests are considerable and interesting in their many possibilities. Table 2-11 shows the eight patterns that could be followed by voters in the three contests. The number of voters ending up in each of the eight categories would, of course, reveal the outcome of each of the races.

The second line of inquiry attempts to sort out the various factors an individual considers in making a choice in a particular contest. The principal factors are the socioeconomic status of the voter; the party affiliation, ideological

27. DeVries and Tarrance, *op. cit.* See also Greenstein, *op. cit.,* p. 41, and Keefe, *op. cit.,* p. 9. Nie, Verba, and Petrocik note that "the decline in partisanship can be measured in three ways: by the proportion who are Independents, by vote switching, and by the expression of negative attitudes toward parties. Each is a different and independent measure. Each moves at the same time, beginning around 1968." Nie *et al, op. cit.,* p. 282.

Table 2-11. Voting Pattern Types for 1972 Contests

	President	*Senator*	*Governor*
(A) Straight Democratic:	McGovern-D	Firebrand-D	Eldersent-D
(B) Split (2 Democratic):	Nixon-R	Firebrand-D	Eldersent-D
(C) Split (2 Democratic):	McGovern-D	Firebrand-D	Toughguy-R
(D) Split (2 Democratic):	McGovern-D	Newcomer-R	Eldersent-D
(E) Split (2 Republican):	McGovern-D	Newcomer-R	Toughguy-R
(F) Split (2 Republican):	Nixon-R	Newcomer-R	Eldersent-D
(G) Split (2 Republican):	Nixon-R	Firebrand-D	Toughguy-R
(H) Straight Republican:	Nixon-R	Newcomer-R	Toughguy-R

Note: More combinations are possible in cases where a voter does not vote on one or more of the three contests. See the discussion and charts in Walter DeVries and V. Lance Tarrance, *The Ticket-Splitter: A New Force in American Politics* (Grand Rapids, Mich.: William B. Eerdsmans Publishing Company, 1972), pp. 127–130.

positions, and specific issue positions of the voter and the candidates; and the voter's reaction to the personalities and campaign activities of the candidates.

Conclusions from a 1968 study that involved several simultaneous samples (the entire nation, four regions, and thirteen individual states) indicated that the two most powerful factors in vote choice were party proximity (that is, the relative closeness of the voter to each of the three presidential candidates

Figure 2-1. Issue Proximity on Control of Violence, 1968 Presidential Candidates

Item: "The government should control riots and violence."

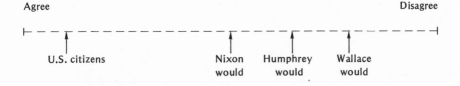

Agree   Disagree

U.S. citizens   Nixon   Humphrey   Wallace
                       would   would   would

Source: Adapted from data in Merle Black, David E. Kovenock, and William C. Reynolds, Political Attitudes in the Nation and the States (Chapel Hill, N.C.: Institute for Research in Social Science, University of North Carolina, 1974), pp. 96–99.

of 1968—Hubert Humphrey, Richard Nixon, and George Wallace—on a party continuum, as perceived by the voter) and issue proximity (the perceived closeness of the voter to each of the three presidential candidates on several issue dimensions such as open housing, peace in Vietnam, law and order, and the cost of living). The idea of issue proximity is shown in Figure 2-1. These approaches have been adapted by Nie, Verba, and Petrocik to suggest linear and geometrical models of attitudinal relationships between voters and candidates. They discuss, speculatively, to be sure, the positions of the presidential candidates in the period 1952–1972 with respect to hypothetical scales categorizing the issue positons of the public; these scales are shown in Figure 2-2. Then they show a battery of five scales relating to the 1972 presidential candidates, representing the issues of government-guaranteed jobs, tax increases on the rich, Vietnam, legalization of marijuana, and urban unrest. The scales show where the public places itself on these five issues and also where the public places the candidates; there is an unusually large distance between the perceived positions of the two candidates, and McGovern was perceived as an "outlying" or noncentrist candidate (see Figure 2-3).

Another way to look at the voting decision is as the sum of evaluations a voter makes about a particular candidate's personal image, his position on various salient issues, and his level of support among various politically relevant

Figure 2-2. Scales Showing Candidate Stands on Issues (generalized)

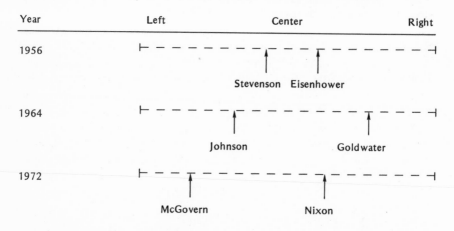

Source: Norman H. Nie, Sidney Verba, and John R. Petrocik, The Changing American Voter (Cambridge, Mass.: Harvard University Press, 1976), p. 309.

Figure 2-3. Public Perceptions of the Positions of McGovern (M) and Nixon (N) on Five Issues of 1972

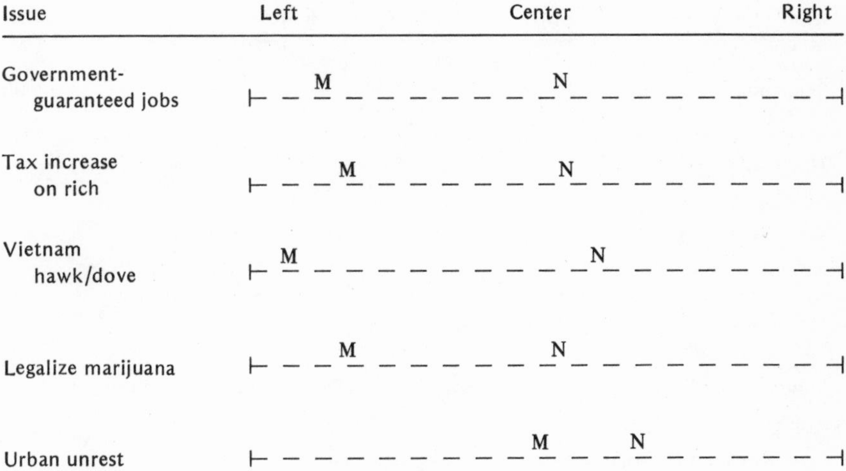

Issue	Left	Center	Right
Government-guaranteed jobs	├ — M — — — — — —	N — — — — — — — ┤	
Tax increase on rich	├ — — M — — — — —	N — — — — — — — ┤	
Vietnam hawk/dove	├ M — — — — — — —	— N — — — — — ┤	
Legalize marijuana	├ — — M — — — — —	N — — — — — — ┤	
Urban unrest	├ — — — — — — — —	M — — N — — — — ┤	

Source: Same as for Figure 2-2, p. 310. The original chart also factored in respondent self-placement, which has not been attempted here.

groups. This is precisely what Ronald Van Doren attempted in his interesting precampaign analysis of twenty-five potential presidential candidates in 1972.[28] Van Doren's approach can be summarized here by extracting the analytical matrices for issues that he presented for the two candidates who evenutally won their respective party's nominations (see Figure 2-4).

A Gallup Poll conducted in 1979 to assess public attitudes toward President Carter and Senator Kennedy illustrated some of the personal characteristics thought to be important in determining how individuals will vote. Carter was more favorably perceived by the public on several characteristics: as being a person of high moral principles, as a religious person, and as a person who displays good judgment in a crisis. Kennedy, on the other hand, was viewed as a person with strong leadership qualities, as a person whose stand on issues was known, as a person with a well-defined program for moving the country ahead, and as a person of exceptional abilities.[29]

28. Ronald Van Doren, *Charting the Candidates '72* (New York: Pinnacle Books, 1972).
29. "Candidates and Character," *Parade* magazine supplement to Sioux Falls (S.D.) *Argus-Leader*, November 4, 1979, p. 14.

Figure 2-4. Another View of the Positions of McGovern (M) and Nixon (N) on Several Issues of 1972

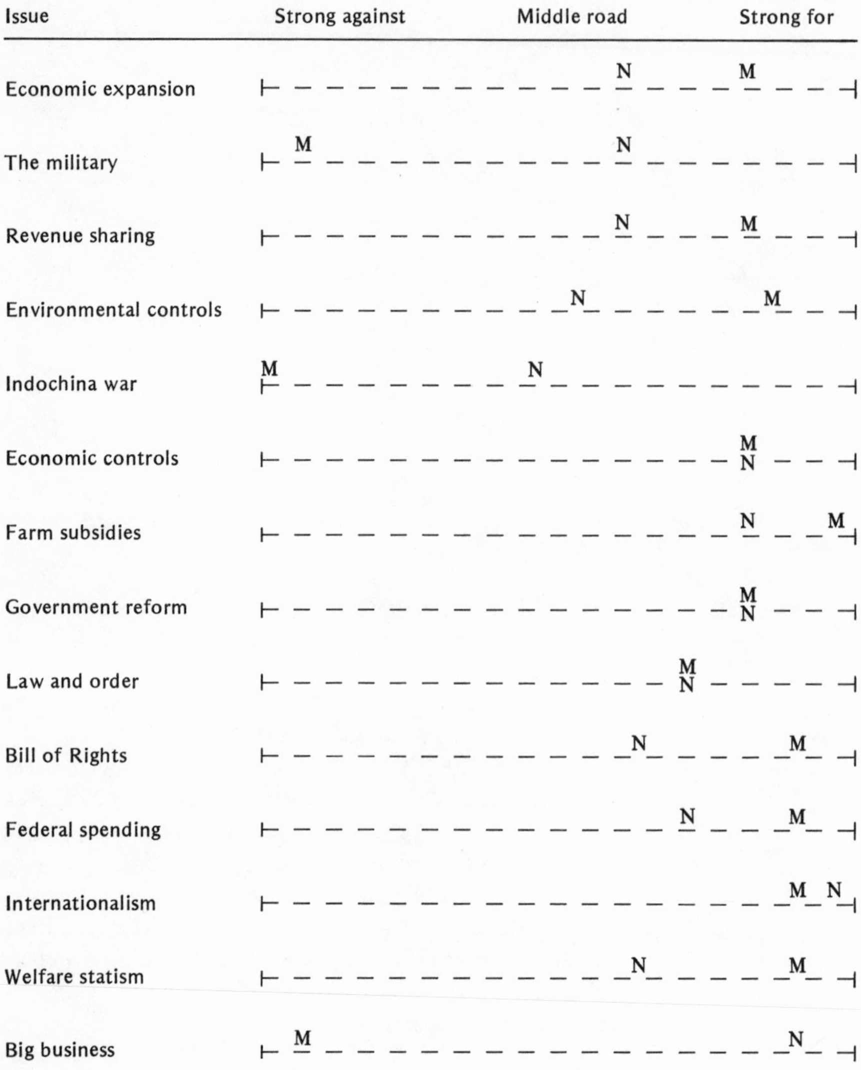

Issue	Strong against	Middle road	Strong for
Economic expansion		N	M
The military	M	N	
Revenue sharing		N	M
Environmental controls		N	M
Indochina war	M	N	
Economic controls			M N
Farm subsidies			N M
Government reform			M N
Law and order			M N
Bill of Rights		N	M
Federal spending		N	M
Internationalism			M N
Welfare statism		N	M
Big business	M		N

Source: Adapted from Ronald Van Doren, Charting the Candidates '72 (New York: Pinnacle Books, 1972), pp. 137, 175.

This line of analysis can be extended, through some admittedly speculative leaps, by referring to the 1978 US Senate campaign in Iowa that involved incumbent liberal Democrat Dick Clark and conservative Republican challenger Roger Jepsen. Basing our judgments at least partly on the foregoing discussion, we might begin by saying that certain factors are critical to the voting decision, and that the percentages assigned to each factor represent, at least roughly, their relative importance in determining the final choice of the voter. Thus we will assume, for purposes of discussion, that party affiliation accounts for 30 percent of the vote decision, that the personal characteristics of the two candidates account for 25 percent, that their positions on major issues account for 30 percent, and that their general ideological orientation accounts for the remaining 15 percent of the decision. The next step is to divide each of the four factors between the two candidates. Since 1978 party registration in Iowa showed the Democrats with a slight edge over the Republicans,[30] Clark is assigned 16 points and Jepsen 14 points for the party factor. Hypothetically, but on the basis of at least observing the two candidates frequently during the campaign, the personal characteristics factor might be divided in Clark's favor, 17 to 8 points. The issues factor is sorted out into three segments, based on the level of debate in the course of the 1978 campaign—20 points for the abortion question, 5 points for the Panama Canal treaty issue, and 5 points for the right-to-work issue (other issues could, of course, be incorporated into this model). Senator Clark supported abortion, supported the treaty, and opposed state right-to-work laws, while Jepsen took the contrary position on each issue. The abortion factor is then sorted out 15 to 5 points in Jepsen's favor, the treaty issue at 4 to 1 in Jepsen's favor, and the right-to-work issue at 3 to 2 in Jepsen's favor; these figures in total give Jepsen a margin of 22 to 8 points on issues.[31] The ideological factor might be divided 10 to Jepsen, 5 to Clark. Summing up the points for Clark and Jepsen on each of the four factors produces a total distribution (Jepsen, 54 percent; Clark, 46 percent) that is close to the actual vote distribution (Jepsen, 52 percent; Clark, 48 percent). The same factors would be at work simultaneously for each of the contests on the 1978 Iowa ballot. That day, voters were also deciding several congressional contests and a gubernatorial contest between incumbent Republican Robert Ray and his Democratic challenger, Jerome Fitzgerald. Issues were

30. The actual 1978 Iowa party registration figures were: Independent, 544,814; Democratic, 541,081; Republican, 471,893.
31. These speculations about the impact of issues could be verified by means of public opinion polls.

much less dramatic in the race for governor, so our voting factors might have split as follows:

Factor	Ray (R)	Fitzgerald (D)
Party (30 percent)	14	16
Personal characteristics (35 percent)	25	10
Issues (20 percent)	12	8
Ideology (15 percent)	9	6
Total (100 percent)	60	40

The actual division of the vote was 59 percent to 41 percent in Governor Ray's favor.[32]

It should be noted that this model does not take into account the name recognition of the candidates at the beginning of the campaign or of quantitative or qualitative differences in the dissemination of campaign messages through the various media; a really superior campaign effort, after all, can change the vote to a degree, beyond the influence of party, personal characteristics, issues, and ideology.

Are the decisions of voters rational? Political scientist V.O. Key, Jr., at the end of a distinguished career, concluded in a posthumous book that they were.[33] More recently, columnist David Broder wrote that the voting in the 1980 New Hampshire Democratic presidential primary conveyed "a reassuring sense of rationality in the voting decisions." Based on the results of ABC News interviews of voters as they left the polls, he decided that: those most concerned about the problems of the poor and elderly went for Kennedy, three to one; those most concerned about inflation and energy favored Kennedy and Brown over Carter; those most concerned about foreign policy favored Carter overwhelmingly; those most concerned about leadership and ability rated Kennedy ahead of Carter; and those most concerned about honesty and stability strongly favored Carter.[34]

32. In the same 1978 election, Iowans elected three Republicans and three Democrats to the US House of Representatives and gave control of both houses of the state legislature to the Republican party—28-22 in the Senate and 56-44 in the House of Representatives.
33. V.O. Key, Jr., with the assistance of Milton C. Cummings, *The Responsible Electorate* (Cambridge, Mass.: Harvard University Press, 1966).
34. David S. Broder, "Voter Turnout—and Turnaround," *Washington Post,* March 2, 1980, p. C7.

This review of voter motivation and behavior is necessarily selective and, to a point, speculative, because political science has not yet become an exact science; in areas where it has become more exact, it tends to be complicated and trivial. It is hoped that new scholarly inquiry will sharpen our knowledge as fundamental political concepts are more rigorously defined and as research findings become better integrated through intelligent and persistent replication.

EIGHT AMERICAN PERSPECTIVES

The reasons for the lack of consistency, clarity, and predictability on the part of American political parties lie essentially in the highly diversified and often contradictory aspirations and beliefs of the citizens. The loosely knit hierarchies and ambiguous policy positions of American parties are direct reflections of a highly volatile and varied citizenry. Politically speaking, Americans don't fit into neat categorical packages. Although Americans are often classifed into groups by scholars and journalists—we may talk, for instance, of the labor vote, the black vote, the farm vote—as individuals we defy these categories. Each American is actually a member of several groups, and these multiple memberships subject us to cross-pressures with respect to every political decision we are called upon to make.

There is a great diversity of ethnic and cultural backgrounds in the United States. Coupled with this is a contrary but complementary phenomenon that Amitai Etzioni has characterized as the essential changelessness of human nature—it is easy enough to change a man's smoking habits from Lucky Strikes to Marlboros, but quite another matter to convince him to stop smoking cigarettes altogether.[35] American attitudes resist both change and order. There is evidence that Americans tend to believe and behave politically most like their families and friends, but it is possible that the person closest in political attitudes to a 63-year-old flower-shop owner in Kalamazoo is a 22-year-old waitress in Seattle, or that the person closest to a New Mexico rancher is a Pennsylvania steamfitter.

One way to visualize the differences that exist is to consider the positions of eight hypothetical persons chosen to represent the diversity of perspectives that characterizes American society.

Consider first a union member working in an automobile plant in one of the large factories located in the industrial belt that includes Buffalo, Cleveland,

35. Amitai Etzioni, "Human Beings Are Not Very Easy to Change After All: An Unjoyful Message and Its Implications for Social Programs," *Saturday Review,* June 3, 1972, pp. 45–47.

Toledo, Detroit, Chicago, and Milwaukee. Much of his political vision comes to him through the modifying lens of his union organization, with its long-standing interest in partisan politics as a means of enhancing the political and economic status of workers. For all that, it is probable that there are many differences between his preferences and the union's. Traditionally liberal in terms of socioeconomic policies at the national level, factory workers as individuals have evidently changed their ideas toward many phases of public policy, as exemplified by the "hard hat" attitudes of the early 1970s, when many union members shunned Senator George McGovern, the Democratic presidential candidate, in favor of President Nixon's reelection. Declines in American automobile production in the face of small-car imports and rising gasoline prices in the late 1970s have also concerned this citizen.

Consider then a retired elementary school teacher in a small New Jersey city. If typical of her vocational group, she would have a liberal orientation with respect to most areas of American national issues, and would in her retirement be enjoying the benefits of the social legislation of the New Deal era. Her view of politics is likely to differ from that of the auto worker because of her geographical location and the fact that she has completed her wage-earning years.

For another angle, consider how the political world looks to a university student in Georgia who is studying architecture, preparing for a career whose success is likely to be affected to a large extent by the amount of public building undertaken by federal, state, or local governments. Any young person is concerned about prospects for gainful employment in the thirty or forty years that will constitute his productive earning period.

A fourth perspective is offered in the case of a cornbelt farmer in western Illinois who farms a half-section of land and is primarily occupied with raising corn, sorghum, and other feed grains that he sells on the grain market or feeds to livestock. He is concerned about the success of a different kind of economic activity, and is probably not interested in problems of industrial centers or ghettos.

A fifth view is offered by a young woman in California whose husband is completing a hitch in the armed forces. How long will she be required to work in order to maintain an acceptable living level for the children she expects to have? What kind of job will her husband be able to find when he is discharged? Where will they settle?

A female bank executive in a small county seat on the high plains of Colorado would have yet another perspective. Will the area's agricultural produce strengthen her bank's position? What role will government farm policy play in the area's economic growth? What will be the effect on her family of proposed changes in state and local tax systems? More personally, what is her own future as a woman in a business that men have traditionally dominated?

And how does the world look to a black retail clerk working in a shopping center in an eastern Texas city? Can he hope to advance as fast as his white counterparts? Will his children have an adequate opportunity for quality education and good jobs?

A dentist in an older New England city is going to be thinking about different components of the political world. He will probably be concerned about the deterioration of the downtown business district where his office is located. Can federal programs save his city? Or would this be an opportune time to move to the suburbs, or to the South? How does he relate to the strong ethnic factions that dominate the region's political and social life?

These sketches suggest that our political life in America is highly diversified because our leaders are obliged to respond to localized needs and preferences; Toledo, New Brunswick, Atlanta, Galesburg, San Bernardino, Fort Morgan, Beaumont, and Worcester are only eight among thousands of American perspectives.

SUMMARY

This chapter highlighted our ambiguous attitudes toward democracy and our political party system, and our rather low levels of voting turnout and interest in politics. The fact that our system is formally open and visible, even inviting, makes us worry even more about voting turnout. Low participation may be said to result from at least three attitudes: (1) impatience with the American political system, the feeling that parties and candidates are not offering clearly different options to the voters, (2) basic distrust of democracy as a method of government, the feeling that most voters do not vote intelligently and that we would be better off letting the experts and the planners make the decisions, and (3) benign neglect, the feeling that one is as well off as can be expected, and that in any case political involvement is not likely to improve one's lot in life.

These feelings to a large extent result from the fact that we are a vast and highly diversified nation, an amalgam of regional cultures. How Americans will vote can be predicted only generally, for all Americans are subject to contradictory political pressures, some pushing the voter toward the Democratic ticket, others toward the Republican side, and a large segment of Americans—the so-called independents and ticket-splitters—do not vote consistently for the same party over the years or up and down the ballot. In making their choices, Americans, in contrast to Europeans, are significantly affected by several factors in addition to the party affiliation of the candidates, namely, (1) the personalities of the candidates, (2) the candidates' stand on intensive, single-issue problems such as abortion or busing and more generalized class interests such as fiscal policy, labor-management policy, trade policy, and welfare policy, and (3) generalized ideological appeals, typically subsumed under the labels "conservative" and "liberal."

Chapter 3
The Party in the Political System

The political party in America is an amorphous institution. As a social structure, according to Frank Sorauf, it has three major manifestations.[1] First, it can be seen as being a part of the electorate, a group of citizens who regularly support and vote for the party's candidates. This aspect was one of the major concerns of the previous chapter. The second manifestation may be seen in the officers (chairmen, committeemen, treasurers) and institutions (conventions, committees, caucuses) of the formal party organization, which exist at each level of government, from the national down through the state, district, county, municipal, township, and precinct levels. These areas will be the subject of chapters 5, 6, and 9. The third manifestation, which is one of the concerns of this chapter, is the party in government. How many Democrats and Republicans are there in office in the federal and various state governments, and how do these partisan public officials behave in office?

We have already seen that American parties have fallen upon hard times, and that an increasing percentage of citizens identify with neither the Democrats nor the Republicans. One reason for this evident disenchantment is that people feel there is simply not much in either party with which they want to identify.

In a more rational political system, where there are policy differences between parties, where these differences are recognized by most voters, where campaigns are waged on the basis of these differences, and where these differences are boldly reflected in the policy decisions that will be made by the party that gains power, parties are strong, visible, cohesive, consistent, responsible, and predictable. These adjectives, unfortunately, do not accurately describe political parties in the United States today.

American parties are widely criticized for being ambiguous and ambivalent with respect to policy. For example, while some Republicans and some Democrats favor stricter control of guns, others oppose it. Furthermore, there is no clear conflict between Democratic and Republican positions on many major issues, such as what to do about the hostages in Tehran, development of nuclear power plants, legalization of abortion, or subsidies for the Chrysler Corporation. Lacking such differences, our parties do not provide adequate

1. Sorauf, *op. cit.,* pp. 9-12.

clues to citizens who have policy preferences and want to vote for candidates or parties who support those preferences.

So, while the American citizen has a clear voting choice every other year—he or she can vote for the Democrat, for the Republican, or for neither—it is by no means clear that the choice carries with it any serious or meaningful implications.

This chapter will survey the general state of American political parties, measuring the relative strength of the two major parties across the years and in different states and attempting to assess the degree and consequences of political ambiguity and inconsistency. These concerns are necessary introductions to the chapters that follow, which will describe our political party institutions, organization, officers, and processes.

THE PARTY IN GOVERNMENT

The purpose of elections is to allow citizens to change the personnel running their government, and thus to affect the direction and perhaps the style of their government. Any free election has the potential to bring drastic change in the government. Elections that result in victory for the incumbent party—as in 1956, 1964, and 1972—ordinarily produce few changes in personnel or in policies. Elections that oust the incumbent executive or legislative majority—as in 1952, 1960, and 1976—invest the new government with the power to pass and to implement new policies.

How have elections changed party control in the federal government since 1929? Over the past fifty years, party control over both the executive and legislative branches of the federal government has shifted twice, in 1932 and 1952. The 1930 election, in which the Democrats won control of the House of Representatives, was a prelude to the broader Democratic sweep of 1932 under Franklin Delano Roosevelt. Roosevelt's New Deal established Democratic dominance of the national government for two decades, except for a brief period of Republican control over the Congress achieved in the 1946 election. Democratic domination at the federal level has continued to this day, the only exceptions being the four terms won by Dwight Eisenhower (1952 and 1956) and Richard Nixon (1968 and 1972). The party control picture is shown in Table 3-1.

Patterns of Control

There have been, in the fifty years since 1929, thirty years of Democratic control of both branches, four years of Republican control (1929-30 and

Table 3-1. Party Control of the Presidency, Senate, and House of Representatives, 1929-1980

Years	President	Senate	House of Representatives
1929-30	Republican	Republican	Republican
1931-32	Republican	Republican	Democratic
1933-34	Democratic	Democratic	Democratic
1935-36	Democratic	Democratic	Democratic
1937-38	Democratic	Democratic	Democratic
1939-40	Democratic	Democratic	Democratic
1941-42	Democratic	Democratic	Democratic
1943-44	Democratic	Democratic	Democratic
1945-46	Democratic	Democratic	Democratic
1947-48	Democratic	Republican	Republican
1949-50	Democratic	Democratic	Democratic
1951-52	Democratic	Democratic	Democratic
1953-54	Republican	Republican	Republican
1955-56	Republican	Democratic	Democratic
1957-58	Republican	Democratic	Democratic
1959-60	Republican	Democratic	Democratic
1961-62	Democratic	Democratic	Democratic
1963-64	Democratic	Democratic	Democratic
1965-66	Democratic	Democratic	Democratic
1967-68	Democratic	Democratic	Democratic
1969-70	Republican	Democratic	Democratic
1971-72	Republican	Democratic	Democratic
1973-74	Republican	Democratic	Democratic
1975-76	Republican	Democratic	Democratic
1977-78	Democratic	Democratic	Democratic
1979-80	Democratic	Democratic	Democratic

1953-54), two years of virtual Republican control (1931-32), two years with a Democratic president (Truman) and a Republican Congress (1947-48), and fourteen years with a Republican president and a Democratic Congress (1955-60 and 1969-76). Each of the shifts brought significant change in policy direction. The 1932 election brought the massive New Deal legislative package of 1933. Republican successess in 1946 and 1952 resulted in strenuous, though generally unsuccessful, efforts to reverse many New Deal initiatives. John Kennedy's election in 1960 brought forth more than oratory, though many of the final policy victories had to wait upon Lyndon Johnson's halcyon years of 1964 and 1965, the years of the Great Society legislation (and Vietnam escalation). Richard Nixon's election in 1968 and Jimmy Carter's victory in 1976 are perhaps less convincing examples of policy redirection following an election that produced change in party control, but even here Nixon imposed economic controls, slowly liquidated our Vietnam involvement, pushed revenue sharing, initiated rapprochement with Red China, and adjusted the ideological balance of the Supreme Court. While noting that election results are often unfavorable to the incumbent party, it is well to keep in mind that federal elections frequently return the same party to power; this has been the result in thirteen elections out of the twenty-five held from 1930 to 1978 inclusive.

State Patterns

Each of the fifty states exhibits the same kind of potential executive/legislative control relationships, with the exception of Nebraska, which has a nonpartisan legislature. Table 3-2 summarizes party control data for selected states over the past twenty years. Here we see several notable patterns. Only Georgia exhibits total one-party domination, with the Democratic party in control of the governorship and both chambers of the state legislature in every biennial period. California and Connecticut have been predominantly Democratic, while Oregon has been Democratic more often than not, but with a larger Republican presence (see Table 3-3). Colorado, New York, Indiana, and Maine have had more Republican that Democratic control at the state level in the past two decades. Oregon and Maine have each experienced a unified state government for only two biennial periods during the twenty years.

The California and New York experiences are especially illuminating. Each state contributed a major Republican political leader—Governor Ronald Reagan of California, a contender for the presidential nomination in 1968, 1976, and 1980, and Governor Nelson Rockefeller of New York, a contender in 1960, 1964, and 1968. Reagan served as governor for eight years, but enjoyed Republican control of both chambers of the state legislature only once, and then

Table 3-2. Party Control of Governorships and Legislature, Selected States, 1961–1979

Year	Governor	Senate	House	Governor	Senate	House
	COLORADO			CONNECTICUT		
1961	Demo	Demo	Demo	Demo	Demo	Repub
1963	Repub	Repub	Repub	Demo	Demo	Repub
1965	Repub	Repub	Demo	Demo	Demo	Repub
1967	Repub	Repub	Repub	Demo	Demo	Demo
1969	Repub	Repub	Repub	Demo	Demo	Demo
1971	Repub	Repub	Repub	Repub	Demo	Demo
1973	Repub	Repub	Repub	Repub	Repub	Repub
1975	Demo	Repub	Demo	Demo	Demo	Demo
1977	Demo	Repub	Repub	Demo	Demo	Demo
1979	Demo	Repub	Repub	Demo	Demo	Demo
	CALIFORNIA			NEW YORK		
1961	Demo	Demo	Demo	Repub	Repub	Repub
1963	Demo	Demo	Demo	Repub	Repub	Repub
1965	Demo	Demo	Demo	Repub	Demo	Demo
1967	Repub	Demo	Demo	Repub	Repub	Demo
1969	Repub	Repub	Repub	Repub	Repub	Repub
1971	Repub	Demo	Demo	Repub	Repub	Repub
1973	Repub	(tie)	Demo	Repub	Repub	Repub
1975	Demo	Demo	Demo	Demo	Repub	Demo
1977	Demo	Demo	Demo	Demo	Repub	Demo
1979	Demo	Demo	Demo	Demo	Repub	Demo

Table 3-2, continued

Year	Governor	Senate	House	Governor	Senate	House
	INDIANA			OREGON		
1961	Demo	Demo	Repub	Repub	Demo	Demo
1963	Demo	Repub	Repub	Repub	Demo	Demo
1965	Demo	Demo	Demo	Repub	Demo	Repub
1967	Demo	Demo	Repub	Repub	Demo	Repub
1969	Repub	Repub	Repub	Repub	Demo	Repub
1971	Repub	Repub	Repub	Repub	Demo	Repub
1973	Repub	Repub	Repub	Repub	Demo	Demo
1975	Repub	Repub	Demo	Demo	Demo	Demo
1977	Repub	Demo	Repub	Demo	Demo	Demo
1979	Repub	Repub	Repub	Repub	Demo	Demo
	MAINE			GEORGIA		
1961	Repub	Repub	Repub	Demo	Demo	Demo
1963	Repub	Repub	Repub	Demo	Demo	Demo
1965	Repub	Demo	Demo	Demo	Demo	Demo
1967	Demo	Repub	Repub	Demo	Demo	Demo
1969	Demo	Repub	Repub	Demo	Demo	Demo
1971	Demo	Repub	Repub	Demo	Demo	Demo
1973	Demo	Repub	Repub	Demo	Demo	Demo
1975	Ind	Repub	Demo	Demo	Demo	Demo
1977	Ind	Repub	Demo	Demo	Demo	Demo
1979	Demo	Repub	Demo	Demo	Demo	Demo

by very narrow margins; in fact, the only times the Republican party could come close to taking control of a legislative chamber were during Reagan's tenure. Rockefeller, on the other hand, suffered Democratic control of the legislature only in the 1965-66 and 1967-68 periods, aberrations which were related to the 1964 Goldwater-Miller presidential ticket that was so notably unpopular in the urban East.

Success in congressional elections does not correlate perfectly with success in gubernatorial and legislative elections. California, which has been solidly Democratic at the state level since Reagan left the governor's chair in

Table 3-3. Party Control in Selected States, by State and by Year, Summary Table

State or Year	Democratic Control	Republican Control	Tied or Independent Control
California	23	6	1
Colorado	8	22	0
Connecticut	23	7	0
Georgia	30	0	0
Indiana	10	20	0
Maine	10	18	2
New York	9	21	0
Oregon	18	12	0
1961	15	9	0
1963	11	13	0
1965	15	9	0
1967	13	11	0
1969	8	16	0
1971	9	15	0
1973	7	16	1
1975	18	5	1
1977	17	6	1
1979	16	8	0

*(based on data in Table 3-2)

1975, has one Democratic and one Republican United States senator, and twenty-five Democratic and eighteen Republican representatives, close to an even standoff. Colorado, Indiana, and New York, all more Republican than California in state races, are less Republican than California in their congressional delegations (see Table 3-4). Obviously, different forces, groups, issues, and candidates are involved in congressional campaigns than in state races, another indication that American parties are anything but monolithic.

Margins of Strength

We have been discussing party strength in terms of which party controls the executive and legislative branches of federal or state government. Two other important dimensions of strength are the margins in seats by which the majority party controls a legislative chamber and the margins, in percentages of votes cast, by which a party wins a specific election.

The party control margins for the Colorado House of Representatives fluctuated considerably in the 1960s and 1970s—the Democratic margin of one seat in 1961 changed in 1963 to a Republican margin of seventeen seats, then back to a Democratic nineteen-seat margin in 1965, then a Republican return in 1967 with an eleven-seat margin that continued in 1969 and 1971 and fell to nine seats in 1973, then a Democratic return to power in 1975 (fol-

Table 3-4. Party Strength in Congressional Delegations for Selected States, 1979-80

	US SENATE		US HOUSE OF REPRESENTATIVES	
State	*Democratic*	*Republican*	*Democratic*	*Republican*
California	1	1	25	18
Colorado	1	1	3	2
Connecticut	1	1	5	1
Georgia	2	0	9	1
Indiana	1	1	7	4
Maine	1	1	0	2
New York	1	1	26	13
Oregon	0	2	4	0

lowing Nixon's resignation) with a thirteen-seat margin, then a Republican resurgence with a margin of five seats in 1977, and finally the 1979 Republican margin of eleven seats in 1979. Variations in party margins in the Georgia lower house have been larger (a sixty-nine-seat swing between 1963 and 1975) but less significant, since the Republican party did not get closer than one hundred thirty-four seats to the Democratic majority over the two decades. Since 1960, Democratic margins in the US House of Representatives have fluctuated between one hundred fifty-five seats in 1965 and fifty-one seats in both 1969 and 1973. Senate margins have also been exclusively Democratic during the twenty-year period, ranging between a high of thirty-six in 1965 and a low of ten seats in 1971.

Large margins in seats can be built on slender election-day voting majorities. Table 3-5 summarizes the closeness of general elections for the US House in 1978; the critical number is the percentage of seats won with less than 55 percent of the vote.

Larger proportions of midwestern and western congressional contests than eastern or southern contests were marginal in the 1960s and 1970s, and, generally speaking, Republican House members are slightly more likely to come from marginal districts than Democrats. The years 1964 and 1974 produced unusually high percentages of marginal contests, and both were Democratic landslide years, precipitated in the first case by the Johnson-Goldwater presidential race and in the second by the Watergate affair and President Nixon's resignation. Republican candidates recouped very well from 1964 in the 1966 congressional contests, but did not recover much of the ground lost in 1976. Urban districts in the 1970s were less likely than suburban, rural, or mixed districts to be marginal. These same urban districts have been the bulwark of Democratic control of the House of Representatives—84 percent of urban

Table 3-5. Election Margins, US House of Representatives, 1978 General Elections

	WINNER'S PERCENTAGE OF VOTE:			
	Under 55	*55 to 59.9*	*60 and over*	*Total*
Democrats	46	36	195	277
Republicans	28	25	105	158
Total	74	61	300	435

Source: Congressional Quarterly Weekly Report, March 31, 1979, p. 573

congressional contests were won by a Democrat in the elections of 1972, 1974, and 1976.[2]

Close election margins do not necessarily weaken the effectiveness of the winning candidate or the cohesion of the winning party. Lyndon Johnson (as senator) and John Kennedy (as president) won office by the slenderest of margins, but were aggressive in office. The Republican party in Congress in 1953-54, when it had narrow control of both chambers, was probably more cohesive than it was in succeeding Congresses after it had fallen out of power. Two examples of the difficulty Republicans had in getting along with themselves were the ousting of Minority Leader Joe Martin of Massachusetts by Charles Halleck of Indiana in 1959, and the subsequent ousting of Halleck by Gerald Ford of Michigan in 1965.

Influences on Party Strength

How can the temporal variances in party strength be explained? In each state there is what might be called a basic partisan disposition that is revealed only partially in the number of persons who register as Democrats, Republicans, or independents.[3] This disposition can change over the years, as the socioeconomic characteristics of the state's residents change in relation to the rest of the nation. This can occur in two principal ways. First, there are changes in the economic activity within the state that affect the political orientation of the population. Second, there are changes in the electorate caused by substantial migration into or out of the state and by the addition of new voters coming of voting age and the subtraction of other voters by death. Virginia and North Carolina have become less Democratic than they were in the 1930s, while the Democratic party has improved its position in Minnesota and Ohio. Thus, a state's basic partisan disposition is affected by events that temporarily increase or decrease the popularity of the major parties. Examples would include the charges of "Communism, corruption, and Korea" leveled against the Truman administration, the unrest in the plains states aimed at Agriculture Secretary Ezra Taft Benson's controversial farm policies, Russia's launching of Sputnik and its advances in Cuba, the presidential candidacy of

2. *Electing Congress* (Washington: *Congressional Quarterly, Inc.,* 1978), pp. 34, 36.
3. The term "independent" is used here to describe persons who are not affiliated with any political party, rather than members of an Independent party, a title which has been used in a number of states by many transient, unallied groups and at the national level by several presidential campaign efforts.

Barry Goldwater in 1964, the Vietnam War, the McGovern candidacy of 1972, and the Watergate scandal. These dramatic events affected party fortunes by moving the percentage of the votes received by the party's candidates up or down as many as ten points in state after state. In some cases, this kind of movement of voting percentages was enough to reverse party control in the state or nation. After the trauma receded in the public consciousness, the partisan vote distribution once again tended to seek its traditional level.

Events of larger significance for the party system—such as the Civil War of the 1860s, the monetary issue of the 1890s, and the New Deal of the 1930s—resulted in more enduring realignments of voters, bringing new parties to the fore, producing new majority parties, changing the composition of the parties themselves.[4]

STATE PARTY SYSTEMS

We have seen that there is wide variation from state to state in political party strength as measured in terms of the number of legislative seats held or in terms of the percentage of votes its candidates received in a particular election. Such quantitative data tell only part of the story; certain qualitative aspects of our political life are far more interesting and significant than the bare bones of vote totals.

Each state has its own cherished political fables and its own unique heroes and characters, events, and persons who stand as symbols to other Americans of the state's political way of life. Illinois points to Adlai Stevenson, Richard Daley, and Everett McKinley Dirksen (even the great orator's name has a mellifluous quality to it); Texas to Lyndon Johnson, "Cactus Jack" Garner, John Tower; New York to Nelson Rockefeller, Jacob Javits, Daniel Moynihan, and Bella Abzug; Kansas to Alf Landon, Frank Carlson, and Robert Dole; Massachusetts to John and Teddy Kennedy, James Curley, John McCormack, and Tip O'Neill; California to Earl Warren, Richard Nixon, Pat and Jerry Brown, and Ronald Reagan; Minnesota to Harold Stassen, Eugene McCarthy, and Hubert Humphrey; Georgia to Richard Russell, Herman Talmadge, and Jimmy Carter.

4. See, generally, Sundquist, *op. cit.*

Each state has a political tradition and culture all its own.[5] Some conduct politics and public business in a notably open and honest way, others
are more secretive and corrupt. Some states have ambitious public programs,
others are content to leave progress to federal or local governments or to whatever private organization wants to make the effort, pay the price, and reap
the rewards. Some state governments are innovative and imaginative, others
are slow to adopt new forms of government or policies. Some are presently
going through the throes of basic realignment of their parties, while others
haven't changed their political orientation or style for several decades.[6] In
some states, party leaders dominate the public officials of their party, while
in other states the public officials are far more visible and significant, and
dominate the party hierarchy. In some, the two parties are contentious during the campaign but seem to be able to cooperate in the general public interest
in policy discussions in the legislature, while in other states the parties are unwilling to get along in the legislature.[7]

The politics of a state may be dominated by a newspaper or media con-
glomerate, by a large corporation (DuPont) or industry (automaking, steel,
oil), by a labor union, by a prominent family, by a permanent political faction,
even by a church hierarchy (Mormon Utah, Roman Catholic Massachusetts).
If a state is not dominated by one particular element, then it is likely that

5. Two noteworthy book-length studies of the political culture of individual states are
   Frank Bryan's *Yankee Politics in Vermont,* (Hanover, N.H.: University Press of New
   England, 1974) and Robert H. Blank's *Regional Diversity in Political Values: Idaho
   Political Culture,* (Washington, D.C.: University Press of America, 1978). Among
   the single-state studies, usually more concerned with party organization, voting pat-
   terns, campaign narratives, or the contributions of key political leaders, are Leon Ep-
   stein's *Politics in Wisconsin,* (Madison: University of Wisconsin Press, 1958), Warren
   Moscow, *Politics in the Empire State,* (New York: Alfred A. Knopf, 1948), and Jack
   E. Holmes, *Politics in New Mexico,* (Albuquerque, N.M.: University of New Mexico
   Press, 1967). Studies comparing a number of states are V.O. Key's ground-breaking
   Southern Politics in State and Nation (New York: Alfred A. Knopf, 1949); Duane
   Lockard's *New England State Politics,* (Princeton, N.J.: Princeton University Press,
   1959); John Fenton's *Midwest Politics,* (New York: Holt, Rinehart and Winston,
   1966); and Neal Peirce's monumental series of which centerpiece was *The Megastates
   of America,* (New York: W.W. Norton, 1972). The concepts of moralistic, tradi-
   tionalistic, and individualistic political cultures were developed and applied in Daniel
   Elazar's *American Federalism: A View from the States,* (New York: Crowell, 1966).
6. For a thoughtful newspaper column summarizing developments in one state, see
   David Broder, "Muskie's Maine: Making a Case for Party Politics," *Today,* October
   26, 1979, p. 11.
7. For a discussion of policy cooperation between parties in Connecticut and of policy
   disputation between parties in Michigan, see Fred Greenstein, *The American Party
   System and the American People,* second edition, (Englewood Cliffs, N.J.: Prentice-
   Hall, 1970), pp. 78-83.

several elements engage in constant conflict for their piece of the political action.

In every state today, both Republican and Democratic parties contest for the presidency, at the least. The Republicans in recent decades have broken up the old Democratic Solid South, at least in presidential elections; in fact, when Senator Barry Goldwater of Arizona was the Republican candidate in 1964, the only states he carried outside his native state were five southern states, the heart of the old Confederacy. Republicans have won several state-wide elections in the South and a few congressional races, but they usually remain out of the running in state legislative and local races there. Before, the South was the home of one-party rule. This did not mean that political competition was dead, only that it took place within the confines of the Democratic party, as factions fought for control. Louisiana has for several decades exhibited a bifactional condition, a year-in-year-out struggle between the Long and anti-Long factions. This competition originated in the 1920s when Huey Long, a Protestant from the northern part of the state, became governor, wresting power away from the Cajun culture of the south. As this suggests, there was a regional and religious dimension to the strife in Louisiana. Some other states, such as Tennessee, Ohio, Illinois, and California, have similarly deep regional differences that are reflected in the voting distribution in most elections. Three of them, Tennessee, Ohio, and California, are also interesting because of the significance of several urban areas in state political contests. In Tennessee, the Mississippi River city of Memphis dominates the western part of the state, the capital city of Nashville sits astride the central section, and Chattanooga and Knoxville are the metropolitan centers of the mountainous east, where Republicans have been strongest. In Ohio, Cleveland, Columbus, and Cincinnati are the traditional bastions of regional influence. Much of California politics has always revolved around conflict between the Bay Area to the north and sunny southern California. Illinois is a state that reflects the importance of community size, rather than region, as the critical political variable; here the essential elements are metropolitan Chicago, suburban Cook county and neighboring counties, and the rest of the state.

But some state factional rivalries have no such geographical or cultural basis; the rival machines operate with roughly equal strength in each county and city. In some one-party states, the factionalism involves several groups, and is usually geared to the popularity of individual political leaders. The Florida Democratic party provided one example of multifactionalism, illustrated in the five-way distribution of the vote in a primary contest.[8] Similar

8. Greenstein, *op. cit.* pp. 71-74.

patterns can be seen frequently when more than three effective candidates became involved in a hotly contested primary. The 1972 Republican senatorial primary in South Dakota offered an example of a multifactional primary in which the candidates were running without the benefit of strict regional, economic, social, or ideological connections—all depended on the relative success of the five candidates in selling their own personalities and qualifications. One looks in vain at the voting returns in other South Dakota Republican primaries to find any connection between the transient factions of 1972 and those of 1970 (when there was a five-way race for the first district congressional seat and a two-way race for the gubernatorial nomination) or 1974 (when there was a three-person race for the nomination for the state's other senatorial seat).[9]

THE PARTY AND POLICY-MAKING

The investigation of how political parties affect policy-making raises the fundamental questions of whether and to what degree Democrats and Republicans in the electorate, in party leadership positions, and in public office differ in their policy objectives. One obvious starting point is to examine the platforms written by national and state conventions and the campaign statements issued by candidates for public office. Parties that appeared to be trailing in popularity have written more specific, controversial planks with more generous promises. As a general rule, national Democratic platforms have been liberal, favoring a larger federal role in the economy and in social welfare programs, while Republican platforms have been more conservative, preaching spending restraint and limited government activity. There are differences between the two major party platforms, differences that are consistent over the years and occasionally quite sharp; Democrats have tended to emphasize labor and welfare issues, Republicans defense and the role of government issues.[10] However, although in some policy fields platform recommendations have a fairly good chance of being enacted into law, it can be questioned whether Democrats and Republicans in Congress have paid very much attention to those platforms in setting their legislative agenda.

9. General election returns give a sense of the strength of the political parties in a given state. Primary election returns for the same election years are helpful in indicating the number, size, and geographical or social base of intraparty factions. Political biographies, political essays, and socially conscious fiction produced in or about the state reflect the state's political-cultural orientation.
10. Gerald M. Pomper, *Elections in America* (New York: Dodd, Mead, 1971), p. 185, and Scott and Hrebenar, *op. cit.,* pp. 232-233.

Perhaps a more critical test of the connection between parties and policy-making is the way legislators vote on critical roll calls. American legislators are by no means consistent in adhering to their party's position (assuming the party has adopted one) when issues come to the vote. Typical congressional roll calls will show some Democrats and some Republicans on both the "yea" and "nay" sides, though some kinds of issues are more likely than others to produce predictable patterns of support and opposition. A few examples of recent voting will suggest the main patterns (see Table 3-6). The first roll call pattern, A, is one in which large majorities of both parties vote in favor of the bill. Type B shows greater majorities of both parties voting on opposite sides, usually resulting in victory for the larger party; this kind of voting pattern is seen in A. Lawrence Lowell's classic definition of a party-line vote: one in which 90 percent of the members of one party vote on one side of the issue and are opposed on the other side of the issue by 90 percent of the members of the opposition party.[11] In the type C roll call, there are sharp divisions within both parties. Type D and type E are those with one party (either the majority or the minority) having a substantial majority on one side of the issue, with the opposition party split about evenly.

For all this variety, there is a strong ideological cast to much legislative voting. The relationship between party and ideology in American legislatures can be illustrated by referring to contemporary voting in the United States Senate covering a fairly large number of issues that have an ideological dimension. *Congressional Quarterly,* whose studies of partisan and ideological voting in Congress are widely disseminated, bases its analysis on the emergence of a "Conservation Coalition" in critical roll calls. Whenever a majority of Republicans and Southern Democrats vote against a majority of Northern Democrats, the "Conservative Coalition" has emerged. The votes of individual members are then said to be conservative if they vote with the "Conservative Coalition" and against the majority of Northern Democrats, who are presumably liberal. Table 3-7 categorizes individual senators on the basis of 1977 voting; Table 3-8 does the same for members of the House of Representatives without identifying individual members. Both tables show strong association between party and ideology in the 95th Congress, but at the same time they identify a number of aberrant cases, that is, the liberal Republicans and the conservation Democrats.

Regularity in legislative voting is a sometime thing, sometimes high, sometimes low to the point of invisibility, but, generally speaking, the party affiliation of the legislator is the best predictor there is of how he will vote.

11. See the discussion of party voting in William Keefe and Morris Ogul, *The American Legislative Process: Congress and the States,* fourth edition (Englewood Cliffs, N.J.: Prentice Hall, 1977), pp. 286-294.

Table 3-6. Types of Party Support Patterns on Roll Call Votes, US Senate, 1979

Type A. Substantial majorities of both parties on same side of issue.

	Democrats	Republicans
Yes	54	28
No	0	9

Yule's Q = +1.00. ϕ = +.40.

(February 26, 1979; nomination of Leonard Woodcock to be US ambassador to China.)

	Democrats	Republicans
Yes	51	31
No	6	9

Yule's Q = +.42. ϕ = +.16.

(March 28, 1979; countervailing import duty waiver.)

Type B. Substantial majorities of parties on opposite sides of issue.

	Democrats	Republicans
Yes	51	0
No	0	38

Yule's Q = +1.00. ϕ = +.1.00.

(February 22, 1979; Byrd/WV motion to kill Stevens amendment on Senate filibuster rule.)

	Democrats	Republicans
Yes	7	35
No	45	5

Yule's Q = –.96. ϕ = –.74.

(March 8, 1979; Percy motion on relations with Taiwan.)

Type C. Both parties considerably split.

	Democrats	Republicans
Yes	20	18
No	32	18

Yule's Q = –.23. ϕ = –.11.

(April 24, 1979; Byrd/Va amendment on budget targets.)

Table 3-6. Types of Party Support Patterns on Roll Call Votes, US Senate, 1979 (cont.)

Type C. Both parties considerably split. (cont.)

	Democrats	Republicans	
Yes	27	16	(May 22, 1979; Byrd/Va amend-
No	28	21	ment on foreign military aid.)

Yule's $Q = +.12$. $\phi = +.06$.

Type. D. Substantial majority of majority party on one side of issue, minority party considerably split.

	Democrats	Republicans	
Yes	52	22	(March 13, 1979; Church amend-
No	3	18	ment on resolution concerning

Yule's $Q = +.87$. $\phi = +.47$.   relations with Taiwan.)

	Democrats	Republicans	
Yes	7	19	(April 30, 1979; Schweiker
No	41	17	amendment on bill to create new

Yule's $Q = -.73$. $\phi = -.41$.   Department of Education.)

Type E. Substantial majority of minority party on one side of issue, majority party considerably split.

	Democrats	Republicans	
Yes	26	25	(April 9, 1979; Supreme Court
No	28	12	jurisdiction over school prayer

Yule's $Q = -.38$. $\phi = -.19$.   cases.)

	Democrats	Republicans	
Yes	25	34	(June 6, 1979; Byrd/Va amend-
No	31	4	ment on termination of mutual

Yule's $Q = -.83$. $\phi = -.46$.   defense treaties.)

Table 3-7. Support for the Conservative Coalition in the US Senate, 1979, by Party

Percentage Support for Conservative Coalition*	Republicans		Democrats	
90–100	McClure ID	Lugar IN		
	Humphrey NH	Helms NC		
	Thurmond SC	Hatch UT		
	Warner VA			
80–89	Jepsen IA	Dole KS	Johnston LA	Boren OK
	Laxalt NV	Domenici NM	Byrd VA	
	Schmitt NM	Garn UT		
	Wallop WY			
70–79	Goldwater AZ	Hayakawa CA	Heflin AL	Pryor AR
	Armstrong CD	Kassebaum KS	Nunn GA	Stennis MS
	Cochrane MS	Young ND	Zorinsky NB	Hollings SC
	Schweiker PA	Tower TX		
	Simpson WY			
60–69	Stevens AK	Roth DE	Stewart AL	Stone FL
	Boschwitz MN	Danforth MO	Talmadge GA	Ford KY
			Long LA	Cannon NV
			Bentsen TX	
50–59	Cohen ME	Bellmon OK	DeConcini AZ	Chiles FL
	Pressler SD	Baker TN	Exon NB	Morgan NC
			Sasser TN	Byrd WV
			Randolph WV	

Table 3-7. Support for the Conservation Coalition in the US Senate, 1979, by Party (cont.)

Percentage Support for Conservative Coalition*	Republicans		Democrats	
40–49	Percy IL	Packwood OR	Bumpers AR	Church ID
			Huddleston KY	Melcher MT
30–39	Weicker CN	Durenberger MN	Eagleton MO	Burdick ND
	Hatfield OR	Heinz PA	Glenn OH	Jackson WA
			Magnuson WA	Proxmire WI
20–29	Mathias MD	Chafee RI	Gravel AK	Hart CD
	Stafford VT		Matsunaga HA	Muskie ME
			Baucus MT	Durkin NH
10–19	Javits NY		Cranston CA	Ribicoff CN
			Biden DE	Inouye HA
			Stevenson IL	Bayh IN
			Riegle MC	Bradley NJ
			Moynihan NY	Metzenbaum OH
			Pell RI	McGovern SD
			Leahy VT	
0–9			Culver IA	Sarbanes MD
			Kennedy MA	Tsongas MA
			Levin MC	Williams NJ
			Nelson WI	

gamma = +.62.

*The "Conservative Coalition" is defined by *Congressional Quarterly* as a roll call vote on which a majority of Republicans and Southern Democrats is opposed by a majority of Northern Democrats. There were ninety such roll calls in the 1979 US Senate. Failure to vote lowers the support score.

Source: Congressional Quarterly Weekly Report, January 26, 1980, p. 198.

Table 3-8. Support for the Conservative Coalition in the US House of Representatives, 1979, by Party

Percentage Support for Conservative Coalition*	Republicans	Democrats
90-100	46	18
80-89	48	13
70-79	25	22
60-69	15	20
50-59	9	13
40-49	5	26
30-39	7	35
20-29	3	30
10-19	0	42
0-9	1	56
Total	159	275

gamma = +.76.

*See Table 3-7 for definition of "Conservative Coalition." There was no data for Speaker O'Neill, who votes at his own discretion.
Source: Congressional Quarterly Weekly Report, January 26, 1980, pp. 196-197.

When a legislator votes contrary to the majority of his party colleagues, it means that some principle or interest is more important to him than voting agreement with his fellow party members. This is not necessarily a bad thing. Majority and party preferences ought to be examined constantly and critically. But too much antiparty behavior in legislative bodies opens the door to more random, casual, or even selfish deviation, which too often seems to be the rule rather than the exception in America. Low party cohesion constitutes a dilemma and a potential danger to the idea of representative government, because it seriously undermines the ability of rank-and-file citizens to affect or even to understand the policy decisions their legislators make in their name.

Table 3-9 shows almost as wide a range of party unity voting in US Senate roll calls as there were in the ideological types discussed earlier. Tables 3-7 and 3-9 show a high degree of association between ideology and party unity (given the liberal bias of the Democratic majority in the Senate, the liberals have the higher party unity scores; for the Republicans, the conservative majority is the "loyal" group).

Table 3-9. Party Unity Voting in the 1979 US Senate

Party Unity Scores	Republicans	Democrats
90-100	Humphrey NH, Helms NC, Garn UT, Lugar IN, Hatch UT, Warner VA	Jackson WA
80-89	McClure ID, Jepsen IA, Armstrong CD, Thurmond SC, Simpson WY, Laxalt NV, Wallop WY	Sarbanes MD, Levin MC, Bradley NJ, Metzenbaum OH, Riegle MC, Williams NJ, Matsunaga HA, Nelson WI, Leahy VT
70-79	Dole KS, Domenici NM, Schmitt NM, Hayakawa CA, Cochrane MS, Boschwitz MN, Roth DE, Schweiker PA, Tower TX	Hart CD, Moynihan NY, Glenn OH, Byrd WV, Muskie ME, Baucus MT, Magnuson WA, McGovern SD, Chiles FL, Culver IA, Eagleton MO, Burdick ND, Bumpers AR, Kennedy MA, Ribicoff CN, Stevenson IL, Durkin NH
60-69	Goldwater AZ, Kassebaum KS, Young ND, Cohen ME, Stevens AK	Randolph WV, Biden DE, Cannon NV, Stewart AB, Huddleston KY, Pell RI, Inouye HA, Melcher MT, Sasser TN, Pryor AR, Church ID, Bayh IN, Bentsen TX, Nunn GA, Hollings SC
50-59	Danforth MO, Pressler SD, Durenberger MN	Exon NB, DeConcini AZ, Ford KY, Johnston LA, Gravel AK, Morgan NC, Stennis MS, Proxmire WI, Stone FL
40-49	Bellmon OK, Heinz PA, Baker TN, Packwood OR	Heflin AB, Talmadge GA, Long LA
30-39	Percy IL, Hatfield OR, Chafee RI, Weicker CN	Zorinsky NB, Boren OK
20-29	Stafford VT, Mathias MD	Byrd VA
10-19	Javits NY	

"Party unity" is defined by *Congressional Quarterly* as the percentage of votes on which a senator votes "yea" or "nay" in agreement with a majority of his party, and a "party unity roll call" is one on which a majority of voting Democrats opposed a majority of voting Republicans. Failure to vote lowers a senator's party unity score.
Source: Congressional Quarterly Weekly Report, January 19, 1980, p. 147.

PARTY AND PATRONAGE

American political parties have the capacity to coordinate the work of the public officials they have helped place in office. This coordination of effort involves not only elected officials, but also those appointed to office by virtue of partisan favor, because at all levels and in all branches of government a considerable amount of political patronage still exists. This appointive patronage includes every federal judge, as well as state and local judges in many jurisdictions, and explains to some degree why lawyers have involved themselves in political party affairs to a greater extent than have members of other professions. Patronage also includes over two thousand key positions of the executive branch of the federal government, scores of jobs on the independent regulatory commissions, and many more in state and local governments as well. Patronage is tempered by the fact that in most cases an executive nomination requires senatorial or state legislative approval. The percentage of federal patronage positions has declined gradually, being displaced by merit appointment based on education, examination, and experience. Finally, there is some patronage involved in appointments to legislative member staff and committee staff positions in Congress and the state legislatures.

Coordinating efforts by parties are visible in several specific aspects. First, party leaders recommend candidates for top cabinet administrative positions in federal and state governments. Second, they recommend candidates for positions lower in the administrative echelons. Third, they coordinate administrative approaches to policy questions and channel ideas from outside experts and influentials to party representatives in the executive and legislative branches. Fourth, they provide a supply of persons to serve on the staffs of legislative members or committees. Fifth, they coordinate legislative approaches to policy questions through liaison between executive and legislative branches, involving legislative committees, individual legislators, administrative officials, outside experts, and party influentials in the process. Finally, they recommend candidates for judicial positions, considering senatorial courtesy, constituency preferences made known through local party leaders, and the recommendations of national or state bar associations.

RELATIONS AMONG PARTY INFLUENTIALS

Public officials and party leaders of the same party interrelate on several levels and in many ways. They are mutually interested in the solution of political issues, the selection of public officials and of party officers, and in such recurring political party affairs as platforms, rules, budgets, and organizational matters. These concerns encompass the national, state, and local levels. Party staffs, like the campaign staffs that are associated with individual candidates, are a frequent conduit of workers, resources, and ideas to governmental agencies. But the connections between party and campaign staffs on the one hand and government office on the other are not as extensive as they were in the days before merit employment systems began to displace patronage appointments.

To review the kinds of relationships that exist among public officials and party leaders, let us speculate about the modes and relative frequency and closeness of contact between these actors; in doing so, we should keep in mind that no state, not even a hypothetical one, can be typical, simply because of the wide variety of population size, types of party organization, and political cultures that exist. The actors to be analyzed are a state's governor, a member of the state's congressional delegation, a member of the state legislature, the party's state chairman, and one of the party's county chairmen.[12]

Figure 3-1. A Chart Showing the Frequency and Intensity of Contacts among Party Influentials.

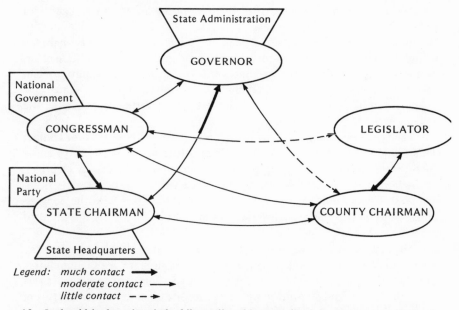

12. It should be kept in mind while reading this generalized description that party officers have positive and meaningful relationships with governors, congressmen, and legislators only when they are members of the same party; a party officer of the "out" party has fewer opportunities for contact with public officials.

In the interests of simplicity and brevity, we will not include in our cast such lesser but often important supporting actors as the governor's administrative assistant, the congressman's press secretary, the head of the state's Department of Public Health (appointed by the governor), the clerk of the appropriations committee of the state legislature (appointed by the party's majority leader), or the party chairman in a critical ward of an important urban center.

The governor is likely to be in most frequent contact with the state legislature, at least while it is in session, because he will be seeking favorable action on his proposals. He is also likely to be in frequent touch with the state's congressional delegation as he seeks favorable consideration of the state's interests in the many areas of federal-state cooperation. Ordinarily, the congressional delegation acts as a communications conduit between state governments and the federal bureaucracy; an important conditioning factor here is the party affiliations of the president, the governor, and the members of Congress from the state. The governor also is likely to have frequent contact with the officials of his own party; the most frequent connection would probably be with the state chairman, followed by the state's members of the national committee, the state central committee and party headquarters staff, and the state convention during its brief period of life.

The member of Congress is likely to be in most frequent contact with party officials, since they are excellent intermediaries between Washington and the people in the congressional district. Contact with the county chairman of the district, the district chairman (if one is designated), and the state chairman is likely to be more extensive than contact with national committee members, the congressional campaign committee, and the state party headquarters. There would likely be moderate contact with the governor, but usually little contact with the state legislature.

The typical state legislator will probably have many occasions for contact with the governor (especially if they are members of the same party) and a good deal of contact with party people, beginning with the county chairmen of the home district and followed by the state chairman and state party headquarters. There would also be some occasions for contact with the congressional delegation if there are federal ramifications in the policy questions of prime concern to the legislator.

The state chairman will necessarily have close ties with the governor (assuming they are of the same party), and also with the state central committee and the state party headquarters, for whose operation he is responsible. He also will be in frequent contact with the national committee members from the state and each of the county chairmen within the state. He is likely to have significant contact with the president, and presidential hopefuls, as election time approaches. Finally, the state chairman will be in frequent contact with the congressional delegation. Of all the influentials in this hypothetical set, the state chairman seems to be the busiest and most crucial contact point.

The contacts of the typical county chairman are, like those of the state chairman, likely to be rather evenly spread. However, given the fact that the county chairman probably does not devote as large a percentage of his time to party affairs as the state chairman does, the contacts will be less frequent and less intense. Of course, if the governor, congressman, or state legislator are not members of the party, there would be no contact with them at all, and the county chairman's political circle would be pretty much restricted to the state chairman, the state headquarters, and his fellow party leaders in the county.

SUMMARY

The constitutional principles of federalism and separation of powers have diversified and decentralized our political system, as they were intended to do. American political parties are probably the most crucial institutions in making our political system work; the party is the common factor that unifies officials from all levels and branches of government and thus, at least potentially, the party provides the glue and the oil that are necessary to hold the system together and to make its machinery work smoothly and expeditiously. There are signs of malfunction too frequently, but it is difficult to see how our system could work at all without the unifying and linking functions performed by political parties. Without them, the connections among popular preferences, national interests, and policy-making would be more remote and less evident than they are.

There is indeed a good deal of ambiguity, ambivalence, and inconsistency in American political parties, but they remain the focal point of electioneering and of organizing legislatures and administrations across the land, and party affiliation is still the best indicator of how citizens will vote in elections and of how legislators will vote on policy questions.

No reform proposals stem directly from this chapter. But the chapters ahead will discuss a number of reforms that should have the effect of strenghtening parties, sharpening ideological and policy differences between them, and increasing the participation of rank-and-file party members in deciding who will lead the party.

Chapter 4

The Campaign in the Political System

The election campaign brings all the political actors, institutions, and movements into focus. Party organizations, candidates and their staffs, media professionals, and interest groups interrelate hecticly for a period of time, as political appeals are perfected and transmitted by rival candidates to specific target groups or to the undifferentiated public.

While the campaign itself may be full of excitement and passion, it is most important that the election game be played fairly. The United States has been notably successful in nurturing an efficient and neutral system of election administration. This success has been due almost totally to the efforts of state and local, rather than federal, officials.[1] The state and local officials in turn were supported in their efforts by the political reform movements of the Progressive era and by those press institutions that valued democracy above chicanery.

CONTEMPORARY CAMPAIGNING

Campaigns are increasingly dominated by specialists whose tools have become virtually indispensible in the running of major, more-than-local campaigns. Chief among such specialists are the following.

The campaign manager. It is the manager's function to organize the total campaign, to hire and coordinate staff, to supervise the collection and distribution of funds, and to be responsible for major decisions in the campaign effort.

1. Typically, the state officer in charge of election administration is the secretary of state. The county-level election administrator is usually an elective officer called the county clerk or the county auditor. These people deal, among other things, with certifying nomination petitions, preparing ballots, registering voters, hiring election clerks and appointing election judges, setting up polling places in each precinct, counting the votes, certifying the winner, and maintaining election and registration records.

The legal adviser. Given the great expansion of federal and state laws regulating campaigns, as well as the large number of party rules, it is necessary to have an attorney review and pass on any doubtful transaction, statement, or activity.

The accountant. The intricate federal and state rules on the collection and spending of funds, and the need to keep posted on their current status, make it imperative that a trained accountant act as or work closely with the campaign treasurer.

The fund-raiser. Campaigns, it need hardly be said, are expensive. Congressional campaigns commonly exceed $100,000 in total costs over the campaign year, and in the larger, more populous states, gubernatorial and senatorial campaigns frequently exceed $1 million.[2]

The media buyer. This person must know the size and special qualities of the audience of each newspaper, magazine, radio station, and television station, as well as which media are appropriate for the transmission of each kind of campaign appeal. Achieving the proper balance and concentration of messages within a finite budget is a delicate matter.

The direct-mail expert. Direct mail is a very important area in political campaigning, and one closely related to the distribution of campaign appeals through the mass media. Some messages are appropriate for mass mailings, in which more can be said than in a thirty-second television spot announcement, though perhaps less dramatically. Other messages can be specially prepared for a specific audience; the acquisition of up-to-date mailing lists for special target groups such as dentists, pro- or anti-abortionists, college students, Republicans (or Democrats) interested in environmental issues, cattle feeders, veterans of the armed forces, or retired teachers can be a critical part of campaign tactics.

The issues expert. Each campaign, at its time and in its place, has a unique set of issues that are important, or can be made so, to the voters. The issues expert senses positive issues for the candidate and develops themes from those issues that the candidate can use to promote his cause.

The public relations expert. This is the person who must retail the campaign, working with and through the press and the advertising specialists. His efforts

2. For the campaign costs of senators and congressmen in 1978, see *Congressional Quarterly Weekly Report,* September 29, 1979, pp. 2157 ff.

include writing speeches, usually in conjunction with the issues expert, and writing the copy for newspaper, radio, and television advertisements.

The public opinion expert. Measuring public opinion, knowing what problems are worrying the voters and how they are reacting to the personalities and the issues, has become a vital professional activity in contemporary campaigns. Experts are needed to plan public opinion surveys among the constituency, to interpret the results, and finally to apply those results to the ongoing dissemination of campaign appeals through the candidate, his workers in the field, and the media.

No two campaigns are alike; they vary in many critical aspects. First, what kind of office is at stake—running for an executive position such as mayor, governor, or president is different from running for a legislative position such as city councilman, state legislator, or congressman or for a special local commission having responsibility for schools or a library or an irrigation district. Is it a municipal, county, district, state, or federal position? The only nationwide election we have is the presidential race; the next level down is the state, and states are as different as Alaska is from Rhode Island or Florida is from Iowa. Statewide elections include those for governor, for US senator, and, in many states, for a half dozen or so state constitutional officers such as the secretary of state, the state treasurer, and the attorney general. Senators and governors have the same constituency, then, but not the same powers, problems, or perquisites. Governors try to become senators, not the reverse. Governors are more likely to run for the House of Representatives than are congressmen to run for governor, but Charles Thone of Nebraska is one recent example of the latter pattern. One important thing about the House is that the power of incumbency has proven to be so great; over 90 percent of representatives choosing to run for reelection in the past two decades have been successful, a far higher ratio than has been enjoyed by presidents, senators, or governors. In the states, most of the constitutional offices turn out to be political dead ends, but a considerable number of attorneys general and lieutenant governors have over the years gone on to higher political positions.

Election Cycles

The election cycle is sometimes an important campaign factor. Seldom are all of a state's major elections held in the same year. In 1980, Americans elected a presidential ticket, thirteen of fifty state governors, thirty-four of one-hundred US senators, and all four hundred thirty-five US representatives. It is possible, theoretically, for all the representatives to be replaced in one election. Because we have short (two-year) congressional terms, every even-numbered year is a congressional election year. Presidential elections occur in years divisible by four. Senators are elected for six-year terms, with the terms arranged so that one-third of the Senate seats are up for election every two years. The one hundred senators are divided into three classes. Class 1 senatorial elections occur in 1982, 1988, 1994, 2000, etc.; Class 2 senatorial elections occur in 1984, 1990, 1996, 2002, etc.; and Class 3 senatorial elections occur in 1986, 1992, 1998, 2004, etc. It will be seen from this that a given senatorial seat's election will coincide with a presidential election every other time. The two Senate seats from a given state are arranged, originally by lot, in one of three possible class patterns: Class 1 and 2 (Delaware, Maine, Massachusetts, Michigan, and Minnesota are examples), Class 1 and 3 (Arizona, California, Connecticut, Florida, and Hawaii are examples), or Class 2 and 3 (Alabama, Alaska, Arkansas, Colorado, and Georgia are examples).

There is great variety in the election schedule for state and local officials, depending on the length of terms of governors, legislators, and local officials and on the particular years in which these terms begin. A typical arrangement is for the governor to serve a four-year term, with the election set in the off-presidential year, to insulate state politics from national politics to some degree. Some states still retain two-year gubernatorial terms, so that their governors are elected as often as their congressmen. A few states elect their governor in an odd-numbered year. States vary in the length and commencement of terms for their legislators; one fairly common pattern is for the members of the upper legislative chamber to have four-year terms, half elected in presidential years, half in off-presidential years, and for members of the lower chamber to have two-year terms.

The variety of terms is even greater at the county and municipal levels. We can see this by reviewing the local elections in South Dakota. There, members of the county commission, composed variously of three or five members depending on the preference of the individual county, are elected to four-year terms on an alternating basis. County commissioners from even-numbered districts are elected in off-presidential years (1982, 1986, etc.), and commissioners from odd-numbered districts are elected in presidential years (1984, 1988, etc.). Six other county officers are also elected to four-year terms: the sheriff, auditor, and register of deeds are elected in off-presidential years, while the treasurer, state's attorney, and coroner are elected in presidential years.[3] Mayors and members of municipal governing boards (councils or commissions) are elected for overlapping two-year terms in a nonpartisan election that is held each year in April. Members of school boards are elected in a nonpartisan

3. *1967 South Dakota Compiled Laws,* 7-8-1, and *1978 Supplement to South Dakota Compiled Laws,* 7-7-1.1

election each June, and the state's nonpartisan judges are chosen in the general election.

Another significant manner in which campaigns vary is in the type of election, by which is meant whether a mere plurality of the votes is sufficient to win, or whether an absolute (over 50 percent) or augmented (say, 60 percent) majority is needed. Also involved here is the number of seats at issue in the district; single-member district races emphasize the individual candidates, naturally, to a greater extent than do multimember district races, which have the further drawback of tending to artificially inflate the percentage of seats won by the majority party.

Other ways in which campaigns differ may be briefly summarized. Is the district population divided into sharply different classes and occupations (heterogeneous) or are the people quite similar to one another in culture and outlook (homogeneous)? Do most of the funds, ideas, and staff for the campaign come from inside the district (endogeneous) or from outside (exogeneous)? Are the candidates warm and friendly or cold and calculating, are they politically wise or politically naive, are they ideologically pure and firm or indifferent and flexible? Does the candidate himself make the critical decisions about the conduct of the campaign, or is he content to let his appointed manager run the show, or does the political party itself or a particular interest group (as a result of its control over funding) direct campaign affairs? Does the campaign center on a particular issue, or on benefits to a specific group, or on the qualities of the candidate? Is the campaign aimed at a specific target group, or a set of different groups, or at the mass public? Was the margin in the previous campaign narrow or wide?

An understanding of these variables, and of how they can affect the outcome, is important if the campaign is going to properly perform its functions in the political system. If one side understands them better than the opposition, it will have a significant advantage both in winning the contest and in acting rationally and positively in office.

MONEY AND POLITICS

The 1970s witnessed a massive effort to publicize and regulate the use of money in politics. It was not that there had been no previous attempts on the federal level to regulate campaign financing; on the contrary, the 1920s produced considerable legislation of this kind. But over the years various ways of getting around the laws had been found, and by the 1950s and 1960s the laws were being honored more in the breach than in the observance. The work of the 1970s, then, was partly a matter of closing loopholes, stiffening standards, and developing an administrative framework that would produce broader compliance.

The new federal laws provided for: (1) public funding of presidential campaigns under certain circumstances, (2) tax credits for political contributions, (3) a check-off system whereby individual taxpayers could place one dollar of their tax liability in their party's presidential campaign treasury, (4) limits on the amount of money that could be contributed to political campaigns by individuals, parties, and nonparty political action groups (PACs), (5) limits on the amount of money that a candidate could spend in campaigning for public office, (6) full reporting and disclosure of contributions to and spending by candidates, and (7) establishment of the Federal Elections Commission (FEC) to administer and enforce the political finance regulations.

The Supreme Court, in Buckley *v.* Valeo,[4] cut away at much of the new regulatory apparatus, declaring that limiting a candidate's right to contribute his own money limited his freedom of speech and his access to the political process guaranteed in the First Amendment and that there were constitutional defects in the methods of naming the members of the FEC. The latter problem was solved by further legislation.

The 96th Congress passed HR 5010, a major but mainly housekeeping updating of federal statutes regulating political finance activity. The bill reduced paperwork, removed the necessity of reporting for small campaigns, allowed more volunteer work, raised the contribution limit above which contributors had to be identified by name, and provided more federal money to the political parties to put on their national conventions.[5]

Although Congress has provided the opportunity for public financing of presidential campaigns, it has not done so with respect to congressional campaigns, because of the fear on the part of senators and representatives that such changes would tend to equalize campaign resources and thus greatly improve the chances of their challengers back home.

Several states—among them, New Jersey, Michigan, Massachusetts, Minnesota, and Wisconsin—have instituted public financing of gubernatorial elections.[6] Minnesota is considering several interesting changes. The state's Ethical Practices Board, in general agreement with the recommendations of Governor Al Quie, suggested: (1) that candidates should be required to raise more small contributions in order to qualify for matching state funds, (2) that overall spending limitations for candidates be eliminated, and (3) that state taxpayers

4. 424 US 1.
5. *Congressional Quarterly Weekly Report,* January 5, 1980, pp. 30-33.
6. Neil Upmeyer, "Campaign Financing: The New Jersey Experience," *FEC Journal of Election Administration,* Fourth Quarter, 1978, pp. 6-8.

be allowed to designate two dollars instead of the present one-dollar to go to a general campaign fund (rather than to be designated to a particular political party).[7]

There are currently a number of campaign finance proposals before Congress that would involve further substantial changes. These proposals suggest several different means of attack on the problem: limiting the amount of money that could be contributed from certain kinds of sources; limiting the total campaign spending of a candidate; equalizing the funds available to contesting candidates; increasing the amounts of money available to candidates or parties through government subsidies; giving such subsidies to more kinds of campaigns; and halting government campaign subsidies altogether.

S. 21, introduced in 1979 by Senator Lowell Weicker (Republican of Connecticut), would terminate the public financing of presidential candiates.[8] Senator Edward Kennedy (Democrat of Massachusetts) introduced S. 1700 in 1979 aimed at reducing campaign contributions to Senate campaigns from nonparty multicandidate committees. Earlier in the year, Senator Kennedy had introduced S. 623 to provide for the public financing of general elections for the US Senate.

S. 1339, introduced on June 13, 1979 by Senator Richard Stone (Democrat of Florida), was an attempt to reduce senatorial campaign contributions by providing a governmental subsidy for candidates when the total contributions to their opponent exceeded certain thresholds.

Senator William Proxmire (Democrat of Wisconsin), on the CBS television program "Face the Nation" on February 10, 1980, proposed in passing the idea that no one be allowed to contribute money to the campaign treasury of an incumbent.

THE IMPACT OF CAMPAIGN MONEY

To understand the impact of campaign spending on election results, let us analyze the 435 contests for the US House of Representatives in 1978.

That election resulted in victories for 277 Democrats and 158 Republicans. Incumbents won in 358 of the districts, challengers in only 19, with 58 of the seats being "open," that is, not contested by the incumbent. The

7. Gerry Nelson, Associated Press dispatch from St. Paul, Minnesota, in Sioux Falls (S.D.) *Argus-Leader,* December 14, 1979, p. 12B.
8. The brief presidential campaigns of Senators Weicker and Larry Pressler (Republican of South Dakota) were aborted largely because of their failure to comply with matching requirements and thus to receive federal subsidies, while millions of dollars went to Democratic and Republican hopefuls with more generous campaign treasuries.

notably high success record of incumbents continued a long-standing phe-nomenon.[9]

Incumbency was a greater advantage to a congressional candidate in 1978 than either having an edge in campaign spending or being a Democrat. Ninety-five percent of incumbents running for reelection were successful, while "only"

Table 4-1. Relationship Between Incumbency and Party Affiliation in 1978 Campaigns for US House of Representatives

	Incumbent Won	Challenger Won	Open Seat	Total
Democrat won	235	5	37	277
Republican won	123	14	21	158
Total	358	19	58	435

Source: Compiled by author from official general election reports from state election officers and campaign expenditure reports from the Federal Elections Commission, published in Congressional Quarterly Weekly Report, September 29, 1979, pp. 2157-2163.

Table 4-2. Relationship Between Party Affiliation and Marginality in 1978 Campaigns for the US House of Representatives

	Democrat Won	Republican Won	Total
Winner's margin larger than ten percentiles	197	118	315
Winner's margin less than ten percentiles	43	23	66
Winner was uncontested	37	17	54
Total	277	158	435

Source: Same as for Table 4-1.

9. In no other major type of American election do incumbents stand such a good chance of winning as in elections for US representative. Senators, governors, and even presidents all have lower success ratios since World War II; while incumbent presi-dents have run for reelection only in 1948, 1956, 1964, 1972, and 1976 (the only unsuccessful effort by an incumbent president), it should be recalled that President Lyndon Johnson's decision not to seek reelection in 1968 was not altogether vol-untary.

83 percent of the candidates who outspent their opponents and "only" 64 percent of the Democratic candidates were successful. Money helps, but not as much as incumbency.

About half of the winning candidates—221, to be exact—spent more than twice the campaign money spent by their losing opponents. Ninety-five other winners spent up to two times more than their opponents and 65 victorious candidates were outspent by the loser. Fifty-four had no opposition in the 1978 general election.

Most congressional elections were not very close in 1978. In 83 percent of the races, the winner's margin was more than ten percentage points.[10]

Tables 4-1 through 4-6 show us more about how these campaign variables relate to one another.

Table 4-1 indicates that Republican challengers had slightly greater success knocking over Democratic incumbents than Democratic challengers had against Republican incumbents; 96 percent of the Republicans running for reelection were successful, compared to a Democratic incumbent success rate

Table 4-3. Relationship Between Party Affiliation and Campaign Spending Levels in 1978 Campaigns for the US House of Representatives

	Democrat Won	*Republican Won*	*Total*
Winner spent more than ten times what loser spent, or loser spent less than $5000	66	26	92
Winner spent from two to ten times what loser spent	70	59	129
Winner spent less than two times what loser spent	60	35	95
Winner spent less than loser	44	21	65
Winner was uncontested	37	17	54
Total	277	158	435

Source: Same as for Table 4-1.

10. This margin of ten percentiles corresponds to the usual measurement of a marginal election as one in which the winner receives less than 55 percent of the votes cast. The number of multicandidate races made the ten-percentile rule more meaningful than the 55 percent standard.

Table 4-4. Relationship Between Incumbency and Marginality in 1978 Campaigns for the US House of Representatives

	Incumbent Won	Challenger Won	Open Seat	Total
Winner's margin larger than ten percentiles	278	5	32	315
Winner's margin less than ten percentiles	30	14	22	66
Winner was uncontested	50	0	4	54
Total	358	19	58	435

Source: Same as for Table 4-1.

of 94 percent. But the Democrats were much better at taking open seats, winning 64 percent of these races.

There was hardly any difference between Democrats and Republicans in the closeness of their races; excluding the uncontested campaigns, 17 percent of the Democratic victories were in the marginal category, compared with 16 percent of the Republican victories (see Table 4-2).

Table 4-5. Relationship Between Incumbency and Spending Levels in 1978 Campaigns for the US House of Representatives

	Incumbent Won	Challenger Won	Open Seat	Total
Winner spent more than ten times what loser spent, or loser spent less than $5000	89	0	3	92
Winner spent from two to ten times what loser spent	111	3	15	129
Winner spent less than two times what loser spent	66	8	21	95
Winner spent less than loser	42	8	15	65
Winner was uncontested	50	0	4	54
Total	358	19	58	435

Source: Same as for Table 4-1.

In terms of money spent, Republican victories were somewhat more prevalent in the second-highest spending relationship category than elsewhere, where they accounted for 46 percent of the cases (see Table 4-3). Overall, Republicans won 36 percent of the races.

Table 4-4 indicates that contested incumbents were far more likely to win by more than ten percentage points (90 percent of them did so) than successful challengers were (only 26 percent won by what is generally considered a safe margin). In the fifty-eight contested open seat races, thirty-two (or 59 percent) were won by a margin of more than ten percentage points.

Incumbents generally had an advantage in campaign money, as Table 4-5 shows. Over two hundred of the incumbents running for reelection outspent their opponents by more than two to one, and another seventy-four outspent their challengers by smaller margins, while only fifty of them were outspent.

Table 4-6. Relationship Between Campaign Spending Level and Marginality in 1978 Campaigns for the US House of Representatives

	Winner's Margin Larger Than Ten Percentiles	Winner's Margin Less Than Ten Percentiles	Winner Was Uncontested	Total
Winner spent more than ten times what loser spent, or loser spent less than $5000	92	0	0	92
Winner spent from two to ten times what loser spent	118	11	0	129
Winner spent less than two times what loser spent	66	29	0	95
Winner spent less than loser	39	26	0	65
Winner was uncontested	0	0	54	54
Total	315	66	54	435

Source: Same as for Table 4-1.

Not surprisingly, as Table 4-6 shows, there was a consistent relationship between money spent and margin in votes. In races where the winner spent less than the loser, 60 percent won by more than ten percentage points; where the winner spent up to twice as much as the loser, 69 percent won by more than ten percentiles; where the winner spent from two to ten times as much as the loser, 91 percent won by more than ten percentiles; and where the winner's spending advantage was even greater, 100 percent won by more than ten percentiles.

PROPOSALS

As noted at the beginning of this chapter, election administration—the business of seeing to the honesty, promptness, and accuracy of casting and counting votes—has not been a serious problem. But one reform that commends itself strongly is that of setting federal standards and definitions in reference to the establishment of political parties and the national registration of citizens for voting purposes.

4-1. To recognize national parties. A federal statute should be written to allow a national political party to be automatically eligible to nominate candidates for president and vice-president, and to have those nominations placed on the general election ballot in every jurisdiction, if that party's presidential candidate received at least 10 percent of the total popular votes cast for president in the last preceding presidential election. In the unlikely event that only one party would qualify on this basis, then it should be provided that the party receiving the second-largest number of popular votes in the previous election would qualify automatically. For the 1972 campaign, the 1968 presidential results would have established the eligibility of the Republican, Democratic, and American Independent (Wallace) parties. For the 1976 and 1980 campaigns, the 1972 and 1976 results would have maintained the eligibility of only the Republican and Democratic parties. The same statute would also provide that parties eligible for the general election would be automatically eligible for the primary ballot in states holding presidential or other federal-office primaries.

Independent, nonparty candidacies for any federal office could be placed on the general election ballot in a particular state by means of a dual process: (1) timely submission to the state's election authority of a petition bearing the signatures of registered voters (irrespective of party affiliation) numbering at least one percent of the total votes cast for that office in the last previous general election, and (2) payment of a $5,000 filing fee to the same state election authority, the fee being refundable if the candidate subsequently won as much as 5 percent of the votes cast in the general election.

Federal legislation should also acknowledge the national convention of recognized parties to be the ruling and responsible authority for each national party and for each state party that claims membership in and uses the name of the national party.

A new party could be automatically established as a national party, entitled to a place on the presidential ballot, if at any given time in the previous four-year period it held as many as sixty governorships and seats in the US Senate and House of Representatives (sixty is roughly 10 percent of the total number of such officials). For the 1984 presidential election ballot, the four-year period would be February 1, 1980 to January 31, 1984.

New parties could also be created and have access to the presidential ballots across the nation through petitions filed with a specified federal agency or officer, such as the FEC. Federal legislation could require, as a basis for the formation of such new parties, that the petitions be signed by persons who thereby declare their support for and membership in the new party and at the same time disclaim membership in any other national party. Petitions for a new party would be required from any three of the following five political groups: (1) twenty US senators, (2) eighty US representatives, (3) ten state governors, (4) three hundred state legislators, and (5) one million citizens, of whom at least ten thousand each would have to be residents of at least ten different states.

Along with each set of petitions would be a governing charter that would, among other things, specify the responsible leaders of the party and the time and place for holding its first national convention. A new party's continued status would depend on its meeting the 10-percent-of-the-popular-vote requirement set forth earlier in this section.

This process of defining a political party should provide a healthy and realistic balance between elite and popular party rule. New parties are not likely to be produced with any regularity, unless there occurs a widely perceived breakdown in the present party system. This does not limit the formation of parties operating only at the state level, but obviously there are powerful reasons why the present two national parties would continue to operate in each state.

4-2. To define national voting eligibility. The right to register and vote in federal elections should be extended to persons who are citizens of the United States, residents of one of the fifty states or the District of Columbia, have attained the age of eighteen years, and who have not been disfranchised under federal or state law because of criminality or insanity.

To vote in a party primary to nominate a candidate for federal office, a person would register with one party under the registration laws of the state, and only persons so registered would be eligible to vote in that party's primary election.[11] Those who favor a more open system should note that an individual may change his or her party membership status by a simple process right up to the registration deadline, which should be no less than fourteen and no more than thirty days before the election. The closed type of primary is by far the most common in the United States. There are at least three alternative systems: (1) allowing each voter to vote in each party's primary, thus giving the voter a hand in choosing the names on all party tickets for the general election ballot, (2) allowing each voter to choose between the parties up and down the ballot, perhaps voting in the Democratic congressional primary contest and in the Republican gubernatorial contest, and (3) allowing each voter, on arrival at the voting place, to choose the ballot of any one party.

States could, if they choose, maintain separate federal and state registration systems, but they would find it convenient to set the same general voter guidelines for elections at all levels. A reasonable degree of discretion could be allowed the states in length-of-residence requirements and registration deadlines before election day,[12] thus allowing local election administrators and party officials to verify doubtful or suspicious cases.

Now we turn to the problem of campaign finance. There are philosophical, ideological, and partisan dimensions to the continuing debate over the propriety of more sharply regulating political funding. Is the financing of election campaigns a proper function of government, or should this responsibility be left to political parties and interest groups? If the idea of tight controls over political finance prevails, how can those who prefer strictly voluntary methods of support fight effectively? If the incumbent majority shapes finance legislation in the interests of their own party, will not the outnumbered minority party be further, and perhaps fatally, wounded?

There are several considerations that should be kept in mind in recommending reforms. A new policy should: (1) not discriminate to the advantage of any particular party, (2) not discourage the development of other parties by artificial tax support of existing parties only, (3) widen political participation and enhance the quality of that participation, (4) result in a general dis-

---

11. For a description of the national voter registration system in Canada, see Jean-Marc Hamel, "Election Administration in Canada," *FEC Journal of Election Administration,* Fourth Quarter, 1978, pp. 4-5.
12. The length-of-residence requirement might be set at no longer than three months, and the registration deadline might be set at no later than two weeks prior to election day.

semination of information about the realities of money in politics, (5) be workable, manageable, sensible, and economical.

Accordingly, the following suggestions are offered with respect to federal legislation on political finance.

4-3. To withdraw federal campaign subsidies. The presidential campaign fund should be terminated because it represents public funding support for a particular party, candidate, or creed. The taxpayer check-off system should also be rescinded; there is plenty of opportunity for an individual to contribute to the party or candidate(s) of choice, and it does not seem necessary or fair for the machinery of government to collect money on behalf of any party or candidate for office. Eugene McCarthy is one outspoken critic of public subsidies; he has said that the federal funding of presidential elections subverts the foundation of our representative system. "The government now controls the process of selecting the new government," he has said. "The American revolution was not financed with matching funds from King George III."[13]

If subsidies of any kind are maintained, then they should be offered to those most in need of them, that is, the challengers who are attempting to unseat incumbents. Incumbents have a relatively easy time attracting campaign contributions, and they are provided by the government with staff, equipment, and travel allowances; thus it would be equitable for the government to provide commensurate help to recognized, responsible opposition candidates. Let there be, then, a direct federal grant, equal to the current salary being enjoyed by the incumbent, to any nonincumbent candidate for the US Senate or House of Representatives who has been duly nominated by a recognized political party or who is on the ballot as a result of petition. Further, let the grant be contingent upon the candidate's success in winning at least 20 percent of the total votes cast in the general election. This same grant for nonincumbent candidates could be applied to state and local campaigns, with the money coming from state or local funds.

4-4. To maintain federal regulatory activities. Full disclosure of political contributions and campaign spending should be continued, with the forms further clarified and simplified so that the data can be distributed and understood as generally and quickly as possible. The FEC should have sufficient independence, power, and funding to competently investigate charges of noncompliance and recommend prosecution as appropriate. At the same time, however,

13. "McCarthy Dismisses Polls as Just Political Distraction," Associated Press dispatch from Washington, D.C., in Sioux Falls (S.D.) *Argus-Leader*, November 7, 1979, p. 12B.

the FEC should be critically reviewed so that it does not become another sprawling bureaucracy beyond the control or comprehension of the public. Graft, bribery, and other forms of corruption should be exposed and punished, of course, but open contributions made without expectation of political reward or repayment should not be limited, nor should campaign spending.

4-5. To enhance the party role in campaign finance. The political party needs to increase its role in the collection and distribution of campaign money. The party, to some extent at least, must displace individual candidates as the primary collector of funds. This could be done in several ways. First, parties might attempt to spread their financial support burden by urging token contributions of, say, one dollar from every registered party member; after all, one dollar from one thousand people is as good as twenty-five dollars from forty people. As a matter of fact, it is better, since one thousand votes is better than forty. Second, parties might require that candidates turn over a percentage of campaign funds to the party treasury. They could stipulate that 10 percent of the funds raised on behalf of an individual running in the primary or running as the party candidate in the general election be turned over to the party, for disposition by its leaders. Third, it could be required that all or a substantial part of money spent by candidates in the general election come from party sources (national, state, or county organizations, or congressional or senatorial campaign committees). Fourth, it could be provided that, except for money from a party organ, no more than 5 percent of a candidate's contributions could come from a particular individual or group whose funds are substantially controlled by the same person, directors, or board. Fifth, state party conventions or committees could have the responsibility of determining the amount of their funds going into the various contests. For example, 25 percent of the funds might be earmarked for the gubernatorial race, 15 percent for the senatorial race, 30 percent for all the congressional races put together, 25 percent for all the state legislative races put together, and 5 percent for the lesser state constitutional office candidates. Sixth, party committees charged with evaluating public officials and candidates for public office (as will be discussed in Chapter 7) might distribute campaign funds among candidates in the party's primary contest, proportionate to each candidate's relative support or level of approval among committee members.

Any of these six possibilities would enhance the role of the party, making it a significant factor in a candidate's money-raising or spending operations. This is probably the surest way to bind the candidate to the party in a more meaningful and enduring manner.

Chapter 5
Organizing the Elements: Party Leadership

Analysis of Party Functions

State Party Organization

The Party Chairman

Leaders and Members

Proposal

Given the theoretical position of political parties in the functioning of American democracy, it would be logical to assume that their leaders at federal, state, and local levels have a great deal of influence over party members who hold public office. But this is the case in only a few states, and then only sporadically. If anything, influence tends to run in the reverse direction: from public officials to party leaders.

The realities of party activity in the United States would probably disappoint and disillusion many observers. In most parts of the nation, the party organization is not very effective, not very visible, not very significant. The role they play is limited largely by restrictions placed upon party leaders by state statutes. These controls arose out of the well-documented antiparty feeling that has permeated the nation since its creation, exemplified so notably in the ideas of James Madison and George Washington. The bulk of statutory restrictions were produced during the Populist and Progressive eras (roughly from 1890 to 1925), most of them originating in midwestern and western states. Notable for their party reform laws and experimentation have been Wisconsin, Minnesota, and Oregon. Wyoming is interesting for its pioneering woman suffrage efforts, South Dakota for its early adoption of the initiative and referendum processes, California for its reform movement that drastically weakened party leadership and cohesion, and Nebraska for its nonpartisan unicameral state legislature. In general, these reforms attempted to reduce the power of party leaders as such and to enhance the influence of the common voters, the party masses. But the real effect of the Populist-Progressive reform effort was to enlarge the role of public officeholders; as the powers of state and city party chairmen declined, the powers of governors, congressmen, and mayors grew. As patronage and other enticements were reduced, American parties concentrated more and more on the functions of recruiting candidates for office and of managing or coordinating their campaigns. Thus, as Frank Sorauf has said, "the electoral preoccupations of the American parties have tipped the scales in favor of party in government and against the party organization."[1]

1. Sorauf, *op. cit.,* p. 135.

Where does leadership exist, at least formally, in our political parties? American party organization consists of three essential elements: (1) conventions, which meet for a day or two every one or two years in most states, and for a week every four years in the case of the national conventions, (2) executive or central committees, which meet several times a year to make decisions concerning party affairs that come up between conventions, and (3) staffs, persons who earn their daily bread in office headquarters. The party conventions will be the subject of Chapter 9; party committees and headquarters staff will be discussed in detail in Chapter 7. In this chapter, we will present an overview of party organization, direction, and leadership.

ANALYSIS OF PARTY FUNCTIONS

State party organizations could be classified on the basis of how well they fulfill certain functional responsibilities, namely, (1) recruitment of candidates for public office, (2) financing and planning the campaigns of all party candidates, (3) providing a permanent and powerful basis for preparing legislative programs and recommending patronage appointments, and (4) resisting the development of sectional, ideological, or personal followings or factions that might reduce the power of the party.[2]

A strong party system is one that is not dependent on other sources of authority and that is effective in achieving its goals. Four dimensions would seem to be critical in measuring the independence and effectiveness of a particular system:

1. Authority—does the party hierarchy have substantial power over party affairs, especially in terms of influence on nominations and the legislative caucus, as well as on the party members in the state's congressional delegation?
2. Concentration—is the power concentrated in central party units, such as the state convention, the state executive committee, or the state party headquarters? Or is the power diffused to district or local levels or to competing factions or factional leaders within the party?
3. Cohesion—is there strong consensus within the party on how current political issues should be solved? Do all its leaders and factions support the same solutions to the same degree? Do legislators of the party

2. The four points are a rearrangement of the functions one would expect to be performed by a "centralized and cohesive party organization," in David Berman, *State and Local Politics,* second edition (Boston: Holbrook Press, 1978), p. 83.

vote together on critical roll call votes all of the time, or at least 75 percent of the time?

4. Democracy—are there frequent and significant opportunities, in the form of meetings, canvasses, systematic polls, or forums, through which individual members can express their preferences on current policy questions, leaders, or public officials?

It is important to keep in mind that parties exist in competition with one another and that the two major parties may differ on one or more of the dimensions listed above. The Democratic party in a given state may have comparatively high authority and cohesion while the Republican party in that same state may have comparatively low authority and cohesion. Looking at a state's laws is only part of the process of analyzing political elements; one must also know the local culture and tradition within which those statutes operate. Then, too, having similar party types does not guarantee similar political results. Fred Greenstein, summarizing the research of Duane Lockard in Connecticut and Norman Thomas in Michigan, noted that powerful cohesive parties in Connecticut produced a competitive situation that resulted in effective policy-making, the parties being able to cooperate in the state legislature, while in Michigan the same kind of parties were unwilling to compromise on legislative issues, a situation that resulted in policy deadlock, confusion, and paralysis. Parties in Michigan were composed of much the same constituent groups as those in Connecticut, but they were combined in different proportions in the two states and thus had different goals.[3] It should further be noted that high levels of party authority and cohesion do not guarantee that the political system will be open or coherent; the typical traditional urban political system involved parties that were sharply opposed to one another and whose decision-making processes were often secretive and devious.[4]

STATE PARTY ORGANIZATION

American parties are mainly occupied with campaign activity and do not attempt to exert much influence on governmental decision-making. There is what Sorauf has referred to as "an insubstantial and even unimpressive quality"

---

3. Greenstein, *op. cit.,* pp. 78-83.
4. For a study of Mayor Daley's Chicago Democratic machine, see Mike Royko, *Boss* (New York: E.P. Dutton, 1971), and a particularly intriguing newspaper column by the same writer based on an imagined colloquy between the late mayor (now in heaven) and his surviving henchmen in Chicago, "Mayor in Sky Appears," Chicago *Sun-Times,* May 11, 1979.

about party organization in this country. Whereas business, government, universities, and other major sectors have evolved large, powerful, and complex bureaucracies, American parties have not done so. In contrast, they are run by amateur part-timers who regard their party work as an avocation. Specialists or full-time professionals are seldom seen in the party apparatus. As noted earlier, the organizations are dominated by party members in public office, especially at the national level.[5] The Democratic national party is showing more signs of breaking this mold than is the Republican, according to Sorauf.[6]

Party leadership and organization vary widely from state to state and change over time, making it difficult to describe, or even to summarize, their overall shape in the United States today. It should be helpful, however, to discuss the outlines of a few types of state party systems to give an idea of the variations that exist. In one type of system the organization enjoys a high degree of authority over party affairs and, partly because of this concentration of authority, supervises a party in which group cohesion and loyalty are high. Connecticut and Michigan, discussed earlier in this chapter, are examples of this. In a second type, power is broadly diffused among different leaders or factions in the state party, but a high degree of cohesion is nonetheless maintained. A third type is one with concentrated authority but low cohesion, a situation likely to produce frequent shifts in leadership and policy preferences on the part of the leaders. A fourth would have diffused authority and low cohesion; the party would have minimal influence on its candidates or on government generally. California is one case in point.

Party organization in the United States is frequently described as a pyramidal arrangement, the national organization placed at the apex of fifty state party units, which in turn rest on a broad base of local organizations. Observers generally conclude that the national party, which can be described as a mere confederacy, is weak and does not control the state and local levels. While the national party does put on the national convention and does direct the

5. Sorauf, *op. cit.* A table in Sorauf's book (p. 63) summarizes the differences between the (American) cadre type and the (European) mass-membership type of parties. The latter have many dues-paying members, undertake ideological and educational as well as electoral activities, are continuously active, possess a permanent professional bureaucracy and full-time leadership, and generally exert influence over party members in the government. The control exercised by public officeholders over party affairs could be reversed if either of two conditions pertained—first, greater party control over political incentives, including control over campaign money, and second, continuation of the current trend by party electorates and activists toward "a politics of issue or ideology." (p. 133)

6. *Ibid.,* p. 133.

work of a permanent national headquarters in Washington, it exerts little control over state parties, has little to do with senatorial or congressional elections (which are partly financed and coordinated by separate campaign committees), and often is scarcely involved in the presidential campaign.[7]

State parties, as noted earlier, come in many varieties, and it is consequently difficult to generalize meaningfully about their relative power. Local organizations are inactive much of the time, and their capacity to dominate party affairs is limited by the dearth of patronage or other rewards for faithful service. Exceptional effort is required at the local level to keep any kind of organized party activity going during noncampaign periods. An energetic chairman, a strong ticket, or a salient issue that has temporarily galvanized and gathered the party faithful are among the resources that can keep local units active and effective.

Relationships within The Party

A more fruitful form of organizational analysis is one that relates the party units (conventions, committees, and chairmen, especially) to other crucial elements, such as the mass membership and the public officials of the party. This approach sharply defines the basic weaknesses of American political parties: the voters have little to say directly about the identity of their party leaders, and those leaders have little influence over party members who happen to be in public office. Figure 5-1 suggests why these seemingly critical relationships are so weak. An interesting comparison to this traditional model of party organization is the model suggested by John Fenton, which features greater party controls over legislators and the congressional delegation (see Figure 5-2).

The primary is widely used for the purpose of choosing delegates to party conventions or members of party committees at the local or state levels. It could also be used, but seldom is, to select party executives directly. Most typically, voters are restricted in the primary election to choosing members of county party organizations, who in turn elect the party officers and delegates to higher committees or conventions. Where the voters do select state convention delegates directly, there is often no opposition and thus no contest. In the South Dakota primary, for example, Republicans and Democrats vote separately in each precinct for (1) a member from their precinct to serve

7. The Republican party's lack of a significant role in President Nixon's 1972 reelection sweep has been cited as one reason for the excesses that led to the Watergate break-in and the Watergate mentality generally. See Theodore White, *The Making of the President 1972* (New York: Bantam Books, 1973), pp. 360-361, and Sorauf, *op. cit.*, pp. 307-308, 312.

Figure 5-1. Members, Leaders, and Public Officials in Political Party Organization

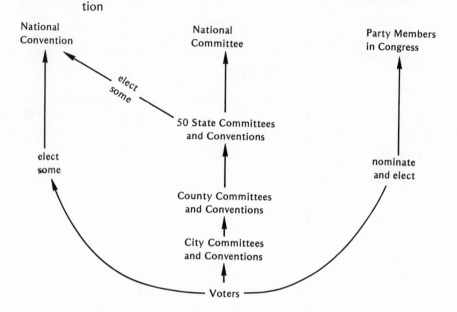

Figure 5-2. Members, Leaders, and Public Officials in a Strong Party Model

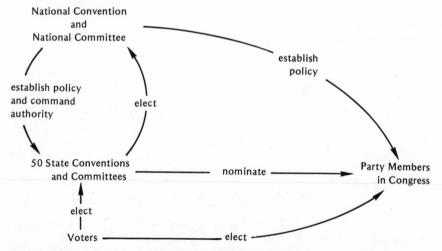

Source: This model was presented under the title "Ideal Organizational Pattern of a Strong National Party" in John Fenton, People and Parties in Politics (Glenview, Ill.: Scott, Foresman and Company, 1966), p. 17.

on the party's county central committee and (2) members from their county to serve as delegates to the state convention scheduled to be held a few weeks later. The choosing of county, state, and national party leaders (such as chairmen, committeemen, committeewomen, treasurers) is ordinarily left to the county committees and state and national conventions.

Figure 5-3. Varieties of Popular Voter Input in the Selection of Party Officers

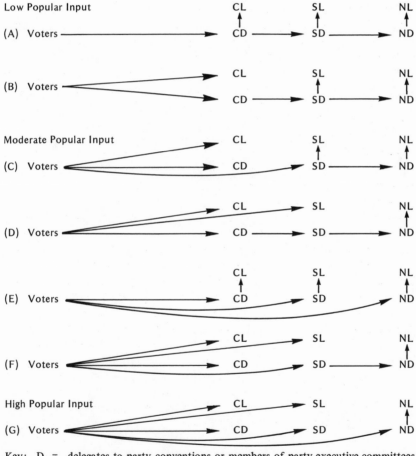

Key: D = delegates to party conventions or members of party executive committees
      L = party leaders, usually chairmen
      C = county
      S = state
      N = national

Seven models are presented in Figure 5-3 to clarify the relationships that exist in various types of party officer selection systems. Model A in the figure is the most authoritarian pattern, in the sense that the mass of party voters would choose the fewest party officers. Model G is the most democratic; the party members would directly elect the largest number of officers (an even more democratic model would have the party voters in the primary choose the national chairman as well as the five other elements).

THE PARTY CHAIRMAN

In discussing party leadership we must take note of the fact that the term can be used to encompass many different kinds of leaders—party members serving in major public office such as governor, congressman, state legislator, mayor; the state or county chairman himself; other party officers; members of party conventions or committees at national, state, or local levels; or merely individuals who are thought to be particularly influential in party affairs.

The executive official of the American political party at all levels has generally been referred to as the chairman. The amount of power wielded by a particular chairman depends on the level of government at which he operates, the party, the state, and the time. In some states, the party chairman has been comparatively powerful and highly visible, but elsewhere he has been more of a figurehead whose functions have been essentially ceremonial and pacifying.

While national party chairmen are generally not as visible as cabinet members or congressional leaders, some of them, by dint of their proximity to the president or of the respect in which they are held by other leaders, do maintain considerable national prestige. Republican Mark Hanna, mastermind of William McKinley's presidential bids of 1896 and 1900 and a senator from Ohio, and Democrat James Farley, political architect for Franklin Delano Roosevelt in the 1930s, are examples of powerful and prominent national party leaders. More recent examples have been Democrats Paul Butler (1955-1960), John Bailey (1961-1968), Lawrence O'Brien (1968-1969, 1970-1972), and Robert Strauss (1972-1976) and Republicans Leonard Hall (1953-1957), Ray Bliss (1965-1969), and Bill Brock (since 1977). They have come from a variety of positions—members of Congress, members of the national committee, state party chairmen, close associates of the party's presidential candidate.

State Chairmen

Turning to the state chairmen, again they are usually not as prominent as members of Congress, governors, or administrative or legislative leaders in the state capital. One study has revealed a good deal about their activities. Republican state chairmen ranked the administration of their state party organization as their most important function; following in the Republican ranking were, in order, promoting the party's image, promoting the party's policies, raising party funds, and (far behind), helping to manage the campaigns of state candidates. The rankings by Democratic state chairmen were in roughly the same order, but there was less distance between the choices; the Democratic order was promoting the party's image, administering the state party organization, raising party funds, promoting the party's policies, and (again last, but not so far behind as in the Republican rankings) helping to manage the campaigns of state candidates. According to Wiggins and Turk, in a majority of states the job of state party chairman was regarded as a part-time position; only 39 percent of the respondents reported that their work constituted a full-time job. Less than one-fourth of the respondents were salaried. The authors characterized the state chairmen as acting more in the role of the head of the board of directors of a national corporation than as the top administrative officer of such a corporation.[8]

Robert Huckshorn began his thorough study of state party chairmen by speculating on why state party organizations generally and state chairmen particularly suffered from such a "lack of visibility." The reasons arose, Huckshorn believed, from four factors: the public wasn't very interested in state politics, the media did not cover state politics uniformly, many important party activities were hidden from public view, and the people who chose the chairman in the first place constituted a small, self-contained group unknown to the public.[9]

Huckshorn identified three main types of party leaders, chairmen who play very different roles in their respective states. The "Political Agent" is essentially the creature of the governor or of some other dominant public official. The agent who happens to serve an activist governor "can wield considerable power and influence." The "In-Party Independent" is usually considered to be the "organizational" leader, while the governor is the "political" leader; their party is in power in the state, but the public official is preeminent in comparison with the party chairman. In many ways, the role of the "Out-Party Independent" is the most interesting and satisfying of the three, for such a state chairman is usually the real power in his party. Further, by definition the "Out-Party Independent" starts at a time when his party is not in control of state government, so there is no way to go but up; any electoral

8. Charles W. Wiggins and William L. Turk, "State Party Chairmen: A Profile," *Western Political Quarterly*, 1970, pp. 327-329.
9. Robert J. Huckshorn, *Party Leadership in the States* (Amherst, Mass.: University of Massachusetts Press, 1976), pp. 1-2.

success for the party makes an "Out-Party Independent" chairman something of a prophet leading his people into the Promised Land.[10]

Changes in the role of state chairmen were emphasized by Huckshorn. The traditional roles of the "old politics"—recruitment of candidates, coordination of campaign strategy, patronage, and the development of issue positions—were highly personal in character and required more of a chairman's time than the newer roles, such as organized fund-raising, public opinion assessment, tapping the expertise of professional political consultants, managing research and data, and improving communication with the party organization. Huckshorn also devoted one chapter to the state chairman's work with the national parties (Chapter 8) and another to how the state organization services the state and local elements (Chapter 9).

Relations with the national party are affected to a large degree by who is living in the White House. The titular head of the party may regard the state parties as important regiments in the national political army (Gerald Ford's attitude), as essentially neutral and relatively unimportant units (George McGovern's attitude), or as downright drags, things to be avoided (Richard Nixon's view).[11] Similarly, a state chairman's reaction to the national party, including its titular head, may range from strong support to intense hostility. Regionalism, ideological differences, and jockeying for position in the next national party convention, where the ambitions of rival presidential candidates will be tested, are among the factors that color the relations between state and national party leaders.

Local Leaders

Contact with the party organization below the state level presents to the state chairman much the same kind of variation and frustration as does contact with the higher level. Most state parties depend heavily on the county organizations for raising the funds to run at least the party's routine affairs, which puts the chairman in a dependent position. Nor have his resources to influence local leaders improved noticeably in recent years; where opportunities for patronage and other political favors have been reduced, so has the potential influence of state chairmen. And only gradually have the party headquarters in the typical state been able to make use of contemporary political technology, with its data banks, access to public opinion information, and capacity for massive and efficient communications. Both state and county

10. Huckshorn, *op. cit.,* pp. 94-95.
11. See the quotations in Huckshorn, *op. cit.,* p. 201.

organizations vary in their effectiveness—they can be very active, or able to perform only routine functions, or totally moribund and worthless. It is possible to have effective state organizations and generally ineffective local organizations, or to have just the reverse. The simplest way to bring about effective political activity would seem to be to find an ambitious and conscientious state chairman, for that pivotal position has the greatest potential for infusing the other levels of the party with the enthusiasm and goals required for a winning effort.

At the local level, party chairmen are generally volunteer, part-time workers, except in urban centers where the headquarters are large and permanently staffed. The county chairman, who in some jurisdictions is chosen in the primary election and in others is selected by the party's county central committee, presides at party meetings, some of which are mandated by state law, carries out the wishes of the central committee, supervises the work of any permanent or volunteer staff, advises state party officials and public officers on local candidates for political jobs, and has many ceremonial and often onerous functions—one of the first local stops made by touring congressmen or governors is to see the county chairman.

LEADERS AND MEMBERS

Parties exist because society seems to be naturally split into groups that argue, more or less constantly, over political or economic advantage. In spite of this, American parties today are generally thought of as agencies of consensus-building, rather than as agencies of conflict. To put it another way, parties spend at least as much time binding their members together or in getting along with the opposition party in legislative chambers as they do in widening the policy splits between them. They seek to find agreeable solutions to current problems, solutions that can be supported by the great majority, if not all party members and legislators. It is true that, to some extent, party leaders dramatize the differences between their policy recommendations and those of the opposing party, but at the same time they seek to diminish internal differences within the party, differences which if not controlled might weaken the party and, indirectly, the candidates who depend on it for support during election campaigns.

These various groups have different ideas about their own importance, about the role of government, and about specific political issues. In a remarkable study completed twenty years ago, Robert McCloskey found that Republican leaders differ quite sharply from ordinary members of the Republican party on many issues, while Democratic leaders and members are much closer to each other (and to the Republican members as well).[12] So, from the standpoint of policy preferences, party leaders (rather than party members) seem to be the elements that establish the interparty differences that do exist in American politics. But even these differences seem to be narrowing; more recent data indicate that the pattern traced by McCloskey has changed somewhat, with Democratic leaders in the 1970s moving away from the positions of the Democratic party rank-and-file.[13] In Chapter 9 we will discuss differences and similarities that exist in the platforms of the Democratic and Republican parties; our purpose here has been merely to suggest that leaders and members of a party do not take the same positions on policy questions all the time.

PROPOSAL

The cultures and laws of the fifty states have produced a high degree of variation in the power and cohesion of state political parties. The general view has it that party operations in America are obscure, confused, even irrelevant. But some states have developed a comparatively advanced degree of internal democracy and participation in party affairs, while at the same time achieving real visibility and influence for the party leaders. This has happened mostly as the result of fortuitous circumstances and the emergence of leaders whose ambitions have centered on party hierarchical position rather than on public office.

A larger and more significant role for the party seems to require this greater power and visibility for its top leaders. Such a development might involve a return, possibly a dangerous or dysfunctional one, to hierarchical patterns of an earlier age.

In suggesting reforms in party organization and operations, care needs to be taken to see that today's changes do not simply continue a cyclic pattern, reproducing a system similar to that of, say, 1920 or 1870. It is hoped that the changes suggested in this chapter, namely, greater mass party control in the selection of party leadership and greater power and visibility for these leaders, will avoid a return to past evils by both concentrating and democratizing party power. The fundamental proposal is one providing for the direct

12. Herbert McCloskey, Paul J. Hoffman, and Rosemary O'Hara, "Issue Conflict and Consensus among Party Leaders and Followers," *American Political Science Review,* 1960, pp. 406-427.

13. Sorauf, *op. cit.,* pp. 292-293.

popular election of party leaders at the county and state levels, in preference to systems in which party leaders are chosen by conventions or central committees that intervene between the officers and the members (see Figure 5-4). The objective is to make the leaders more responsible to the mass membership and more powerful with respect to other party institutions and influentials.

5-1. To choose party directors National conventions would, as they do presently, choose the national director[14] of the party, and the expectation is that the party's presidential nominee would in effect make the selection unilaterally, to be confirmed by the convention. The state director would be chosen by plurality vote in the primary election, candidates for state director having had their names placed on the primary ballot by means of a nominating petition signed by at least one hundred registered party members in the state or through

Figure 5-4. Political Party Structure (Model)

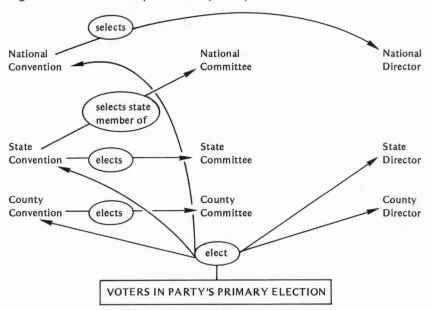

Note: Other organizational levels could be established, such as multicounty district organizations or municipal organizations. Apportionment of convention seats to component units would be based on the distribution of the vote for the party's presidential ticket in the most recent election, using the formula of equal proportions. See text for fuller explanations.

14. To avoid the awkward word "chairperson," and to avoid any sexist overtones, the title "director" is suggested here to designate the party's chief executive officer.

formal endorsement by the state executive committee filed not less than four and not more than eight weeks prior to the date of the primary election. If more than three candidates file for the position of director, the state executive committee would be required to reduce the list of candidates to three; this winnowing process should proceed in such a way that the three candidates having the greatest amount of support on the committee are certified for the primary ballot. If no person files as a candidate for state director, then the state party convention meeting subsequently to the primary election would be empowered to elect a director by majority vote; if more than two candidates are nominated in the state convention, then the candidate(s) receiving the fewest votes would be dropped from each ballot until a majority vote is achieved.

The state director would be a full-time, well-paid executive, whose salary and working arrangements would be determined by the state convention; the salary could not be diminished during an incumbent's uninterrupted service. The state director would appoint other state party officers, such as the state treasurer, on approval of the executive committee. National and state directors would supervise arrangements for party conventions, chair the conventions, and present a speech detailing the state of the party and its prospects for success in upcoming election campaigns. Party directors could be involuntarily removed from party office only by formal action on the part of 75 percent of the chairmen or executive committees at the organizational level next below them (that is, it would require county-level action to remove a state director, state-level action to remove a national director). Elective, paid state directors would increase popular, as opposed to elite, control of the party and would at the same time enhance the power of party leaders vis-à-vis office holders such as governors, congressmen, and state legislators.

The county director would be chosen in the party's primary election. Delegates to the state convention would be chosen by party voters in the same primary. Candidates for county director and for county delegate(s) to the state convention would be placed on the primary election ballot by submission of a nominating petition containing the signatures of a number of registered voters equal to or exceeding 5 percent of the votes cast in the previous election in the county for the party's candidate for president. If no person files as a candidate for county director, then the county convention would be empowered to select the director by majority vote at the postprimary convention; if more than two candidates are nominated for county director at the county convention, then the candidate(s) receiving the fewest votes on each previous ballot would be dropped from the next ballot, and voting would continue until a majority is achieved. The county director would name other party officers and precinct captains. Vacancies in any of these offices would be filled by the county executive committee within one month of the occasion of the vacancy.

If, however, a primary election is not held in a given state, then the choice of state or county party director would devolve upon the state or county party authority.

The comprehensive approach to party reform proposed here would establish structures that would be essentially the same in each state, that would encourage greater popular participation in party affairs, that would democratize the party system, and that would make the party director much more visible, powerful, and significant than party chairmen presently are in this country. The approach would base party decisions more squarely on the preferences of the majority of its members. It would more clearly locate and define the responsibility for action or inaction in government, thereby strengthening rational, responsive, and responsible self-government.

Chapter 6

Running the Show: Party Committees and Staffs

The National Committees and Staffs

State Committees and Staffs

County Committees

Caucuses and Other Party Elements

Proposals

It is no easy task to hold together the American political party long enough every two years so that it can perform its basic functions of nominating its candidates, activating its partisans, coordinating its campaigns and supporting operations, and getting its voters to the polls in November. The national and state party conventions attract a good deal of attention for the few days they meet. Their work is visible and their impact is significant. But for more than 99 percent of the time, the parties are administered and coordinated by executive committees and headquarters staffs that have little power and receive correspondingly little attention from the press or the public.

Not that the work of the national party organizations is unimportant. They must provide what integration can be had in the hurly-burly of a national political campaign. The headquarters staff is presented by the national convention with a presidential ticket, a platform, and a few generalized directives; then quite suddenly the convention is over and the staff must begin to sort out its goals and responsibilities and tools from among the rubble. It is inevitably difficult to coordinate the work of the national convention with that of the national committee and headquarters staff when the convention is in existence for only a short time, and the same is true of integrating party effort between state conventions and state committees and staffs. In our political system, a state organization must simultaneously concern itself with the presidential campaign in the state, a campaign for governor, a campaign for US senator, campaigns for a dozen seats in the US House of Representatives, campaigns in perhaps 150 legislative districts, and campaigns for perhaps a half dozen or more courthouse positions in 60 or more counties. It is no wonder that chaos threatens the party at every turn in the campaign trail. In the campaign itself, as in a number of related operations, there is a great need to integrate the work of candidates, staff members, and volunteers among the national, state, and local levels, and within each separate level as well. Such integration is most likely to come from party committees and the permanent staffs they direct.

119

THE NATIONAL COMMITTEES AND STAFFS

The national committees and the headquarters staff they administer are creatures of the national convention. A recent undated bulletin from the Republican National Committee shows the dependent position of the national committee quite clearly:

> The Republican National Committee is created by no law, either state or federal. The National Convention is the highest Party authority. In fact, there is no authority either for the creation or continuance of a National Committee. Any National Convention could, by the adoption of a resolution, do away with the National Committee.
>
> Since the successive National Conventions create the National Committee, as a Committee, and ratify the members thereof, no state law can do more than provide a method for electing members of the Committee.

The chief executive officer of the party is the national chairman, elected by the national convention, usually following the recommendation of the party's presidential nominee. Republicans choose a co-chairman (of the opposite sex) and a secretary-treasurer from and by the national committee membership.

Like the Republicans, the Democrats recognize the national convention as "the highest authority" of the party, subject to the provisions of the national party charter.[1] The Democratic National Committee is responsible for party affairs between conventions, which includes issuing the call to the national convention, conducting the party's presidential campaign, filling vacancies on the presidential ticket, formulating and disseminating policy statements, choosing the national party officers (including the chairperson), and filling vacancies therein. The national committee is composed of the chairperson and the highest ranking officer of the opposite sex of each state party organization, two hundred additional members apportioned to the states on the same basis as delegates to the national convention (provided that each state shall have at least two such additional members), three Democratic governors, two Democratic senators, two Democratic congressmen, six national Democratic party officers, three Democratic mayors, three members of the Young Democrats of America, three Democratic county officials, the president of the National Federation of Democratic Women, and up to twenty-five additional members from the territories or abroad.[2] Article Four of the charter also provides for an executive committee, whose size, composition, and terms are to be determined by

1. Article Two, Section 2, *Charter of the Democratic Party of the United States.*
2. Article Three of the Democratic party charter.

the national committee, with the stipulation that no fewer than half of the executive committee members shall be selected from regional caucuses of members of the national committee. The executive committee is required to meet at least four times a year.

There is still a good deal of validity in a study of national committees undertaken nearly two decades ago, which concluded that their members had

Figure 6-1. Organization of Republican National Committee Staff

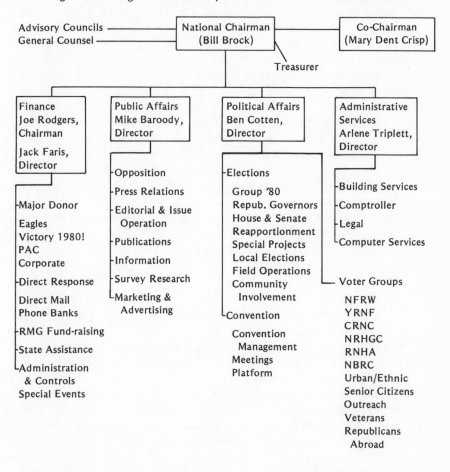

Source: Adapted from a chart headed "Departments, Divisions and Programs of the RNC," Chairman's Report, Republican National Committee—1980 (Washington, D.C.: Republican National Committee, no date), p. 5.

"very little collective identity, little patterned interaction, and only rudimentary common values and goals."[3] The national committee was characterized as a group that met principally for ceremonial or newsmaking purposes, an almost haphazard list of persons chosen by separate processes in each state.

The major functions of the national party organization are to conduct research on issues, public officials, and governmental institutions; to advise and help coordinate campaign staffs across the nation; to help states strengthen their separate party organizations; to develop publicity for party candidates and issues dear to its collective heart; to organize and bring into the party effort various groups, especially minorities; to raise and spend money; and to organize and conduct the national convention and any other interim party meeting. As individuals, members of national committees are often consulted on campaign plans, are asked to advise others of political developments in their state that may have general significance, and are called on to moderate conflicts or make decisions having to do with party rules, leaders, meetings, and efforts.

Both national parties maintain headquarters in Washington, D.C., the Democrats at 1625 Massachusetts Avenue, N.W., about six blocks north of the White House, and the Republicans at 310 First Street, S.E., about two blocks from the Capitol. The size of the Republican party's headquarters staff is about four hundred full-time employees, as of early 1980. The accompanying chart gives an idea of the major functions performed by the Republican organization and of the relationships among functional elements of the party.

STATE COMMITTEES AND STAFFS

State party headquarters come in all shapes and sizes. Some have a large office and a permanent staff numbering scores of employees; others, even today, have no more than one room with two desks.

The functions commonly performed by state party headquarters include coordination of party organizations; maintaining rosters, rules, and financial records; planning and arranging for state or regional party conventions and meetings; and serving as a depot for the storage and distribution of information and campaign supplies. The office and staff are usually administered by an executive secretary, appointed by and responsible to the state party chairman.

To describe the organization and operation of one state party headquarters, though not necessarily a typical one, may give a picture of what it is like to be involved in party administration.

3. Cornelius P. Cotter and Bernard C. Hennessy, *Politics Without Power: The National Party Committees* (New York: Atherton, 1964), p. 39.

In the late 1970s, South Dakota's Republican state headquarters was located in a four-room suite in a small office building across from the St. Charles Hotel in Pierre, within a couple of blocks of the state capital building. The reception room was occupied by a clerk who served as both receptionist and typist. Another room was used by the administrative assistant to the state chairman, an official who in other states might have had the title of executive director or executive secretary of the state party. A supply room also included space for the party bookkeeper, an indispensable person in today's world of complex financial reporting regulations, both federal and state. Later, another official was added to the supply room roster, a state organizational director whose salary was paid by the Republican National Committee but whose equipment, travel, and related expenses were covered by the state central committee. Finally, a conference room was available for meetings of the state executive committee, and served frequently as an area for the seemingly endless piling-folding-stuffing-mailing operations that political staffs become involved in.

The administrative assistant, Roger Meier, a young man with midwestern newspaper experience, ran the day-to-day affairs of the party. He was under the direction of Leo Thorsness, a former Vietnam prisoner of war who had run for the US Senate in 1974 against George McGovern and who was later to run for the US House of Representatives in 1978, losing eventually to Democrat Thomas Daschle in a race so close that it was not finally decided until the South Dakota Supreme Court completed a statewide recount of the ballots late in 1979.[4] Thorsness had chosen Meier with the approval of the state executive committee. Thorsness himself had been selected by the state central committee in March 1976 over Ronald Jensen of Sioux Falls (party rules do not provide for the automatic sucession of the vice-chairman in the event of a vacancy in the chairmanship).

Executive Committees

The executive committee in South Dakota is composed of about two dozen members, including party legislative leaders and state officials, representatives chosen by county chairmen in eight regions, three appointees of the state chairman, and the chairmen of the Women's Federation, the Young Republicans,

4. The final official vote margin for Daschle was 110 votes. Daschle had served in the House throughout 1979, but an adverse decision by the state supreme court would probably have resulted in his replacement by Thorsness. The House Committee on Administration delayed a final decision until the court's recounting process was completed, a process stipulated by South Dakota law. The first district congressional seat was open in 1978 as a result of incumbent Larry Pressler's decision to seek the US Senate seat vacated by James Abourezk, who wanted to retire after one term.

and the Teen-Age Republicans. The executive committee meets at least once each quarter. Its parent is the Republican state central committee, composed of the state committeeman and committeewoman from each county as well as the county chairman of each county, resulting in an unwieldy body of nearly two hundred members. The state central committee is required by law to meet at least once each year, but the usual practice is to meet twice, once at the annual state fair in Huron in late summer, and one other time, in even-numbered years on the Sunday morning after the close of the biennial state convention. The main regular function of the state central committee is to consider changes in the rules governing party activity in the state.

In 1977, with the encouragement of Charles Bailey, regional field manager for the Republican National Committee, Thorsness and Meier inaugurated planning activities for the party that were undertaken by two smaller ad hoc committees of about half a dozen members each, composed partly of members of the executive committee itself and partly of nonmembers. It was thought necessary to include persons not on the executive committee in order to widen the contacts of the two groups and to tap outside expertise. The planning committee met for two or three days in September 1977 to put together an "election plan for 1978." This document then became the basis for the work of the second committee, the budget committee, which met for two days in October 1977 to work out a budget for 1978, setting income goals and providing funds for such areas as a state organizational director, a newsletter, and a legislative campaign program. Both the plan and the budget were subject to review and final approval by the executive committee.[5]

The operation of the Democratic state headquarters in Tennessee is even more modest than that of the Republican one just described. The state headquarters is composed of two rooms in an office building adjacent to the state capital and legislative offices in downtown Nashville. It is manned by a full-time volunteer senior citizen and by a "part-time" (a euphemism, since he often spends more than forty hours per week on the job) state executive director, Bart Gordon, a lawyer who resides in nearby Murfreesboro. Gordon has no party headquarters budget, and must deal with an opposing Republican state headquarters of larger size and greater sophistication. Gordon is responsible to, and carries out the directives of, the state chairman, who lives in Memphis. The chairman is in frequent contact with the headquarters, but he does not direct the day-to-day office details. He is chosen by the state central committee which is composed of one man and one woman from each of thirty-three

5. These observations on the work of the state executive committee are based largely on information obtained from Roger Meier in an interview in the Washington, D.C., office of Senator Rudy Boschwitz, February 6, 1980.

state senatorial districts. Formerly, the executive director was also elected by the state central committee, but now he is appointed by the chairman, which seems to make for a closer working relationship. The circumstance that seems to have the most to do with the level of activity of party officials in Tennessee is whether or not the party controls the governorship.[6]

State Central Committees

State central committees or smaller executive committees are the elements that exert party control and administer routine party affairs in the long periods between meetings of the state convention. (Like its national counterpart, the state convention exists for a very short period of time, but it does make most of the big decisions.) Occasionally the committee must take emergency action on an important matter, such as a vacated nomination (see Chapter 7).

State central committees are chosen in a variety of ways. Members may be picked by voters in the primary election; where this method is employed, intraparty factionalism is invited, but contested races for the state central committee (and for the convention) are not common. Another method is to have the choice made by the party's convention or central committee operating at the next lower level, usually the county convention or county central committee. Again, systematic competition for these positions is not characteristic of recent decades. Another method, committee selection by state convention, is usually based on the same unit representation system employed by the convention itself; that is, a state convention whose members are chosen by county units selects a central committee chosen from those same units. The same person could serve as a member of the state convention and a member of the state central committee.

There is also great variety in how state parties constitute their central committees. The party could chose an equal number of representatives from each county—a single member (as in South Carolina), or a male and female member, or a committeeman and committeewoman plus the county chairman (as in South Dakota).[7] Or the party could choose one (or more) members from each congressional district (as in Illinois) or from each legislative district (as in New York). This system has the advantage of automatically building in population equality in party organizations, since congressional and legislative

6. Telephone interviews with Bart Gordon, executive director of the Tennessee Democratic party, Nashville, Tennessee, March 10-11, 1980.
7. In South Dakota, however, the county representatives do not have equal voting power. The votes a particular county casts in the state central committee, as in the state convention, are exactly proportional to the county's share in the statewide vote cast for the party's gubernatorial candidate in the previous election.

districts must be fairly apportioned in terms of population. Another variant is to make the chairman and vice-chairman of each county members of the state central committee, ex officio. Wisconsin provides for two members from each congressional district, chosen by convention. Finally, there are mixed systems of central committee composition, in which the membership is chosen from delegates to the state convention, party candidates for and holders of major offices in the state, the national committee members from the state, county chairmen, and others appointed by county or state chairmen or conventions.[8]

Irregular Nomination Decisions

An example of a state central committee decision, one that was to prove highly significant for Republican fortunes in the state over the next two decades, was provided by the meeting of Nebraska Republicans at the Cornhusker Hotel in Lincoln in July 1954, following the sudden death of US Senator Hugh Butler.[9] The committee by acclamation chose Roman Hruska, then a member of the US House of Representatives, to be the Republican nominee to succeed Butler, in preference to former US Representative Howard Buffet.

Just three years earlier, members of the Republican committee for the third congressional committee were faced with the necessity of choosing a nominee to succeed US Representative Karl Stefan, who had died in office. Members from the twenty-four counties in the district, covering the northeast and east-central parts of the state, convened in Columbus to determine the relative strengths of three candidates. It took several ballots before Norfolk oil dealer R.D. Harrison narrowly defeated South Sioux City jeweler Merle Haynes in the committee meeting. Harrison went on to win the 1951 special election, and to win reelection in 1952, 1954, and 1956, before being swept out of office by the Democrats' agrarian upsurge of 1958, largely based on the unpopular farm policies of Agriculture Secretary Ezra Taft Benson.

8. Sorauf, op. cit., pp. 69-72.
9. Butler's death was preceded in April by the more unexpected death of US Senator Dwight Griswold. Griswold had died early enough so that candidacies could be filed for his replacement in the upcoming primary election. Governor Robert Crosby of North Platte appointed Mrs. Eva Bowring of Merriman as Griswold's temporary replacement, and himself became a candidate for the Republican nomination for the full term, along with US Representative Carl Curtis of Minden (the eventual winner), State Chairman (and later Representative) David Martin of Kearney, former Representative Terry Carpenter of Scottsbluff, and three minor candidates. Butler's death came too late to allow nomination through the regular primary, although some controversy did develop over former Representative Howard Buffet's attempt to file nomination petitions with the Secretary of State late one Friday afternoon.

Another example of an irregular committee decision occurred in South Dakota in 1962 when Joe Bottum was chosen by the Republican state central committee to be the party's nominee for the US Senate, following the sudden death of Senator Francis H. Case in June, just a few days after the South Dakota primary election in which Case had won nomination for a third term. The assembled Republicans chose Bottum in preference to five other candidates: US Representative Ben Reifel, former Governors Sigurd Anderson and Joe Foss, Attorney General A.C. Miller, and former House Speaker (and future Governor) Nils Boe. It required twenty long ballots on a hot summer day for the necessary majority to be reached. It seems pertinent to comment at some length on the consequences of such sudden and extraordinary involvement of a usually invisible party group in such a critical selection process.

The committeemen and committeewomen were not chosen with such a specific task as nominating a senatorial candidate in mind. The committee was a group with numerous and complicated internal associations, having to embark on a task which few if any of its members had ever taken part in or even considered prior to the sudden occurrence of the Senate vacancy. There are several sides to the question of how party nominees should be chosen, in regular or irregular circumstances. Supporters of the committee method, as used in the nomination of Joe Bottum, would probably base their arguments on the idea that 134 central committee members, being experienced in party politics and knowing the candidates more intimately than might the average citizen, would choose a better candidate than would the general party electorate. The notion might also be advanced that the discrete committee group would be more likely to withstand the temptation to choose a candidate strong on popularity and personality but weak on substantial qualifications and experience. Supporters of the general election method, on the other hand, would probably base their arguments on the agrarian-democratic idea of open nominations participated in by the general party membership. They might also say that a candidate chosen by the general membership of the party would be more acceptable to the public.

Supporters of committee nomination would have a difficult job attempting to prove that when the committee members assembled in Pierre they had a definite idea of which candidate they preferred, based on their experience in politics and their acquaintance with the individual candidates. A discrete committee may indeed make such a choice in such a way, but there is little evidence in the case studied here that this committee did so. The voting patterns from ballot to ballot indicate that most of the members were not decisive about their preference. Thus one is left to wonder about the rationality of committee decisions when important issues or offices are at stake. Of course, nomination responsibilities for small party groups raise the risks of bribery and corruption and the specter of the smoke-filled room, as well as the risk of dysfunctional confusion and factionalism.[10]

The executive committee is a recent addition to party organization in the United States, growing out of the traditional system in which state central committees were sometimes composed of several hundred members. With many states choosing two or three members from each county, state central committees of more than one hundred members were the rule. Rather than use such large and unwieldy groups, many state parties have developed, to either replace or at least supplement the central committee, smaller executive committees of perhaps one or two dozen members (see the discussion of contemporary party operations in South Dakota earlier in this section). These smaller groups can meet regularly to consider routine party business in a much more expeditious and probably harmonious way than was possible with the cumbersome state central committee.

Frank Sorauf's conclusions about the formal organizational structures that have been created by the state legislatures will round out this discussion of state party organization. First, he finds that parties are viewed almost exclusively by the legislatures as electoral organizations, which are to serve as "an auxiliary of the state's regulation of nominations and elections."[11] Secondly, he shows that parties are viewed as skeletal organizations, as cadres to be run by a small number of party officials, in which large numbers of activists are not expected to participate. Thus, parties are to be democratic and open to all members, with small cells of activists unable to make decisions without referral to all members who wish to take part in the party's primary.[12] A third point is that parties are not strictly hierarchical, though they may appear on paper to be so. For instance, in some states the state central committee is elected directly by the voters, rather than being selected by the layer of county committees that lie between the voters and the state committee. Party power seems to concentrate at the base, rather than at the apex of the organizational pyramid. "The result," according to Sorauf, "is to build into party organizational structure a great deal of localism and distaste for statewide direction."[13]

10. For a fuller discussion, see my *The Nomination of Joe Bottum* (Vermillion, S.D.: Governmental Research Bureau, 1963). Bottum was defeated by George McGovern in the November general election.
11. Sorauf, *op. cit.*, p. 71.
12. It is instructive here to consider the use of local party caucuses that take part in certain kinds of party decisions or discussions, as in the Iowa caucus system that has played an increasingly significant role in the presidential campaigns of 1976 and 1980.
13. Sorauf, *op. cit.*, p. 72.

COUNTY COMMITTEES

There is considerable potential for variety in the size and complexity of county-level party operations, just as there is at national and state levels. Consider the fact that Cook County, Illinois, contains a population of upwards of 5,493,766, while the population of Arthur County, in the sand hills of western Nebraska, is only 606. A ward organization in Chicago is larger and more complex than most county and many state organizations.

Typically, a party county organization is headed by a county chairman. Serving with the chairman is a county vice-chairman,[14] to act in the absence or incapacity of the chairman. A secretary or clerk is commonly chosen to keep minutes, maintain party records and membership lists, and take care of other clerical and correspondence duties. A treasurer is responsible for raising money to meet the county's quota for the state party treasury, accounting for receipts and expenditures, and distributing funds to various local campaign efforts.

The party's county officers are usually appointed by the county chairman or selected by the county central committee. The central committee is generally elected in the primary, each precinct choosing a man and a woman, or perhaps just one person, to serve on the committee. In large counties, the ward (a combination of several voting precincts) is the critical unit of election for members of the county central committee.

The correlation between political party organization and the formal organization of governmental units is not exact. The essential elements of state political party organization are the state and county organs. Depending on state statute or party rule, the state and county level organizational elements may be supplemented by supervisory units at the precinct, ward, special district, legislative district, judicial district, or congressional district levels.

CAUCUSES AND OTHER PARTY ELEMENTS

Some states make considerable use of another organizational element, the caucus. In Arkansas, for example, most of the Republican delegates to the 1980 national convention were chosen on February 2 in party caucuses at the congressional district level (this will be further discussed in Chapter 8). Iowa makes particularly dramatic use of the caucus. Its statutes provide for precinct caucuses to meet in late winter to begin the process of collecting local

14. Perhaps vice-chairwoman is the proper term, since there is often a rule that the second-in-command be of the opposite gender from the chairman.

sentiments and presidential candidate preferences. These caucuses gave tremendous boosts to Jimmy Carter's political aspirations in both 1976 (when
he was a not-very-well-known presidential possibility until he did so well in
Iowa) and 1980 (when as the incumbent president he showed impressive
strength in withstanding the challenge of Massachusetts Senator Edward
Kennedy).[15] In Iowa, these precinct caucuses are the fundamental political
unit, with their decisions being passed on up the organizational line to county,
district, and state meetings. The critical thing is that anyone may attend these
precinct caucuses, and hence access to the party decision-making machinery
is notably open and unstructured. The caucus system makes it possible for
both elite and mass groups to dominate party affairs. It is the danger of elite
manipulation of caucuses that most worries observers of American party processes. Of course, it requires strong and widely distributed support to convert
precinct preferences into national convention delegates or party nominations
or policy resolutions, but the system is geared to accommodate local manifestations of interests and concerns.

James MacGregor Burns, speaking at the 1979 annual convention of the
American Political Science Association in Washington, D.C., called for more
widespread use of Iowa-type, grass roots party caucuses as a vehicle for revi-
talizing American political parties specifically and American politics generally.
Burns was sanguine about the prospects of having regular town meetings all
across the country to discuss the problems of the day and their solution. It
is a question, of course, of how many citizens would be enthusiastic enough
about a given topic to attend such meetings.

A word is in order about other uses to which the term "caucus" has been
put. We have been talking about caucuses authorized by state statute or party
rules. The word has also been used in at least three other ways. "King Caucus"
refers to a time in early American history when the members of the dominant
party in Congress[16] met to determine the candidates for president in succession to Thomas Jefferson (James Madison in 1808, James Monroe in 1816,
and John Quincy Adams in 1824). The term is also commonly used to describe
clandestine meetings of a few party influentials to make critical decisions about

15. See Martha Angle and Robert Walters, "Does Iowa Sing Ted's Song?" Sioux City
    (Iowa) *Journal,* October 30, 1978, and Jules Witcover, *Marathon: The Pursuit of
    the Presidency, 1972-1976* (New York: Signet Books, 1977), pp. 145, 199-375
    passim.
16. The party has been variously referred to as the Democratic-Republican, the Demo-
    cratic, the Republican, and the Jeffersonian party. In spite of the modern Demo-
    cratic party's attachment to Thomas Jefferson, the party he headed in the first
    decade of the nineteenth century was the one Andrew Jackson opposed in establish-
    ing the Democratic party that still exists.

local leadership positions and nominations for public office, especially late in the last century—the era of the smoke-filled room. A third meaning is more contemporary, signifying the convening of all members of the party in a given legislative body for the purpose of electing party floor leaders and whips and determining the party position, if any, on upcoming legislative issues. These legislative caucuses generally operate independently of the national or state conventions and of the president or governor, even when the chief executive is a member of the same party. The congressional caucuses are more independent of party or executive control than are most state legislative caucuses.

Finally, there are a number of ancillary and auxiliary groups outside the regular party apparatus that developed to allow the party and its candidates to have closer relations with specific population clusters that are thought to have at least the potential of political clout. Such groups can be organized on a national basis, as is the Republican party's liberal-oriented Ripon Society, or on a very localized basis, as is the Stanton Square Neighborhood Democratic Council. Examples of ancillary groups include ethnic, religious, ideological, vocational, senior citizens, veterans, gender, and youth organizations (see Figure 6-1 for some examples in the Republican party).

PROPOSALS

6-1. To establish party committees. The national committee of a political party would be composed of one member from each state and the District of Columbia, who would be chosen by the state convention, and ten persons from the nation at large to be broadly representative of the national party, nominated by the party's presidential candidate and approved by the national convention. Terms on the national committee would be four years, beginning on the first day of September of presidential election years. The national committee would be chaired by the national director, who would be chosen by the national convention on the recommendation of the party's presidential candidate. The national committee would meet at least four times per year, on call of the national director. Each member would have one vote, the director voting only in case of a tie, and a simple majority of members present and voting would carry any motion, with one exception—when the national committee is balloting to fill a vacancy in the party's nominee for president or vice-president or in the office of party director, a special majority would be required. Such vacancies could be filled only if two conditions are met: (1) a majority of national committee members present and voting concur, and (2) state members representing states having at least half the national party strength as measured by the popular vote in the most recent presidential election concur as well.

The state executive committee would be composed of the state director and from seven to twenty-three other members chosen by the state convention, distributed among congressional or legislative districts in order to equitably represent the state's population. Terms could be set at either two or four years, depending on local preference and the state's terms for governors and state legislators. The state executive committee would meet at least two times each year, on call of the state director.

The county executive committee would be composed of the county director, elected in the primary, and from five to thirteen other members chosen by the county convention; members would be distributed among cities and rural areas so as to equitably represent the county's residents.

Executive committees for multicounty districts could be made up of members of county executive committees in the district, as determined by the respective county executive committees. The voting power of the county in district executive committee meetings would be proportional to the party vote in the county as a fraction of the party vote in the district as a whole.

Municipal executive committees, if mandated, could be formed by members of the county executive committee who reside in the municipality, all having an equal vote on the municipal committee.

6-2. To define the powers of party committees. The powers of national, state, county, and other committees would be specified. These powers would be similar from level to level, and in each case they would be determined by the party convention and exercised in the periods when the convention is not in session.

First, as already mentioned, party committees would be empowered to fill vacancies in the directorship of the party and in nominations for public office. Prior to primary elections, committees would have the power to endorse candidates for nomination for public office and to evaluate all such candidates by means of approval voting. These two proposals will be discussed further at the end of Chapter 7.

The other basic functions of party committees would include the following:

1. to oversee the administration of party business and the activities of its officials and staff;
2. to coordinate and support the campaign efforts of candidates within their respective levels, and with other levels of the party organization;
3. to plan and supervise arrangements for the party convention and for other meetings at their level of operation;
4. to maintain liaison with and among party officers and party members in public office at their level; and
5. to see that party officers fulfill their responsibilities.

The conduct of party affairs at any level seems to require the appointment of several officers to serve under the director. These would include an assistant director, who could act for the director in case of absence or inability and would succeed as director in case of death, permanent inability, or resignation; a secretary, who would maintain the records of the party, keep track of its official activities, issue calls for meetings, maintain membership lists, and handle correspondence; and a treasurer, to handle party receipts and disbursements and to record all financial transactions. The above officers and others at any level, such as research director, campaign coordinator, membership director, sergeant at arms, publicity director, and so forth, would be appointed by the director with the approval of the executive committee of that level.

6-3. To establish regular county caucuses. The county director would be required to call a county caucus at least once each year, with the caucus of the even-numbered year coming at least two months prior to the date of the primary election. All registered members of the party would be invited. At these meetings, members would be encouraged to express ideas or preferences as to problems, policies, prospective candidates, and other issues.

Notice of the caucus would be placed in the official newspaper of the county and released to all news media at least ten days before the meeting. The caucus notice would be sent to all members of the county executive committee and of the last county convention at least ten days prior as well. The caucus would be scheduled to meet at a place and time convenient to the largest number of members.

The county director would preside at the meeting, and the secretary would keep minutes. Any resolutions adopted by majority vote of the members present and voting, if at least twenty-five members are present, would be transmitted promptly to the state chairman of the party and to any other public or party official so designated in the resolution, along with an endorsement by the county director showing the circumstances of the meeting, the vote, and the director's personal position with respect to the resolution.

Such a caucus is not designed to be a representative body in a strict sense, but to afford an opportunity for social and political activity on the part of all party members that goes beyond the mere act of voting in a primary or general election.

Chapter 7
Choosing the Candidates: State and Local Party Nominations

Recruiting candidates to run for public office, and selecting the single nominee for each office to carry the party's banner in the general election, are probably the two most critical functions performed by American political parties. Elsewhere in this book there are discussions of the formation and leadership of the party institutions that are involved in the nominating process. This chapter looks at the means by which parties determine their nominee. Attention will focus on primary elections and the conventions, committees, and caucuses that come into play in various circumstances. Presidential nomination processes are covered in the next two chapters.

THE PARTY PRIMARY

The primary election is only one method a party may use to select its officers (see Chapter 5) and its nominees for public office, but it is the method most commonly used and the one that best reflects democratic ideals. In theory, a primary election extends the idea of majority rule in general elections to the choice of party candidates by a majority of the party's voters in the primary election.

Primaries are best known as the means of choosing the party's candidates to run in November. As such, their use goes back nearly a century in some states, where they were developed as part of the effort to wrest control of party affairs from urban machines and party bosses. The bosses had long dominated access to political office through their control over the selection of nominees, choices made in the proverbial smoke-filled rooms that were the setting for so much of American political activity in the late nineteenth and early twentieth centuries.

State Primaries

There are several methods used for nominating state officers.[1] Most states use the direct primary. Five (Alabama, Georgia, Indiana, South Carolina, and

1. See *The Book of the States, 1978-79* (Lexington, Ky.: Council of State Governments, 1978), p. 241, and *Congressional Quarterly Weekly Report,* February 25, 1978, p. 511.

Virginia) leave the question of whether there will be a primary election to the respective political parties; usually in these states the major candidates are nominated in a party primary, while the party convention makes the other nominations. In two states (Kansas and Michigan) some nominations are made in convention, others in the primary; in Michigan, the only state office at issue in the statewide primary is the governorship. In New York, nominations are by primary or by central committee selection. Several states use a combination of convention and direct primary mechanisms. In Colorado, there is a preprimary designation assembly under which a primary is avoided if the designee receives more than 80 percent of the assembly votes. In New Mexico, a candidate must receive at least 20 percent of the convention votes or use the petition process to gain a place on the primary ballot; New York has a similar plan, with 25 percent of the convention vote as the eligibility threshold. In Utah, there is a preprimary convention assembly; if the designated candidate receives at least 70 percent of the vote, there is no primary. In Connecticut, a combination of convention and primary is employed. There, the nominees for senator are selected by state convention, but any losing candidate who receives 20 percent of the convention vote may request a primary. In North Dakota, the Democratic party convention in June 1980 endorsed candidates prior to the state's September primary. In Iowa and South Dakota, candidates are nominated if they receive at least 35 percent of the vote in the primary; otherwise, the decision is made at the subsequent state convention, which may consider only the two top vote-getters in the primary.

These special voting quotas and thresholds add to the burden of election administrators and judges. Ordinarily, certification of election returns comes into question only when a candidate's plurality is very close; when the vote is not close, the losing side is unlikely to request the expensive and often unpopular recount process. But, as noted, often a standard other than plurality is involved. Representative John Anderson, Republican of Illinois, called for a recount of the 1980 Republican presidential primary in New Hampshire because the rules there specified that a candidate would receive two national convention delegates if he polled 10 percent of the Republican vote; the first count showed Anderson only 176 votes short of the 10 percent threshold.[2]

State primaries are held at a time determined by the state legislature. In 1978, Illinois held the earliest primary, in March. Nine states held their primary in May, eleven in June, eight in August, twenty in September, and one (Hawaii) in October. Nine southern or border states (Alabama, Arkansas, Florida, Georgia, Mississippi, North Carolina, Oklahoma, South Carolina, and Texas) where the Democratic party has traditionally been dominant, provide

2. "Campaign Notes: All Quarter-Million Votes in N.H. Must Be Recounted," *Washington Post,* March 2, 1980, p. A4.

for a runoff primary if no candidate receives a majority in the first primary. In Louisiana, all candidates run in a single nonpartisan primary; if none receives a majority of the vote, the top two candidates irrespective of party face each other in the general election. If a candidate receives a majority of the vote in the nonpartisan primary, he runs unopposed in the general election.

The primary schedule for 1980 was quite similar, even with the addition of the presidential races; the most dramatic difference was the New England primaries of late February and early March. In 1980, Illinois had its primary for gubernatorial and congressional nominations in March, Pennsylvania in April. Nine states used June, and in addition North Carolina, Texas, Arkansas, Mississippi, and South Carolina scheduled their runoff primaries in the same month. Seven states used August, twenty used September (plus runoffs in Georgia, Oklahoma, and Alabama), and Florida provides for a runoff as late as October.

Simple and Quota Pluralities

There are a variety of conditions under which winners of primaries are declared. In some cases, a simple plurality—receiving more votes than any other candidate—is sufficient. Sometimes a specified plurality floor is required. As noted earlier, in South Dakota a candidate must receive 35 percent of the vote to win nomination for governor, US senator, or US representative. As a result, a candidate's chance of securing the nomination decreases as the number of candidates (which is virtually unlimited) increases. Some observers have suggested a sliding quota plurality, in which the winning quota would depend on the number of candidates running. In Alabama, a winner is declared only if he wins a majority of the votes cast in the primary, and if no one receives such a majority, a runoff must be held a few weeks later between the top two candidates.

In the 1978 Democratic primary in Alabama, on September 5, no candidate for any one of the three top offices obtained the required majority. In the race for the gubernatorial nomination, Forest James, a former Republican state committeeman, surprised almost everyone by winning 28 percent of the vote, while Attorney General Bill Baxley received 24 percent with backing from labor and blacks, thus edging out former Governor Albert Brewer, who had been expected to lead in the primary.

In the race to fill the last two years of the term to which the deceased Senator James Allen of Alabama had been elected in 1974, his widow, Maryon Allen, who had been appointed to her late husband's seat by Governor George Wallace, led State Senator Donald Stewart by only 60,000 votes and was deprived of a hoped-for clear majority because of the presence of a third contender, Dan Wiley.

Meanwhile, in the race for the full Senate term to replace the retiring John Sparkman, former state court justice Howell Heflin just missed receiving a majority of the vote in a seven-candidate primary and outpolled his chief opponent, US Representative Walter Flowers, by about 120,000 votes.[3] As a result of the inconclusive primary, a Democratic runoff was held September 26, with James, Stewart, and Heflin the victors: James with 55 percent over Baxley in the race for governor, Stewart with 57 percent over Mrs. Allen in the short-term Senate race, and Heflin with 65 percent over Flowers in the full-term Senate race.[4] Each Democratic nominee eventually defeated his respective Republican opponent in the November general election.

It is possible to imagine a requirement that nomination be based on an augmented majority, that is, one greater than 50 percent. Such a rule would probably be based on an effort to overcome party regionalism or factionalism, in that it would necessitate a broad consensus of support. This would be akin to the pre-New Deal rule in the Democratic national convention that the presidential nominee receive the votes of two-thirds of the delegates, which gave the Democratic South virtual veto power over the presidential ticket. The percentage level required for declaration of a winner would presumably be affected by the patterns of intraparty regionalism or factionalism perceived by the policy-makers. In general, one would assume that a high percentage requirement for nomination would tend to reduce the number of candidates. But some may enter a contest in the hope of preventing a specific opposing candidate or faction from achieving the augmented quota, rather than in the hope of winning.

Most states holding primary elections have closed primaries wherein only registered members of the party may participate. In such states, independent voters ordinarily have no vehicle for expressing candidate preferences, and hence are virtually disfranchised in primary elections. Three states, Alaska, Louisiana, and Washington, have blanket primaries allowing a voter to vote for candidates of more than one party. Eight states (Idaho, Michigan, Minnesota, Montana, North Dakota, Utah, Vermont, and Wisconsin) make party registration a private thing, with voters receiving the ballots of all parties, but being restricted to voting for candidates of one party only.[5]

Filling Vacancies Via Primaries

In the previous chapter we described the special role taken by party central or executive committees in nominating candidates for major office in the wake

3. "Alabama Primary: A Day of Surprises," *Congressional Quarterly Weekly Report*, September 8, 1978, p. 2423.
4. *Congressional Quarterly Weekly Report*, September 30, 1978, p. 2680.
5. *The Book of the States, 1978-79, op. cit.*, p. 241.

of an unexpected vacancy caused by the death or resignation of a public official, when the vacancy occurred after the deadline had passed for filing for a place on the primary election ballot. By such central committee action, as we have seen, Roman Hruska and Joe Bottum secured their party's nomination for seats in the United States Senate. Several states have provided election machinery that allows the vacated nomination to be filled by voters in a primary election. Florida lost two veteran US senators, Park Trammell and Duncan U. Fletcher, in the spring of 1936, too late for a Democrat to become a candidate for the senate nominations (Florida was operating under the double-primary rule, with a first primary scheduled for June 2 and the runoff for June 23). Lacking any statutory authority, the Florida Democratic State Executive Committee on June 30 called for special primary elections to be held August 11 and September 1. The Florida Supreme Court subsequently approved this procedure on July 23.[6] Eventually, Claude Pepper of Tallahassee and Charles O. Andrews of Orlando were elected and took their Senate seats in January 1937.

For certain irregular or unscheduled vacancies in Georgia, a primary election is held in which voters of all parties take part, with a second election between the top two candidates if no one wins a majority of the vote. This occurred in 1977, following US Representative Andrew Young's resignation to become US ambassador to the United Nations in the Carter administration. Civil rights leader John Lewis and Atlanta city council president Wyche Fowler, Jr., finished one/two in the March 15 special election, dashing the hopes of Republicans, who had entered just one serious candidate in the open primary with the idea of winning a position in the expected runoff election. Fowler received just under 40 percent of the vote, Lewis 29 percent, and State Senator Paul Coverdell, the Republican hopeful, 22 percent, with the other nine candidates trailing far behind. The Rev. Ralph Abernathy, former head of the Southern Christian Leadership Conference, was the fourth-ranking candidate, with only 5 percent of the vote. In the runoff election on April 5, Fowler defeated Lewis, receiving 62 percent of the vote.[7]

Another variant of the nomination process following an irregular vacancy in office is the California system. Congressmen Leo J. Ryan, Democrat representing the eleventh district, was shot to death in November 1978 in Guyana while investigating "The People's Temple," an agricultural commune. An election was held March 6, 1979, with five Democratic candidates, five Republican candidates, and one candidate from each of two minor parties. Under California law, a candidate would have been elected outright in the first special election had he received a majority of all the votes cast. The

---

6. State ex rel. Andrews *v.* Gray, 169 So. 501, 125 Fla. 1 (1936).
7. *Congressional Quarterly Weekly Report,* March 19, 1977, p. 486, and *ibid.,* April 9, 1977, p. 657.

leading Democratic contender, G. W. Holzinger, formerly a Ryan aide, received 23.2 percent of the total vote, while the leading Republican, Bill Royer, a San Mateo county supervisor, received 21.5 percent. As a consequence, a runoff was held April 3 among the top vote-getters from each party, namely, Holzinger, Royer, and the two minor party candidates (who in the primary had together received less than one percent of the votes cast, and yet qualified for the runoff). In the April runoff, Royer was elected to succeed Ryan.[8]

In another example, J. Bennett Johnston was elected to his second term in the US Senate in the September 16, 1978 Louisiana primary because he was able to win an absolute majority of all the votes cast. He received 59 percent of the vote, compared to the 41 percent received by Democratic State Senator Louis Jenkins (of course, in a two-way race, one candidate is bound to receive a majority of votes).[9]

Primaries and Party Factionalism

Austin Ranney has called the direct primary the most radical political party reform in American history.[10] Primaries exist for the purpose of allowing rank-and-file members of the party to exercise a powerful role in selecting its officers and nominees for public office. But, on the negative side, there is much evidence to show that holding direct primaries may also encourage intraparty dissension, strife, and factionalism. Multicandidate primary contests can seriously divide a party, permanently as well as temporarily, and a two-candidate race can have bitter consequences. Losing candidates or their supporters may be so offended or outraged by their loss that they will refuse to lift a finger to help the nominee in the general election campaign, and in some cases elements of the losing side may even turn their resources to helping the other party.[11] But it is possible for parties or individual candidates to emerge from the primary with more unity and energy than before, especially if the campaign has been waged on a high level of discourse and competition. The trick is to avoid personal attacks and to minimize sectional, factional, or ideological rivalries that might leave lasting irritations. For the winner, the primary campaign can be of significant help in publicizing his name and his position on issues, in shaking down his campaign organization, and in cementing

---

8. *Congressional Quarterly Weekly Report,* March 10, 1979, p. 413.

9. *Congressional Quarterly Weekly Report,* September 23, 1978, p. 2571.

10. Ranney, *Curing the Mischiefs of Faction, op. cit.,* p. 121.

11. Donald Bruce Johnson and James R. Gibson, "The Divisive Primary Revisited: Party Activists in Iowa," *American Political Science Review,* March 1974, pp. 67–77. See also the earlier article by Andrew Hacker, "Does a 'Divisive' Primary Harm a Candidate's Election Chances?" *American Political Science Review,* March 1965, pp. 105–110.

political alliances and securing financial support.[12] Of course, the same benefits may accrue to losing candidates in future campaigns.

OTHER NOMINATING SYSTEMS

Primary elections do not settle all the basic decisions that are made in respect to party leaders and nominees. Conventions and other elements such as committees, conferences, and caucuses are also employed, as discussed elsewhere. But in this section it is important to point out how primaries can fit into the electoral sequence in a particular state. Some primaries occur before party conventions; here, the electoral function of the convention is to nominate candidates for lesser offices rather than for the major ones and to resolve nomination contests where no candidate has received the required percentage of votes in the primary. In other states, there are preprimary conventions or assemblies. The electoral function of such meetings is to endorse one candidate in preference to others.

Colorado, Minnesota, and New York offer illustrative examples. In Colorado, a primary is held if a second candidate, having sufficient strength in the party organization, challenges the one designated by the party. Such a primary occurred in September 1978 when State Senator Ted Strickland won the gubernatorial nomination over Dick Plock, and US Representative William Armstrong defeated Jack Swigert for the US Senate nomination.[13] Minnesota Democrats in June 1978 endorsed Senator Wendell Anderson and US Representative Donald Fraser for the two Senate seats (one of which was open due to Hubert Humphrey's death earlier in the year), but in the September primary the Democratic voters chose Robert Short in preference to Fraser; both Anderson and Short were defeated by Republicans in November. New York's challenge primary system, enacted in 1967, provided for endorsement of candidates by county, district, or state comittees several weeks prior to the primary. If no one were to challenge the endorsed candidate, he or she automatically became the

12. An empirical study of primary election results in South Dakota during the postwar period showed little connection between the closeness of the vote in the primary and the candidate's success in November. The gamma score for the thirty-five races covered was a modest +.26. Of course, a close primary may not be bitter, and a bitter primary may not be close; it is the bitterness, not the closeness, that hurts subsequent party effort. See Alan L. Clem and Kenneth J. Meier, "Another Look at the Effects of Divisive Party Primaries: The South Dakota Experience, 1946–1974," *Public Affairs* (University of South Dakota, Governmental Research Bureau), August 1975, pp. 1-4.

13. Rhodes Cook "Right vs. Right in Colorado," *Congressional Quarterly Weekly Report,* September 16, 1978, p. 2474.

party nominee. But if a challenging candidate who had received 25 percent support in the earlier committee balloting were to petition for a place on the primary ballot, then the final decision would be deferred to the primary.[14]

Historically, especially in the post-Federalist Congresses, congressional party caucuses played the major role in presidential candidate selection. This system was substantially changed as a result of Andrew Jackson's presidential campaigns and the development of the new Democratic party in the 1830s. But the practice of using state legislative party caucuses lingered. Party caucuses in the sense of smoke-filled back rooms were dominant as nominating devices in the last decades of the nineteenth century. The tendency in this century, however, has been to systematize the organs of party government, such as county, district, and state committees and conventions, and to democratize the choice of their members and delegates.

THE SPECIAL PROBLEM OF VACANCIES

Vacancies in office are fairly infrequent, but when they occur they signal the beginning of important and often confused decision-making periods.

Four types of vacancies are of concern to this study. First are those in public office, such as the Alabama, California, Florida, Georgia, Nebraska, and South Dakota cases described in Chapter 6. In the case of the presidency, the Constitution, especially the Twenty-fifth Amendment (1967), states that such vacancies are to be filled by the vice-president, and vacancies in the vice-presidency are to be filled by presidential nomination of a replacement, on approval by the two houses of Congress. The events of the second Nixon administration are still fresh in our memories. Vice-President Spiro Agnew, who had served as vice-president through Nixon's first term, resigned early in the second term while under fire concerning bribery allegations during his former tenure as governor of Maryland. President Nixon then nominated US Representative Gerald Ford of Michigan, his party's floor leader in the House, to replace Agnew as vice-president. When in August 1974 Nixon himself resigned the presidency, the first person in history to do so, at a time when

---

14. Robert F. Sittig, "The Voter's Voice: New York's 'Challenge' Primary Passes First Test in Democratizing Nominating Process," *National Civic Review*, September 1969, p. 356.

the House Judiciary Committee was moving toward a vote of impeachment against him, Ford became president, and then subsequently appointed Governor Nelson Rockefeller of New York to replace him as vice-president.

Vacancies in the US Senate are surprisingly common, a function in part of the long Senate term and the somewhat greater age of senators. In the period 1919–1965, 18 percent of all full terms in the Senate were not completed by the person elected to them.[15] One idiosyncrasy worth noting is that, while Senate vacancies may under the Seventeenth Amendment (1913) be filled by gubernatorial appointment, at least until the next scheduled general election, vacancies in the House may be filled only by a special election. States have by constitution or statute provided for succession to a vacated governor's chair; indeed, the lieutenant governor was created very largely in the image of the vice-president.

The second kind of vacancy is one involving not the public office itself but the party nomination for that office. When an incumbent dies in office or resigns before the expiration of the term but after being nominated for re-election, vacancies in both the office and in the party's nomination are created, as in the Florida, Nebraska, and South Dakota cases discussed earlier. Of course, vacated nominations may also happen to the challenging party and in open seat contests as well. In 1962, when Bill Day of Winner resigned his Democratic nomination for the office of attorney general of South Dakota, the Democratic state committee chose Thomas E. Poe, Jr., of Vermillion to replace him on the ballot.

The third kind of vacancy occurs when a party officer, such as the national committeeman, the state chairman, or the county chairman, fails to complete the term for which he was elected. It is commonly the duty of the central or executive committee of that level to name a replacement to complete the term.

Finally, there is the much rarer and generally less significant situation in which a particular party officer is elected in a primary and more than one candidate is mandated by state statute or party rule.

Although vacancies in office or in nomination don't occur often, they can lead to decisions that have lasting consequences for the party as well as the entire political system. Some states have quite casual approaches to such situations, and others have more sophisticated (and sometimes very intricate) processes ready to handle the emergency. Attention needs to be given to proposals to improve the means of filling vacancies, looking toward the proper balance between efficiency and economy on the one hand and responsibility and democracy on the other.

15. See the present author's "Popular Representation and Senate Vacancies," *Midwest Journal of Political Science,* May 1966, p. 66.

PROPOSALS

Party executive committees at all levels should be encouraged to critically evaluate all phases of partisan activity. They could share with the party's convention the job of evaluating the performance of public officials, as will be suggested in Chapter 9. They could perform a critical function in primary election campaigns by assessing the relative merits of the various candidates for public office or party leadership, thus enhancing the power and prestige of the party organization. At the same time, however, it is proposed that control of party nominations for major office remain in the hands of party members voting in the primary election.

7-1. To nominate candidates for federal office in a party primary. As will be detailed in proposals at the end of Chapter 8, party members would indicate their presidential preference in a primary election. Candidates for the United States Senate and House of Representatives would also be nominated in a closed party primary. The same primary would be the vehicle for the election of party directors (see Chapter 5) and of delegates to state or county conventions (see Chapter 9). It is also recommended that states require parties to nominate their candidates for governor and the state legislature by means of the primary election.

7-2. To approve candidates. Party committees should be required to review candidates for party or public office. The national committee would concern itself with senatorial and congressional candidates, the state executive committees with state legislative candidates and the state's own congressional delegation, and the county executive committees with candidates for county offices. The device of approval voting, by which each member of the committee would indicate whether he approves or disapproves of each candidate, is available as a new, convenient, and simple way to assess the relative acceptability of several candidates for the same nomination or position. It is entirely possible that a majority of all the electors might approve all of the candidates, in which case the candidate approved by the highest percentage of voters would have the strongest endorsement.[16]

The approval voting system will be better understood by means of a hypothetical case involving a party's prospective candidate for a particular

16. For a full explanation of approval voting, see Steven J. Brams and Peter C. Fishburn, "Approval Voting," *American Political Science Review,* September 1978, pp. 831–847. See also Brams, "Approval Voting: A Practical Reform for Multicandidate Elections," *National Civic Review,* November 1979, pp. 549–553, 560.

congressional district. The executive committee for the district, meeting a few weeks before the primary, finds that three persons, Frederic Fremont, Harriet Hastings, and Kenneth Kearney, have petitioned to be the party's nominee. The three are invited to submit written statements to the committee, covering their backgrounds, their qualifications for public office, and their views on the issues and challenges that face the district and the nation. The candidates would also be asked to present their cases before the committee in person. After the statements have been read and the presentations concluded, each committee member would indicate whether the candidates appear to be sufficiently qualified, intelligent, and industrious to handle the responsibilities of the office. In effect, the committee member is asked whether he would support the candidate in the general election campaign should that candidate win the nomination. Assuming that twenty-two committee members take part, the results might look like this:

> Kenneth Kearney—nineteen members approving, three members not approving;
> Harriet Hastings—fifteen members approving, seven members not approving; and
> Frederic Fremont—ten members approving, twelve members not approving.

The primary ballot would list the results of approval voting for each candidate, so that the voters have clear evidence of the relative acceptability of each candidate to the party leaders. Voters, of course, could accept or reject the committee's evaluations. Thus, without forcing the leaders to narrow their choice to a single endorsed or approved candidate, this process allows them to show their preferences to the voters.

The tabulation of approval voting might have one further use. In primary contests where no candidate receives the required percentage quota of votes, as will be discussed in Chapter 9, the leading vote-getter in the primary could be certified as the nominee if he received the approval of at least 60 percent of the executive committee. If the leading candidate failed to receive the quota in the primary and was not approved by 60 percent of the executive committee in the preprimary approval process, then the nomination would be made by the postprimary party convention (see Proposal 3, Chapter 9).

7-3. To fill vacant offices. Presidential vacancies, as noted earlier, are filled by processes established in the Constitution. It is recommended that states fill gubernatorial vacancies by similar provisions, substituting the office of lieutenant governor for the vice-president.

Vacancies in the US Senate or House of Representatives should be filled only by means of an election.[17] A vacancy occurring between July 1 and October 5 of a congressional election year (that is, any even-numbered year) would be filled in the regular general election. A senatorial or congressional vacancy occurring at any other time would be filled by a special election to be held not less than sixty and not more than ninety days from the date of the vacancy.

For a nomination for a vacated office that is to be filled at a regular general election, a primary would be held on the Tuesday nearest twenty days from the date the vacancy occurred. In cases where a special election is required, the primary would be held on the Tuesday nearest thirty days from the date of the vacancy, with the deciding special election coming not less than thirty and not more than sixty days after the primary.

Candidates for special senatorial or congressional elections would get their names on the ballot by means of nominating petitions signed either by three members of the party executive committee at the appropriate level (state or congressional district) or by one thousand registered members of the party. The executive committee would exercise its approval voting responsibilities in elections to fill vacancies just as in other elections.

Vacancies in a state legislature would be filled by the district or county executive committee of the party that held the seat prior to the vacancy. Vacancies in a state elective office other than the governor and lieutenant governor would be filled by gubernatorial appointment, subject to legislative approval. Vacancies in county or municipal office would be filled by the respective governing board or council. These state and local replacements would serve only until the next election at which such officers would be regularly elected.

Admittedly, the above provisions for state and local replacements depart somewhat from the principle of democratic or popular control of public offices, but it is felt that the expense and confusion entailed by special election processes would not be warranted by the fairly limited stakes involved.

7-4. To fill nomination vacancies. Vacancies in a party nomination for congressional, state, or local office would be filled by the party executive committee of the appropriate level. However, states wishing to do so could,

17. Such a policy would require a slight change in the Seventeenth Amendment, which provided for direct election of US senators but at the same time allowed states to empower the governor to make temporary appointments lasting until the next general election. Individual states could achieve the same effect by withdrawing or not granting that gubernatorial power.

for vacancies in Congress, require use of a primary to designate the party's nominee within the limits of the process described in Proposal 3 above. Note that here we are speaking of a circumstance in which only one party has a vacant nomination, which might or might not involve a vacated seat; in Proposal 3, we were discussing cases where the seat had been left vacant, calling for nominations from both parties.

Vacancies in party office, or in nominations for party office where rules require a competitive primary, would be filled by the party executive committee of the appropriate level.

7-5. To provide for nominations by convention. There are no provisions in these propsals for nominations by county conventions, and the presidential nominations made by national conventions will be covered in later chapters, but there are two cases in which state conventions would act as the nominating agent for the party. The first involves the nomination of party candidates for state office who, under the laws of the state, are not nominated in the primary election (in many states, this would include a number of constitutional officers such as the lieutenant governor, the attorney general, the secretary of state, the state treasurer, etc.). The second involves the resolution of a nomination contest where the results of the primary have not been conclusive, as sometimes happens when an augmented plurality is required. For example, if it is required that a candidate must receive 35 percent of the primary vote to win nomination for a specified office, and if no candidate receives that quota, then the subsequent party convention must make the final choice between the two candidates receiving the most votes in the primary.[18]

18. A number of states have established such plurality quotas as a means of reducing factionalism in the state party and of assuring that whoever is nominated has the support of a sizeable part of the state. It should not be forgotten that in a race among six candidates, a mere 17 percent of the vote could be sufficient to constitute a plurality. In South Dakota, one of those requiring 35 percent of the primary vote, five candidates ran for the 1972 Republican nomination to succeed Karl Mundt in the United States Senate—former State Senator Robert Hirsch, former Attorney General Gordon Mydland, Rapid City banker Charles Lien, Humboldt farmer Ken Stofferahn, and Sious Falls businessman Thomas Reardon. The five men finished in that order in the primary, but Hirsch's 27 percent of the votes was insufficient for outright nomination. The state convention a few weeks later chose him over Mydland; Hirsch subsequently lost in November to Democrat James Abourezk. Abourezk himself had narrowly avoided such a convention vote two years before when, running for the second congressional district Democratic nomination, he barely exceeded the 35 percent quota in a contest with Rapid City's Don Barnett and former state legislator Elvern Varilek.

Table 7-1.   Percentage of Primary Vote Required to Win Nomination, Depending on Number of Candidates Entered

Number of Candidates	Primary Vote Percentage Required for Nomination
2	50
3	40
4	35
5	30
6 or more	25

The arguments for augmented plurality quotas in party nominations are persuasive (for example, that they tend to reduce intraparty factionalism). However, rather than set a single quota irrespective of the number of candidates, a sliding quota could be established, making it somewhat easier for a candidate to achieve nomination in cases where a large number of candidates have entered. Such a sliding scale is displayed in Table 7-1. In any event, the choice of the subsequent convention should be limited to the two candidates receiving the most votes in the primary.

The national convention should continue to choose the party's presidential ticket (this topic is considered in Chapter 8). State conventions would nominate the party's ticket for lesser state constitutional officers such as secretary of state, state treasurer, state auditor, and attorney general, and would also, as noted above, resolve inconclusive primary contests. County conventions would have no regular nominating role; nominees for partisan district, county, or municipal public office would be chosen by simple plurality vote in the primary.

Chapter 8

Testing Presidential Hopefuls: Presidential Primaries and Delegate Selection

Perhaps the greatest recurring miracle of democracy is that every four years Americans can accomplish the election of their president. The system by which this miracle is accomplished is tortuous, protracted, capricious, bewildering, and not altogether democratic. Unfortunately, interest in reforming any of the several elements of the presidential selection system, which just before and during the year-long campaign sometimes rises to quite a high point, dwindles and evaporates as soon as the contest is over. Only a calamity seems likely to threaten us sufficiently into reaching a consensus on national electoral reform, and one may doubt whether today's system could actually endure such a crisis.

COMMENTARIES ON THE SYSTEM

Why is the presidential selection process so awkward and confusing? Because, in essence, we have fifty different systems of assessing the popularity of various presidential candidates or electing delegates to the national conventions that will finally choose the Democratic and Republican nominees. As William Barry Furlong has said, "Presidential campaigns seem to be designed by the inane for the insane."[1] Writing of the maze of state presidential primaries, Jules Witcover has described presidential politics as "an insiders' game that even many of the insiders cannot follow." He is not very optimistic that anything will be done to simplify the system: "It would be helpful . . . if a way could be found to assure uniform rules for the primaries . . . . But the chances of achieving much uniformity are slim."[2]

Evidence of how one state's idiosyncrasies can affect the presidential selection system crop up unexpectedly, dramatizing its crazy-quilt nature. In the autumn of 1979, rebellious Massachusetts Democrats were exempted from national party rules so that the state could hold an early primary, and thus

1. William Barry Furlong, "The Wild, Wild Year of Politics 1980," *Saturday Evening Post,* January/February, 1980, p. 12.
2. Jules Witcover, *Marathon* (New York: Signet Books, 1977), p. 693.

perhaps boost the candidacy of Senator Edward Kennedy. In justifying the request for exemption, Massachusetts House Speaker Thomas McGee told the national party's Compliance Review Commission that Democratic party leaders in Massachusetts had been unsuccessful in their efforts to convince Democratic members of the state legislature that the primary should be moved from March 4 to March 11, the date specified by the national party as the earliest on which a presidential primary could be held in 1980.[3] In January 1980, the Wisconsin Supreme Court told the Democratic National Committee that it could not require the state's presidential primary, scheduled for April 1, to be open only to Democrats.[4] With national and state-level party officials and federal and state-level legislators, administrators, and judges involved in making or applying presidential selection policy, it is no wonder that we have the mess we do. What is a wonder is that we have had so few problems and disputes.

The problems brought about by the confusion of state presidential primaries have prompted an experienced political scientist, Donald Herzberg, to recommend that we "bring back cigar-puffing political kingmakers and their smoke-filled rooms" to displace the present fourteen-month campaign season with its "hyped-up primaries and confusing caucuses." Herzberg voiced the belief that the presidential primaries and caucuses have damaged the two-party system far more than they have helped it, and that delegates to national conventions should not be committed to one candidate or to a single issue.[5] This illustrates the basic dilemma of the presidential nomination process—to open up the system and give ordinary party members a significant role, to let the general popularity of the various candidates be given free expression through primaries, seems to strip party leaders of much of their power to influence affairs and at the same time makes it more likely that the nomination process will divide, rather than unite, the party leadership in the nation and in the states.

According to David Broder, the "problems of the presidential selection system are symptomatic of the problems afflicting our politics."[6] Writing in the early stages of the 1980 campaign, Broder emphasized three faults with

3. Associated Press dispatch from Washington, D.C., "Kennedy Country Gets Early Test," in Sioux Falls (S.D.) *Argus-Leader,* November 17, 1979.
4. United Press International dispatch from Madison, Wisc., "Wisconsin High Court Sets Stage for Battle on Democratic Delegates," in *Washington Post,* January 20, 1980, p. A10.
5. Interview with Donald Herzberg of Georgetown University by Rudy Maxa, "Tired of Caucuses, Primaries Already? This Political Pro Says It Was More Fun Back in the Era of the Smoke-Filled Room," *The Washington Post Magazine,* January 20, 1980, p. 4.
6. David Broder, "It's Party Time Again," *The Washington Post Magazine,* February 24, 1980, pp. 6–13. Much of the piece is devoted to reflections on the earlier Iowa caucuses; Broder is hopeful that the resurgence of party enthusiasm in Iowa is the beginning of a reversal of "two decades of decay." *Ibid.,* p. 9.

the system—that there are far too many primaries, that there is too much dependence on television, and that the primaries work against rather than for a united party effort.[7] Broder noted that the fragmentation he saw in presidential selection processes was part of a more pervasive fragmentation in national politics, where congressional decision-making authority has become decentralized, where interest groups have proliferated, and where single-issue causes have become dominant in many races.[8]

One of the most compelling and anguished commentaries on the primary system was made by a onetime presidential candidate, US Representative Morris Udall, Democrat of Arizona, in the wake of the 1976 Democratic primaries that served to catapult Jimmy Carter to the nomination over Udall and several other hopefuls:

> We had thirty primaries, presumably all of them equal. After three of those primaries, I'm convinced, it was all over. The die was cast. Just imagine the whole process being completed by Carter who wins New Hampshire by 29 percent to my 24, he comes in fourth in Massachusetts, and then he beats Wallace by three percentage points in Florida. In the ensuing two weeks he shot up twenty-five points in the Gallup Poll, almost without precedent, by winning two primaries and coming in fourth in another one.
>
> If there was a state in America where I was entitled to relax and feel confident, it was Wisconsin. I'd been there thirty times and I had organization, newspaper endorsement, and all the congressmen and state legislators. Well, I take a poll two weeks before the primary and he's ahead of me, two to one, and has never been in the state except for a few quick visits. That was purely and solely and only the product of that narrow win in New Hampshire and the startling win in Florida. And he won there only because everybody wanted to get rid of George Wallace.
>
> It's like a football game, in which you say to the first team that makes a first down with ten yards, "Hereafter, your team has a special rule. Your first downs are five yards. And if you make three of those you get a two-yard first down. And we're going to let your first touchdown count twenty-one points. Now the rest of you bastards play catch-up under the regular rules."[9]

---

7. Broder in passing did remind his readers of the many useful features of presidential primaries—they test a candidate's campaign organization, they force a candidate to address issues unfamiliar to his home area amid widely different cultures and settings, and they test a candidate's qualifications, emotional stability, and stamina. *Ibid.*, p. 10. For a list of six arguments against any sort of presidential primary, some touched on elsewhere in this chapter, see Sorauf, *op. cit.,* pp. 284–285.

8. Broder, *op. cit.,* p. 11.

9. Witcover, *Marathon, op. cit.,* pp. 692–693.

VARIETIES OF PRESIDENTIAL PRIMARIES

The use of presidential primaries goes back to the early years of this century, as individual states sought ways to reduce the power of old-line political machines and to enhance the importance of candidate popularity among the mass of party members. Primaries did not become common until after World War II, nor really dominant in terms of nomination choice until the 1960s. Four states, Florida, Wisconsin, Pennsylvania, and Oregon, pioneered in developing the processes by which individual members could play a formal role in choosing their party's nominee. By 1912, twelve states had a presidential primary law, and fourteen more joined the primary bandwagon by 1916; however, in ensuing years several states dropped the experiment, and national attention did not ordinarily focus on individual primaries as it does now. It is well to remember that the candidacies of Eisenhower, Stevenson, Kennedy, and Nixon did not depend absolutely on success in primaries, and that Kennedy, after all, won only a small handful of them in 1960. In the 1970s, success in primaries had become the *sine qua non* of nomination, as the experiences of George McGovern, Gerald Ford, Jimmy Carter, and Ronald Reagan attest.

The variety of American presidential primaries can be bewildering. For one, Democratic primaries are under growingly stringent restraints imposed by the Democratic national party, and the Republicans have a few national standards that must be considered by state legislatures and party organs in establishing a presidential primary. More importantly, the rules and conditions of the presidential primaries in the several states are determined by the respective state legislatures. However, the courts have ruled that party charters and rules are superior to state statutes if they involve federal questions such as the process by which party nominations for federal office are made.[10]

10. Cousins *v.* Wigoda, 419 U.S. 477 (1975). The Supreme Court noted that allowing each of the fifty states to determine the qualifications and eligibility of delegates to national party conventions could "destroy the effectiveness of the National Party Convention as a concerted enterprise engaged in the vital process of choosing Presidential and Vice-Presidential candidates—a process which usually involves coalitions cutting across state lines. The Convention serves the pervasive national interest in the selection of candidates for national office, and this national interest is greater than any interest of an individual state." (p. 490). The Court emphasized (footnote 4, on pp. 483–484) that it was intimating no views on such questions as: (1) whether the decisions of a national political party in the area of delegate selection constitute state or governmental action, and, if so, whether or to what extent principles of the political question doctrine counsel against judicial intervention, (2) whether national political parties are subject to the principles of the reapportionment decisions, or other constitutional restraints, in the methods of delegate selection and allocation, and (3) whether or to what extent national political parties and their nominating conventions are regulable by, or only by, Congress. For a general commentary on the decision, see "Supreme Court Establishes National Party Conventions Superior to State Election Law," *Electionews,* IV, February 1975, pp. 1–2.

Since there is not sufficient space here to describe the presidential primary system for every state, our discussion will focus its attention on the major types. There are several factors that need to be considered in attempting to classify contemporary presidential primaries.

First is the question of citizen access to the voting booth. In most states, primary elections are open only to registered party members; this is the "closed" primary system. But in others, the primary is also open to nonparty members.

Second is the matter of the candidate's access to the ballot. In twenty-one of the 1980 presidential primaries, the candidate obtained his place on the ballot on his own initiative. In fourteen primaries, the names of nationally recognized candidates were placed on the ballot by state officials. In three primaries, candidates must respond affirmatively to their nomination by state officials, or pay a filing fee to be listed.[11]

A third factor is the timing of the primary and of the filing deadline. Early primaries, notably New Hampshire's, have an importance far beyond the number of delegates to be selected because they occur early in the primary season (as lamented by Morris Udall in the section above). But late primaries can be of critical significance in those cases where no outstanding front-runner has come forth in the early stages. With the primary season stretching out over more than three months, the cast of characters can undergo considerable revision; this leads to anomalous circumstances such as the 1976 Democratic development, when Senator Frank Church of Idaho and Governor Jerry Brown of California mounted bids to head off Jimmy Carter, but entered too late to contest for delegates in several of the last primaries. In the South Dakota primary, for instance, Brown and Church were not on the ballot, but Udall and Senator Henry Jackson of Washington were, even though their candidacies had collapsed. In 1980, two primaries were scheduled in February, ten in March, four in April, thirteen in May, and nine in June. Filing deadlines were generally set about two months before the primary, but in a few states it was as short as one month or as long as three months.

The number of delegates at stake is the fourth factor to be considered. All things being equal, the larger the number of delegates being chosen, the more important the primary, but all things are not equal. We have already noted the attention given to certain primaries simply because they are so early. There are other questions involved: whether the distribution of delegates is at-large, by district, winner-take-all, or proportional. Raw population is the principal determinant of the size of the state delegation to the national convention, but slight variations occur in Democratic and Republican delega-

11. This discussion of presidential primary rules and practices comes largely from the article "How Presidential Primaries Operate in Each State in the 1980 Campaign," *Congressional Quarterly Weekly Report*, February 2, 1980, pp. 284–285. See also Sorauf, *op. cit.*, pp. 275–278.

tions due to differences in party strength from state to state, in the size of the respective national conventions, and in party success in recent state elections. In any event, on the matter of size alone, the primaries in New York, where 282 Democratic and 123 Republican delegates are chosen, or in California, with its 306 Democratic and 168 Republican delegates, are more significant than the primaries in Vermont (12 Democrats, 19 Republicans) or Montana (19 Democrats, 20 Republicans).

Fifth, are the delegates bound by the results of the primary? In the great majority of state primaries, they are, but the delegates themselves are selected outside the primary by the presidential candidate or by a party organ such as a committee or caucus. This is the case in forty-four of the seventy different primaries scheduled in 1980, twenty-three of thirty-four Democratic primaries and twenty-one of thirty-six Republican primaries. In eleven primaries, the presidential preference is binding and most of the delegates themselves are elected in the primary. In five, the presidential voting is advisory only, and the delegates are selected outside the primary. In seven cases, the voting is advisory as to the presidential candidate, and most delegates are elected in the primary. Finally, in three cases, there is no presidential preference voting at all, but most delegates are chosen in the primary.

The sixth factor has to do with the method by which the delegates are allocated among the presidential candidates. Here, too, one method is in a clear majority, but we can see real differences between the two parties. In forty-four out of the seventy primaries, the delegates are awarded to presidential candidates in proportion to their share of the primary vote. Twenty-nine of the thirty-four Democractic primaries are of this type, while only fifteen of the thirty-six Republican are; this is one reflection of the much stronger role the Democratic national party takes with respect to delegate selection. The second variety is called the loophole primary, in which many of a state's delegates are elected by districts, and in many cases the decision is on a winner-take-all basis. The loophole device can, of course, produce far different results in terms of delegates won as compared with the results of the allocation of seats based on statewide percentages. Two Democratic primaries (Illinois and West Virginia) are of this kind, as are nine Republican primaries. The third variant, used only in six Republican primaries, involves a mixture of statewide and district elections, with all of them on the winner-take-all basis. Two state Republican primaries use the statewide, winner-take-all rule that used to be the model for all presidential primaries. Three, Louisiana, Texas, and Vermont, constitute a fifth variety among Republican primaries in that they involve some combination of district or statewide allocation. Finally, in three Democratic and one Republican primary, there is a nonbinding presidential preference vote with delegates chosen to reflect candidate strength in a separate caucus process.

Table 8-1. Presidential Primaries in 1972

State, Date	Democratic	Republican
New Hampsire, March 7	Muskie 46, McGovern 37	Nixon 68, McCloskey 20, Ashbrook 10
Florida, March 14	Wallace 42, Humphrey 19, Jackson 14	Nixon 87
Illinois, March 21	Muskie 63, McCarthy 36	Nixon 97
Wisconsin, April 4	McGovern 30, Wallace 22, Humphrey 21, Muskie 10	Nixon 97
Massachusetts, April 25	McGovern 53, Muskie 21	Nixon 81, McCloskey 14
Pennsylvania, April 25	Humphrey 35, Wallace 21, McGovern 20, Muskie 20	Nixon 83, Wallace 11*
Dist. Columbia, May 2	Fauntroy 72, unpledged 28	(no primary)
Indiana, May 2	Humphrey 47, Wallace 41, Muskie 12	Nixon 100
Ohio, May 2	Humphrey 41, McGovern 40	Nixon 100
Tennessee, May 4	Wallace 68, Humphrey 16	Nixon 96
North Carolina, May 6	Wallace 50, Sanford 37	Nixon 95
Nebraska, May 9	McGovern 41, Humphrey 34, Wallace 12	Nixon 92
West Virginia, May 9	Humphrey 67, Wallace 33	Unpledged 100
Maryland, May 16	Wallace 39, Humphrey 27, McGovern 22	Nixon 86
Michigan, May 16	Wallace 51, McGovern 27, Humphrey 16	Nixon 96
Oregon, May 23	McGovern 50, Wallace 20, Humphrey 13	Nixon 82, McCloskey 10
Rhode Island, May 23	McGovern 41, Muskie 21, Humphrey 20, Wallace 15	Nixon 88
California, June 6	McGovern 44, Humphrey 39	Nixon 90, Ashbrook 10
New Jersey, June 6	Chisholm 67, Sanford 33	unpledged 100
New Mexico, June 6	McGovern 33, Wallace 29, Humphrey 26	Nixon 89
South Dakota, June 6	McGovern 100	Nixon 100

*Write-in candidate.

Data are percentages of the total votes cast in the party primary; only candidates receiving at least 10 percent of the vote are listed.

Source: Congressional Quarterly, *Guide to US Elections,* 1975, pp. 346 ff.

Table 8-2. Presidential Primaries in 1976

State, Date	Democratic	Republican
New Hampshire, Feb. 24	Carter 28, Udall 23, Bayh 15, Harris 11	Ford 49, Reagan 48
Massachusetts, March 2	Jackson 22, Udall 18, Wallace 17, Carter 14	Ford 61, Reagan 33
Vermont, March 2	Carter 42, Shriver 28, Harris 13	Ford 84, Reagan 15
Florida, March 9	Carter 35, Wallace 31 Jackson 24	Ford 52, Reagan 47
Illinois, March 16	Carter 48, Wallace 28, Shriver 16	Ford 58, Reagan 40
North Carolina, March 23	Carter 54, Wallace 35	Reagan 52, Ford 45
Wisconsin, April 6	Carter 37, Udall 36, Wallace 13	Ford 55, Reagan 44
Pennsylvania, April 27	Carter 37, Jackson 25, Udall 19, Wallace 11	Ford 92
Dist. Columbia, May 4	Carter 40, Udall 26, Fauntroy 22, Washington 11	(no primary)
Georgia, May 4	Carter 83, Wallace 12	Reagan 68, Ford 31
Indiana, May 4	Carter 68, Wallace 15, Jackson 12	Reagan 51, Ford 48
Nebraska, May 11	Church 39, Carter 38	Reagan 54, Ford 45
West Virginia, May 11	R. Byrd 89, Wallace 11	Ford 54, Reagan 44
Maryland, May 18	Brown 48, Carter 37	Ford 58, Reagan 42
Michigan, May 18	Carter 43, Udall 43	Ford 64, Reagan 34
Arkansas, May 25	Carter 63, Wallace 17	Reagan 63, Ford 35
Idaho, May 25	Church 79, Carter 12	Reagan 74, Ford 24
Kentucky, May 25	Carter 59, Wallace 17, Udall 11	Ford 50, Reagan 46

Table 8-2. Presidential Primaries in 1976 (continued)

State, Date	Democratic	Republican
Nevada, May 25	Brown 53, Carter 23	Reagan 66, Ford 28
Oregon, May 25	Church 34, Carter 27, Brown 25*	Ford 50, Reagan 45
Tennessee, May 25	Carter 78, Wallace 11	Ford 49, Reagan 49
Montana, June 1	Church 59, Carter 25	Reagan 63, Ford 34
Rhode Island, June 1	unpledged 32, Carter 30, Church 27	Ford 65, Reagan 31
South Dakota, June 1	Carter 41, Udall 33, unpledged 13	Reagan 51, Ford 43
California, June 8	Brown 59, Carter 21	Reagan 65, Ford 34
New Jersey, June 8	Carter 58, Church 14	Ford 100
Ohio, June 8	Carter 52, Udall 21, Church 14	Ford 55, Reagan 45

*Write-in candidate.

Data are percentages of the total votes cast in the party primary; only candidates receiving at least 10 percent of the vote are listed.

Sources: For Democratic primaries, *Congressional Quarterly Weekly Report,* July 10, 1976, pp. 1806–1807; for Republican primaries, Richard M. Scammon and Alice V. McGillivray, *America Votes 12* (Washington: Election News Center and Congressional Quarterly, 1977), p. 27.

To sum up, in both parties most national convention delegates are chosen in a way that reflects popular party preferences for the presidential nominee. In 1980, according to *Congressional Quarterly,* 76 percent of the Republican and 71 percent of the Democratic delegates were chosen through the primaries. But nearly all the Democratic delegates will be apportioned among the presidential candidates to reflect the candidates' support, while most of the Republicans will be chosen through some sort of winner-take-all system.[12]

Tables 8-1, 8-2, and 8-3 review the sequences of presidential primaries in 1972, 1976, and 1980 to clarify what has been happening recently in the preliminary stages of the long presidential election process.

12. See the chart entitled "Party Differences in Allocating Delegates,"*Congressional Quarterly Weekly Report,* February 2, 1980, p. 288.

Table 8-3. Presidential Primaries in 1980

State, Date	Democratic	Republican
New Hampshire, Feb. 27	Carter 47, Kennedy 37	Reagan 50, Bush 23, Baker 13, Anderson 10
Massachusetts, March 4	Kennedy 65, Carter 29	Bush 31, Anderson 31, Reagan 29
Vermont, March 4	Carter 73, Kennedy 26	Reagan 30, Anderson 29, Bush 22, Baker 12
South Carolina, March 8	(no primary)	Reagan 55, Connally 30, Bush 15
Alabama, March 11	Carter 82, Kennedy 13	Reagan 70, Bush 26
Florida, March 11	Carter 61, Kennedy 23	Reagan 56, Bush 30
Georgia, March 11	Carter 88	Reagan 73, Bush 13
Illinois, March 16	Carter 65, Kennedy 30	Reagan 48, Anderson 37, Bush 11
Connecticut, March 25	Kennedy 47, Carter 42	Bush 39, Reagan 34, Anderson 22
New York, March 25	Kennedy 59, Carter 41	(no primary)
Kansas, April 1	Carter 57, Kennedy 32	Reagan 63, Anderson 18, Bush 12
Wisconsin, April 1	Carter 56, Kennedy 30, Brown 12	Reagan 40, Bush 31, Anderson 28
Louisiana, April 5	Carter 56, Kennedy 22, no preference 12	Reagan 74, Bush 19
Pennsylvania, April 22	Kennedy 46, Carter 46	Bush 52, Reagan 44
Texas, May 3	Carter 56, Kennedy 23, unpledged 19	Reagan 52, Bush 47
Dist. Columbia, May 6	Kennedy 62, Carter 37	Bush 66, Anderson 27
Indiana, May 6	Carter 68, Kennedy 32	Reagan 74, Bush 16, Anderson 10
North Carolina, May 6	Carter 70, Kennedy 18	Reagan 67, Bush 22
Tennessee, May 6	Carter 75, Kennedy 18	Reagan 74, Bush 18

Table 8-3. Presidential Primaries in 1980 (continued)

State, Date	Democratic	Republican
Maryland, May 13	Carter 47, Kennedy 38	Reagan 48, Bush 41
Nebraska, May 13	Carter 47, Kennedy 38, unpledged 11	Reagan 78, Bush 16
Michigan, May 20	unpledged 53, Brown 34, LaRouche 13	Bush 57, Reagan 32
Oregon, May 20	Carter 58, Kennedy 32, Brown 10	Reagan 55, Bush 35, Anderson 10
Arkansas, May 27	Carter 60, unpledged 18, Kennedy 18	(no primary)
Idaho, May 27	Carter 62, Kennedy 22, no preference 12	Reagan 83, Anderson 10
Kentucky, May 27	Carter 67, Kennedy 23	Reagan 82
Nevada, May 27	Carter 38, no preference 34, Kennedy 29	Reagan 83, no preference 10
California, June 3	Kennedy 47, Carter 37, unpledged 11	Reagan 81, Anderson 14
Mississippi, June 3	(no primary)	Reagan 89
Montana, June 3	Carter 52, Kennedy 37, no preference 11	Reagan 87, Bush 10
New Jersey, June 3	Kennedy 56, Carter 37	Reagan 81, Bush 18
New Mexico, June 3	Kennedy 46, Carter 42	Reagan 64, Anderson 12, Bush 10
Ohio, June 3	Carter 51, Kennedy 44	Reagan 81, Bush 19
Rhode Island, June 3	Kennedy 68, Carter 25	Reagan 71, Bush 18
South Dakota, June 3	Kennedy 48, Carter 46	Reagan 82
West Virginia, June 3	Carter 62, Kennedy 38	Reagan 86, Bush 14

Data are percentages of the total vote cast in the party primary; only candidates or "tickets" receiving at least 10 percent of the vote are listed. Data in some cases are based on incomplete or unofficial returns.

Source: Wire service press dispatches and various editions of the *Congressional Quarterly Weekly Report.*

OTHER METHODS OF DELEGATE SELECTION

Of the 5,325 Republican and Democratic national convention delegates chosen in 1980, 1,432 (or 27 percent) were selected by a party organ (convention, committee, or caucus) operating at one or more levels or stages (state, district, county, or precinct).[13]

Delaware chooses its national convention delegates at the state conventions of the two parties; delegates to the 1976 state conventions were elected in the June 5 primary. Maine followed the same pattern in 1976, but here the delegates to the state convention were chosen in municipal caucuses in February.

Arkansas Republicans in 1980 chose their nineteen delegates to the national convention in two stages. In early February, party members met in district caucuses across the state to choose a total of twelve delegates; six were named for Ronald Reagan, four for Howard Baker, one for George Bush, and one was uncommitted. Two weeks later, the final seven members of the Republican delegation were chosen at a meeting of two hundred ten members of the state committee in Little Rock. The committee chose four uncommitted delegates and one each pledged to Reagan, Bush, and John Connally. Thus the final delegate count was Reagan seven, uncommitted five, Baker four, Bush two, and Connally one.[14]

Iowa

Iowa's caucus system has attracted increasing public and media attention in recent presidential elections. Iowa has a multistaged system of delegate selection, based on local precinct caucuses held in the late winter of the presidential election year. Both parties in 1976 held caucuses in each precinct of the state on the evening of January 19. Any resident of the precinct who would be eligible to vote by election day and who had a "concern about the political process and a legitimate interest in one of the parties" could attend a party caucus. The Democrats nominated and voted for presidential candidates, and any candidate who received as much as 15 percent of the precinct vote became entitled to a proportionate representation at the subsequent county conventions. Supporters of various candidates clustered in separate corners of the meeting area, and envoys would work between these groups to

13. For a capsule description of delegate selection procedures in each state in 1976, see the *National Journal,* December 6, 1975, p. 1668.
14. Special dispatch from Little Rock, Ark., "Arkansas GOP Selects Seven Final Delegates," in *Washington Post,* February 17, 1980, p. A4.

encourage swapping and switching of votes. Precincts were apportioned one delegate for every forty votes cast in the precinct for the previous Democratic gubernatorial candidate. Delegates could run on an uncommitted basis, and groups winning less than 15 percent of the precinct vote could merge with other groups to establish their claim to representation at the next stage in the process. Only supporters of Governor George Wallace of Alabama were bound to vote for him at the subsequent county stage, since other presidential candidates had not extracted such pledges. The Republican rules allowed a winner-take-all result if a majority at the precinct caucus agreed. Republicans also expressed their opinions on twenty-two different issues, such as school financing, energy conservation, local option taxes, reduction of the federal budget, selling wine in grocery stores, and marijuana penalties.

More than a month elapsed between the precinct caucuses and the county conventions. These conventions (held on February 28 by Republicans and on March 6 by Democrats) elected delegates to the next stage of the election process. For the Democrats, this was the congressional district convention on April 10, and the final stage was the state convention on May 29. For the Republicans, there was no congressional district stage; their state convention was held June 18–19. Democrats chose most of their delegates to the national convention at the congressional district convention, and chose the remainder at the state convention. Republicans picked all of their national convention delegates at the state convention. While the Iowa caucus system certainly places a premium on local participation, it has been criticized because those who show up for the precinct caucuses, numerous as they may be in some cases, seldom constitute a significant percentage of the precinct's party membership, and this makes the caucus system smack of elitism. George McGovern in 1972 and Jimmy Carter in 1976 both got a jump on their rivals by assiduous organization of a grass-roots precinct caucus program across the state of Iowa.

Caucuses such as Iowa's are intriguing institutions. They require a large investment of time by candidate staffs and by those citizens who attend, and for the latter they require a semi-public declaration of choice rather than a simple, secret marking of a ballot in the privacy of a voting booth. Caucuses are usually an exercise in elite rather than mass democracy, for in 1976 only about 7 percent of Iowa Democrats and 4 percent of Iowa Republicans turned out for them. As the *Washington Post* concluded in an editorial: ". . . in Iowa, a committed, competent 'grass root' is worth more than the most creative, colorful television advertising campaign. Just because it's a caucus and not a primary."[15]

15. "Iowa Does Not Have a Primary," *Washington Post,* January 16, 1980, p. A20.

Virginia

Virginia, which does not have voter registration by party, is not authorized by either political party to hold a presidential primary. Delegates to national conventions are chosen by a complex, multistage process of local and congressional district meetings. For Democrats in 1980, the first step consisted of mass meetings at the local level beginning in March, from which delegates were selected to congressional district and state conventions. A newspaperman has described the confusion as follows:

> The Democratic mass meeting resembles a schoolyard full of kids choosing sides for a game of tag. Participants align themselves by presidential preference or in uncommitted groups. For a group to win representation, it must have at least 20 percent of the total caucus. For instance, if one hundred persons attend the mass meeting at Kenmore Intermediate School in Arlington and only nineteen congregate for Brown, that group must disband and join another group that has at least twenty people or leave the room.[16]

The second step was the ten congressional district conventions in April; each of these chose five delegates for the national convention. The final step was the state Democratic convention in Richmond, May 16–17, where the final fourteen national convention delegates were picked.

Virginia Republicans began with mass meetings, party canvasses, or conventions at the local level in early spring, from which representatives were selected to attend congressional district and state conventions. In some areas of Virginia, Republicans imposed a second stage, seen by some as an attempt to enhance the influence of party regulars more likely to persevere; Republican delegates who were elected at local meetings had to be reelected at a county meeting before they were eligible for the district convention. Ten congressional district conventions in May each chose three national convention delegates, and the final ten national delegates were selected by the Republican state convention in Richmond, June 6–7.

RECENT PRESIDENTIAL PRIMARY REFORM BILLS

The current presidential primary system is rather whimsical about whether, where, when, and how primaries are to be held. Thus one of the main concerns of legislation introduced in Congress in recent years has been to bring a substantial degree of uniformity to the system. Ideas to reform the presidential primaries seem to fall into three categories.

16. Denis Collins, "Scrambling for Delegates: Presidential Politics in Virginia," The Virginia Weekly section, *Washington Post*, March 6, 1980, pp. Va. 1– Va. 2.

Setting Federal Standards

The first idea is simply that states holding a presidential primary must conform to certain federal standards. Such a plan was introduced in 1979 in the House of Representatives by two unsuccessful presidential candidates of the 1970s, Representatives John Ashbrook (Republican of Ohio) and Morris Udall (Democrat of Arizona). Ashbrook's bill, H.R. 1169 in the 96th Congress, provides that: (1) states holding a primary must do so on the second Tuesday of either March, April, May, or June of the presidential election year, (2) voters will be eligible to vote only in the primary of their registered affiliation or, if there is no such affiliation, in the primary of only one party, (3) candidates will receive no delegate votes unless they receive at least 10 percent of the primary votes (the threshold rule), (4) the delegates themselves are to be chosen and apportioned to candidates after the distribution of the primary vote, (5) the Federal Elections Commission (FEC) will designate the presidential candidates, and all of them shall be listed in all states having a primary (other candidates can also get on the ballot in a particular state by filing a petition signed by one percent of all the voters in the state in the previous election).

Regional Primaries

The second idea, originally proposed by Senator Bob Packwood (Republican of Oregon), involves holding regional primaries. Introduced as S. 964 in the 96th Congress by Packwood and his Oregon colleague, Mark Hatfield, it allows states to determine whether or not they wish to hold a presidential primary, but if a state does so choose, its primary date must be set in accordance with the region to which the state has been assigned. There would be five regions and five given dates (the second Tuesdays of March, April, May, June, and July). As with the first reform idea, the primary would be essentially closed, and the FEC would identify the candidates whose names would appear on the ballot. An alternative to the Packwood-Hatfield bill, introduced as H.R. 125 by Representative Charles Bennett (Democrat of Florida), sets up six rather than five regions and calls for the primaries to be held from the last Tuesday of March to the second Tuesday of June. Bennett's six regions: (1) New England and New York, (2) seven Middle Atlantic states and the District of Columbia, (3) the Southeast plus Puerto Rico, the Virgin Islands and the Canal Zone, (4) the Great Lakes and northern Great Plains states, (5) the Southwest, and (6) western and Pacific states, plus Guam. Representative Richard Ottinger (Democrat of New York) has a further variant on the regional idea that would require each state to hold a presidential primary (H.R. 4212). As in the Packwood-Hatfield plan, states would be grouped in one of five regions, and the FEC would draw lots to assign those regions to the five Tuesdays (beginning with the first Tuesday of April and ending with the twelfth subsequent Tuesday). Delegates would be bound for two ballots in the national convention. There would be a filing fee of $10,000 for each region, which would be refunded by the FEC if the candidate received at least 2 percent of the party vote in the region.

One National Primary

The third proposal is for a direct national presidential primary to be held in every state on a specified date. This idea has had several sponsors over the years, and goes back to a bill introduced in 1911 by Representative Richmond Hobson (Democrat of Alabama), which proposed a direct national primary to replace the national party convention method of nominating presidential candidates. The version introduced in 1979 by Senator Lowell Weicker (Republican of Connecticut), S. 16, sets the first Tuesday of August as the national primary day. Voting in a primary is restricted to registered party members and to independents choosing to vote in that party's primary and in no other. Candidates would have their names placed on the ballot by filing a petition containing the names of party members numbering at least one percent of the total votes cast for all candidates in the preceding presidential election. A majority of all the votes cast would establish the nominee; failing that, a runoff would be held on the third Tuesday following the first primary, between the two candidates who had received the most votes. Candidates would be restricted from receiving or spending campaign money before the first day of January of the presidential election year. Two variations of the basic Weicker bill were introduced in the 96th Congress. In H. R. 1904, Representative Douglas Applegate (Democrat of Ohio) set the election date as the first Tuesday after the first Monday of May, stipulated that candidates would qualify for the ballot by regions, and that whoever received the most votes would be nominated. In H. J. Res. 81, Representative Neal Smith (Democrat of Iowa) provided that to receive his party's nomination, a candidate would have to get at least 40 percent of the primary vote; failing that, a runoff would be held six weeks later between the top two finishers. The Smith bill set the primary election day as the second Saturday after the first Monday in July.

Several drawbacks to a national presidential primary have been pointed out by politicians, journalists, and scholars. First, such a primary would not coincide with the date of other primary elections in most states, forcing the states either to change the date of their gubernatorial, congressional, and legislative primaries or to have two primary election dates. Second, the cost of a national primary campaign focused on one day would be terribly high, so that for most candidates financial considerations would be the critical element in the decision to run. Third, the petition route to qualifying for the ballot is awkward at best and susceptible to fraud at worst. Fourth, the importance and visibility of the national conventions would be severely reduced.[17]

PROPOSALS

Restructuring the national presidential primary system must be done carefully, for otherwise it might be even more chaotic than it is now. The reformed system ought to provide:

1. maximum opportunity for participation of party members, with some provision for the involvement of unaffiliated, independent voters;
2. a workable process for placing presidential candidates on the ballot, perhaps by means of petition, filing fees, thresholds and other negative quotas, or designation by responsible officials, because a ballot with three dozen candidate names makes for too much democracy;
3. timeliness, with any critical decisions about delegates or presidential preferences being made no earlier than April 1 or no later than June 30 of presidential election years;
4. flexibility, for accommodation of other primaries in a given state, to avoid the necessity of expensive second primaries;
5. a responsible method of binding delegates in their convention voting to the preferences of party members as expressed through a primary election in the state;
6. fairness to all kinds of parties and candidates, which would militate against holding presidential primaries only in randomly chosen states where certain candidates would be bound to have an advantage because of region, ideology, or ethnicity;
7. standardization, so that a citizen of Oregon could move to Michigan or South Carolina and not be lost in the complexities of the new state's electoral system; and
8. democratic methods of choice, whether a primary election is involved or not, so that delegates not chosen in a primary would have to be selected by members of responsible, visible, elective party or public organs.

17. For further commentary and descriptions of earlier primary proposals, see Austin Ranney, *The Federalization of Presidential Primaries* (Washington: American Enterprise Institute, 1978).

It is not intended to produce a nomination system in which the winner, or even a clear favorite, is necessarily identified long before the national convention. The proposals below seem no more likely than the present sytem to produce a preconvention choice, and both present and proposed systems are less likely to single out such a nominee than the former system in which the winner-take-all rule applied in most primaries and momentum was therefore the fundamental fact of political life. Even then it was seldom the case that primary elections could be called the decisive stage in the ultimate choice of the national ticket. (It is worth recalling that in the wake of the Illinois primary on March 18, 1980, Jimmy Carter and Ronald Reagan appeared to have their respective party nominations sewed up.)

8-1. To establish a national presidential primary system. States and other units holding a presidential primary would be required by federal statute to comply with certain federal standards. Voters would be able to indicate their preference for president, thus simultaneously voting for that candidate's slate of delegates to the national convention.

Prior to March 10 of each presidential year, the FEC would be required to publish a list of no more than eight presidential candidates for each qualifying party. The FEC would compile such a list from among those who had declared their interest and who had received some general support as evidenced by press reports, endorsements from prominent leaders, or the results of current, reputable, scientific public opinion polls. Candidates so named would be eligible to submit to the election authority of each state a list of national convention delegate candidates equal to the number of seats apportioned to that state, and by doing so would automatically be allotted a place on that party's presidential ballot in every voting jurisdiction of the nation. The FEC could update the candidate lists up to two times, prior to April 10 and prior to May 10, to reflect changing conditions. Other candidates could obtain a place on the ballot in individual states by paying a filing fee of $5,000 (to be refunded if the candidate subsequently were to receive at least 2 percent of the votes cast in the state's party primary), and by submitting a petition signed by a number of registered party members equal to 2 percent of the number of votes cast for that party's presidential ticket in the state in the most recent presidential election. In addition, there could be any number of uncommitted slates, which would obtain their ballot position by the same means just described. A slate of delegates committed to a particular presidential candidate would have to be certified by that candidate or his designated agent in the state; in the unlikely event that two slates were to be filed in behalf of the same candidate, only the one filed first would be valid. Slates of delegates would have to be submitted to the state election authority at least thirty but not more than sixty days before the primary election.

The victorious delegates would be determined by a modification of what is known as the list system. A slate would have to receive at least 10 percent of the statewide vote to qualify for representation on the state's delegation. Numbers of delegates would be apportioned among the qualifying slates on the basis of the distribution of the statewide vote, excepting from the calculation those votes received by candidates who failed to obtain 10 percent of the votes. If Candidate X wins, say, five delegates, the top five names on his slate would be elected. Further details are given in the second proposal.

With this system, it is likely that a state's delegation to the national convention will contain support for several presidential hopefuls. However, because of the threshold rule, it would be possible for a state to send a delegation totally committed to one candidate. If it were desired to give further support to an overwhelmingly favored candidate in a given state and to encourage reduction in the number of candidates, it might be provided that a presidential candidate would be awarded all the state's delegates if specified percentage quotas are reached; the quota would be a sliding one, depending on the number of candidates in the primary (see Table 8-4). A simpler and more satisfactory way to accomplish the same ends would be to raise even higher the threshold required to qualify for any delegates, perhaps to 15 or even 20 percent rather than the 10 percent threshold proposed above.

Each state holding a presidential primary would be required to do so in April, May, or June of the presidential election year. A later date would shorten the long presidential season somewhat (a salutary objective, to be sure), but with national conventions being held in July and August, the primaries must be finished in time to allow necessary arrangements to be made. If neither party held its national convention before August 15, then the primaries could be set back a little later. The exact date of a state's primary would be determined by the state legislature, but no more than six would be allowed to hold their presidential primary on a given day. If the same day is chosen by more than six states, that day would be awarded by the FEC to the first six states to submit the required date-setting resolution; these would

Table 8-4. Winner-Take-All Quotas for Presidential Primaries

Number of Candidates on Ballot	Percentage of Primary Vote Required to Qualify for All Convention Delegates
2	85
3	75
4	65
5 or more	55

have to be submitted to the FEC before February 1 of presidential election years, and would stay in effect from one election year to another until rescinded by its legislature. That is, if the state of Illinois were to choose, and be assigned, the third Tuesday in May as the date of its 1984 primary, Illinois would con- tinue to be assigned the third Tuesday in May as long as it wished to keep that date. This would help to stablize the state's electoral schedule over the years.

One of the several advantages of this presidential primary system is that the list of candidates, once it had been issued by the FEC, would be considerably standardized and stabilized. There would not be the capricious pairings that developed among Democratic hopefuls in 1972, when McGovern and Muskie opposed each other in New Hampshire, followed by a Wallace-Humphrey- Jackson confrontation in Florida, a Muskie-McCarthy contest in Illinois, a McGovern-Wallace-Humphrey-Muskie struggle in Wisconsin, and so on. A candidate would have a chance to rebuild his momentum in the wake of early setbacks and disappointments, rather than feel he had to pull out, though of course nothing in this proposal would cause either the popularity or the treasury of an also-ran candidate to stay high. One problem that would remain is that of late candidacies. When Gerald Ford was thinking of entering the Republican race in the middle of March 1980, he was confronted by the fact that at that date it would have been possible for him to enter no more than a dozen Republican primaries.[18]   Another problem that should be noted is that federal campaign finance subsidies and state primary laws work against the interests of parties and candidates other than those of the Democratic or Republican persuasions.

8-2. To establish a delegate selection mechanism. It was convenient to cover some of this process in the previous proposal. As indicated, in states holding presidential primaries, there would be two stages in the delegate selection process: first, putting together slates of prospective delegates for each candi- date and, second, counting the primary votes for the various slates to see how many delegates would be awarded to each one.

To win any delegates, assuming the winner-take-all quota has not been reached (see Table 8-4), a slate would have to receive at least 10 percent of the vote in the state party's presidential primary. Delegates would be chosen in direct proportion to the distribution of primary votes among slates receiving at least the 10 percent floor. For example, let us say that the state party has

18. See Haynes Johnson, "A Sense of Crises Unresolved, Future Uncertain," *The Washington Post,* March 16, 1980, p. A3.

been apportioned twenty-two delegates, and that the results of the primary voting are as follows:

Committed Slate "A"	483,111
Committed Slate "B"	409,832
Uncommitted Slate "Z"	277,090
Committed Slate "C"	93,904
Committed Slate "D"	77,442
Uncommitted Slate "Y"	48,484
Committed Slate "E"	23,400
Committed Slate "F"	19,305
Total votes cast	1,382,568

Eliminating from consideration the votes cast for slates failing to reach the 10 percent floor (138,257 votes, since 1,382,568 votes have been cast), the proportion of votes going to successful slates would be:

Committed Slate "A"	43.13 percent
Committed Slate "B"	36.59 percent
Uncommitted Slate "Z"	20.28 percent
Total	100.00 percent

Finally, the number of delegates selected from each slate would be:

Committed Slate "A"	10
Committed Slate "B"	8
Uncomitted Slate "Z"	4
Total delegates	22

Thus the top ten candidates from Slate "A," the top eight candidates from Slate "B," and the top four candidates from Slate "Z" would become delegates to the national convention.

8-3. To provide for delegate selection in nonprimary states. For states not using a presidential primary, national convention delegates would be chosen in June in the following fashion (see Table 8-5). Twenty percent of the delegates would be chosen publicly by random selection from a register containing the names of all members of the current year's state convention who consent to serve as national convention delegates. Ten percent of the delegates would be chosen in the same way from a register containing the names of all county directors of the party. Thirty percent of the delegates would be chosen in the same way from a register containing the names of all delegates to the several county party conventions of the same year. Fifteen percent of the delegates

Table 8-5. National Convention Delegates to be Chosen from Various Components, Given Various Sizes of State Delegations in Nonprimary States

Component	Quota	DELEGATION SIZE					
		280	120	50	28	12	6
State convention delegates	20%	56	24	10	5	2	1
County directors	10%	28	12	5	3	1	1
County convention delegates	30%	84	36	15	8	4	2
Members of congress and state legislators	15%	42	18	8	4	2	1
(subtotal)		(210)	(90)	(38)	(21)	(9)	(5)
State chairman designees	balance	70	30	12	7	3	1
Total		280	120	50	28	12	6

would be chosen in the same way from a register containing the names of all party members serving in Congress or in the state legislature. Fractional remainders of .50 or more in delegates would have the effect of adding one seat to that category. Remaining delegates would be chosen by the state chairman. Any replacements or alternates would be selected from the same register and by the same means. If there are insufficient numbers of qualifed and consenting persons in a given category, the balance of delegates for that category would be obtained equally from among the other three categories. If the numbers are still not sufficient, quotas would be filled by the state convention (if in session) or the state executive committee. No candidate for delegate could appear on more than one register, and each of the five components would be entitled to at least one delegate.

The effect of this proposal is to force states to choose between holding a presidential primary meeting clear federal standards and having the national convention delegates chosen randomly from among the political leaders of the state. This would eliminate caucuses that can easily be dominated by unrepresentative activists or elites at the expense of the party interest and of the true preferences of the mass membership of the party.

8-4. To bind the convention voting of committed delegates. Federal statute would establish the binding nature of the state presidential primaries with respect to slates committed to a specific candidate. Delegates so bound would be required to support and vote for that presidential candidate on the first ballot, and after that up to and including the third ballot as long as the candidate continues to be supported by at least 20 percent of the convention, and unless the candidate were to withdraw from the nomination contest or were to release the bound delegates in writing to the presiding officer of the convention. Such withdrawal or release of bound delegates could occur before the convention is convened or before any ballot at the convention, including the first. To recap what was said in earlier sections, uncommitted delegates would be free to vote for any presidential candidate on any ballot; the same rule would apply to delegates released from their commitment. The vice-presidential candidate would be selected by the convention following current practices, and it is expected that the preference of the presidential candidate would, as at present, strongly determine the choice of running mate. The vice-presidential nominee would succeed in event of a vacancy in the presidential nomination, and the national committee of the party would be empowered to choose a replacement for the vice-presidential nomination in event of a vacancy in that position.

A majority vote of all delegates would be required to win the party's presidential and vice-presidential nominations. Within that framework, party rules could answer such questions as whether or not to provide for the forced dropping of the names of low-ranking presidential candidates after a specified number of ballots, for the purpose of assuring that convention balloting would reach a nomination decision without undue delay.[19]

19. At the 1924 Democratic National Convention, it required more than 100 ballots to nominate John W. Davis of West Virginia.

Chapter 9
Setting the Goals: Party Conventions

Nomination Battles

Platform Battles

Other Convention Battles

Proposals

The convention is the fundamental element, the constituent assembly, of the American political party. It is the most visible and most powerful of all the party organs.

The functions that party conventions perform are well known and need only be itemized at this point. First, conventions endorse or nominate candidates for public office, and in some cases have the responsibility of resolving inconclusive primary contests for nomination for public office. Second, they select party officers, most notably the chairman. Third, they write the party's platform, which presents the party's positions on the major issues of the day and thereby seeks to attract public support for its ticket. Fourth, they plan ahead for the party's organizational life, making decisions that direct the work of the party staff in the months and years ahead, including plans for the next convention.

Some party conventions have been more democratically chosen than others. Generally, conventions are most democratic, in the sense of how delegates are chosen, at the local and state levels; at the national level, the selection of delegates has not always been determined by an open vote among rank-and-file party members. As the models presented in Chapter 5 attempted to show, the degree of democracy existing in American party organizations varies widely from state to state and from level to level.

Judith Parris has proposed a set of guidelines for what national conventions should be and do.[1] They should: (1) represent the party's presidential constituency, that is, allocate seats on the basis of the distribution of the party vote in the past, (2) reflect candidate preferences of the rank-and-file members, and thus primary election results should have a powerful voice, (3) be efficient in their deliberations, (4) restrict the process of drafting the platform to a fairly small group, and then plan to use the document as a policy guide for party members in Congress, and (5) be fair in terms of media coverage and commentary, giving full opportunity for objective reporting. These guidelines were suggested in the context of national conventions, but they would also serve well for the formation and conduct of state and local party conventions.

1. Judith Parris, *The Convention Problem* (Washington: Brookings Institution, 1972), pp. 177–179.

The following sections review the most dramatic actions taken at national conventions over the past generation or two. The reader should keep in mind that similar kinds of activity have taken place in 100 state conventions. Also, the reader should note that party nominations at the state and local levels were covered in Chapter 7; this chapter will discuss the presidential and vice-presidential nominations made by the national conventions.

NOMINATION BATTLES

Since the second quarter of the nineteenth century, national conventions have been the critical element in the nomination of each party's presidential ticket. The identity of the party's candidate for president has generally been quite predictable. A study by Donald Matthews concluded that the eventual nominee had been clearly favored for the nomination at the beginning of the election year in fifteen cases out of twenty in the period 1936-1972.[2] Of course, because of the power of incumbency, this predictability is greater for a party which has control of the White House (see Table 9-1). In 1976, President Ford's renomination by the Republican party was severely challenged by Ronald Reagan, and Jimmy Carter's eventual nomination by the Democrats was by no means a foregone conclusion in January. For 1980, President Carter's renomination looked much more secure in January than it had four months earlier, and the Republican picture was even less clear in January, when George Bush did surprisingly well against Ronald Reagan in the Iowa caucus straw voting.

In 1940, Democratic President Franklin D. Roosevelt was running for an unprecedented third term, and received his third nomination by acclamation. On the Republican side, Wendell Willkie of Indiana, a newcomer to presidential politics, trailed Thomas Dewey of New York and Robert Taft of Ohio on the first two convention ballots, but went ahead on the fourth ballot and secured the nomination on the sixth.

Four years later, Roosevelt received his fourth nomination even though Senator Harry F. Byrd, Sr., of Virginia received nearly 100 votes on the one ballot taken, and Dewey won the Republican nomination on the first ballot.

In 1948, President Harry Truman defeated Senator Richard Russell of Georgia on the first ballot, 947½ to 263. The Republicans that year, expected to win handily in November, had three serious candidates, Dewey, Taft, and

2.   Donald R. Matthews, "Presidential Nominations: Process and Outcome," in James D. Barber (ed.), *Choosing the President* (Englewood Cliffs, N. J.: Prentice-Hall, Inc., 1974), p. 54.

Table 9-1. Predictability of Presidential Nominations Since 1936

	Expected Candidate Was Nominated	New Candidate Emerged as Nominee
Party was in power at beginning of year	Roosevelt '36 Roosevelt '40 Roosevelt '44 Truman '48 Eisenhower '56 Nixon '60 Johnson '64 Nixon '72 Ford '76	Stevenson '52 Humphrey '68
Party was not in power at beginning of year	Landon '36 Dewey '44 Dewey '48* Eisenhower '52* Stevenson '56 Kennedy '60 Nixon '68	Willkie '40 Goldwater '64 McGovern '72 Carter '76

*Senator Robert Taft was listed as co-favorite in both 1948 and 1952.

Source: 1936–1972 data from Donald R. Matthews, "Presidential Nominations: Process and Outcome," in James D. Barber (ed.), *Choosing the President* (Englewood Cliffs, N. J.: Prentice-Hall, 1974), p. 54.

Harold Stassen, former governor of Minnesota; they finished 434-224-157 respectively on the first ballot, and Dewey won his second Republican nomination on a unanimous third ballot.

In 1952, when Truman decided not to try for another term, there were major nomination struggles in both party conventions. Among the Democrats, four candidates each received more than 100 votes on the first ballot—Senator Estes Kefauver of Tennessee, 300½; Senator Russell, 267½; Governor Adlai Stevenson of Illinois, 248½; and former Governor Averill Harriman of New York, 126. Stevenson won the nomination on the third ballot, after Harriman and several minor candidates dropped from the race. The Republican battle was mainly between General Dwight D. Eisenhower and Senator Taft, with some support going to Stassen, former Governor Earl Warren of California, and General Douglas MacArthur. Eisenhower won a close first ballot victory over Taft.

Four years later, the nominees were the same with Stevenson's main competition coming from Harriman and Senator Lyndon Johnson of Texas.

In 1960, Vice-President Richard Nixon succeeded to the Republican presidential nomination, though it required a preconvention "treaty" with New York Governor Nelson Rockefeller to ensure it, while Senator John F. Kennedy of Massachusetts defeated Johnson, 806 to 409, on the one ballot taken at the Democratic convention.

President Johnson was nominated for a full term by acclamation in 1964. Senator Barry Goldwater of Arizona won the hotly contested Republican nomination with 883 first ballot votes against 214 for Governor William Scranton of Pennsylvania and 114 for Rockefeller.

In the wake of President Johnson's 1968 decision not to seek nomination for a second full term and the assassination of Senator Robert Kennedy of New York on the night of the California primary, Vice-President Hubert Humphrey won a first ballot victory over a fellow Minnesotan, Senator Eugene McCarthy, and South Dakota Senator George McGovern at the riot-torn 1968 convention in Chicago. The Republicans nominated Nixon over Rockefeller and Reagan (the before-switching first ballot count gave them 692, 277, and 182 votes respectively).

Senator McGovern won the 1972 Democratic nomination, gaining 1728.35 votes compared to the 525 received by Senator Henry Jackson of Washington, the 381.70 received by Governor George Wallace of Alabama, and the 151.95 received by Representative Shirley Chisholm of New York. President Nixon was routinely renominated by the Republican convention.

Former Governor Jimmy Carter of Georgia swept to victory at the 1976 Democratic national convention, leading Representative Morris Udall of Arizona and Governor Jerry Brown of California 2238½ to 329½ and 300½ on the first ballot (before switches). On the Republican side, President Gerald Ford's troops had their hands full turning aside the Reagan challenge, 1187 to 1070. In 1980, President Carter and Reagan each won their party's nomination on the first ballot.

Characteristics of Nominations

This review of presidential nomination outcomes since 1940 suggests several "rules of the game":

1. Eligible incumbents who seek it invariably win their party's nomination.
2. Most contests (seventeen of the twenty) are decided on the first ballot. No party has won in November that had more than one ballot for the presidential nomination.
3. Very seldom are there more than two candidates who receive more than 100 votes on any convention ballot; in other words, the convention is the final stage in a long process, wherein most candidates have been weeded out before the convention opens.

4. A high degree of intraparty competitiveness at the convention lowers a ticket's chances of success in the November election. Eisenhower's victory in 1952 after the hard-fought nomination contest with Taft is the only exception to this rule in the period we are considering.
5. There is little difference between the two parties in levels of competition, whether the competition is measured by the number of candidates receiving 100 or more votes on any ballot or by the number of ballots required to reach a nomination verdict.
6. Outsiders—that is, persons not part of the party's central power structure—can be nominated. Willkie, McGovern, and Carter were nominated, and Kefauver came close.

In their analysis of presidential nominations, William Keech and Donald Matthews have classifed the choices as consensual, semi-consensual, and non-consensual. A consensual nomination was one in which any opposition to the eventual nominee had evaporated by the time the convention opened. Three Democrats—Roosevelt in 1936 and 1944 and Johnson in 1964—and five Republicans—Kansas Governor Alf Landon in 1936, Dewey in 1944, Eisenhower in 1956, and Nixon in 1960 and 1972—were considered consensual nominations. A semi-consensual nomination was one in which the nominee survived the primaries, entered the convention as the front-runner, and was nominated on the first ballot. In this category were four Democrats (Roosevelt in 1940, Truman in 1948, Stevenson in 1956, and Kennedy in 1960) and one

Table 9-2. Nomination Competition Level and Outcome of November Presidential Elections, 1940–1976

November Outcome	Level of Convention Competition*		
	Low	Moderate	High
Ticket won	Eisenhower '56 Nixon '72 Roosevelt '40 Roosevelt '44 Johnson '64	Nixon '68 Truman '48 Kennedy '60 Carter '76	Eisenhower '52
Ticket lost	Dewey '44 Nixon '60	Dewey '48 Goldwater '64 Stevenson '56 Humphrey '68 McGovern '72	Willkie '40 Ford '76 Stevenson '52

*Based on number of ballots and closeness of vote.

Republican (Nixon in 1968). To that classification the present author would
be inclined to add the names of Democrat Jimmy Carter and Republican
President Ford in 1976. A nonconsensual nomination was one with no front-
runner, where amateurs were likely to get involved, where several ballots may
have been required, and where candidate strength fluctuated widely over the
course of the primary season. Examples include three Democrats—Stevenson
in 1952, Humphrey in 1968, and McGovern in 1972—and four Republicans—
Willkie in 1940, Dewey in 1948, Eisenhower in 1952, and Goldwater in 1964.[3]

PLATFORM BATTLES

The platform expresses a political party's view of the state of the nation.
Drafting and debating the platform resolutions give the party an opportunity
to sort out its policy preferences and to publicize them to the nation at large.

Observers have amassed a good deal of conventional wisdom about American political party platforms, which might be summarized along the following
lines:

1. There are some differences between Democratic and Republican platforms. Labor-management relations, the role of government in the
   economy, budgetary and fiscal policy, and welfare policy are among
   the issues that perennially and predictably divide the two parties. In
   many other areas, there is little or no difference in platform statements.
2. Policy differences in platforms are often muted because both parties
   try to appeal to the broadest possible segment of the population,
   and at the same time to avoid offending any significant segment.
   This attempt to be all things to all people distinguishes American
   political style from that practiced in European democracies.
3. There are important disputes within each party in the drafting and
   debate of the platform, and these often are related to the fortunes of
   the rival candidates for the presidential nomination.
4. Both parties are sensitive to special interest groups and to mass public
   opinion in writing their platforms.
5. There is considerable attention to both short-term, immediate issues
   and to longer-term programs and goals.
6. There is little expectation on anyone's part that the platforms will
   significantly influence federal government policy for the next administration or the next Congress, irrespective of which party controls
   either the executive or legislative branch.

3. William R. Keech and Donald R. Matthews, *The Party's Choice* (Washington: Brookings
   Institution, 1977), pp. 160–212.

Occasionally, fights over the platform become the central drama of the convention. Sometimes this is because the platform fight is closely intertwined with the outcome of the presidential nomination maneuvering. In other cases, this happens because the nomination is a foregone conclusion, and consequently press and public attention shifts to other convention happenings.

In 1896, the Democratic party argued mightily over the monetary issue. The old guard of the party, prominent in President Grover Cleveland's second administration, were unable to secure acceptance of a gold plank, which lost 303-626. Attention shifted to the alternative silver plank, accepted in the wake of perhaps the most dramatic speech in convention history, the "Cross of Gold" speech by Nebraska's William Jennings Bryan, who was to become the presidential nominee himself (and not only in 1896, but in 1900 and 1908 as well).

A highlight of the 1932 Republican national convention was the plank calling for state option on liquor policy, defeated 460-690.

A notable turning point in recent US history was the adoption, by a close 651-582 vote, of a strong and controversial civil rights plank pushed by Mayor of Minneapolis Hubert Humphrey at the 1948 Democratic convention.

The 1964 Republican convention produced the GOP's version of an internal civil rights struggle when the attempt by Pennsylvania Senator Hugh Scott to strengthen the civil rights plank—and thereby to sidetrack the Goldwater bandwagon—went down to defeat, 409-897.

In 1968, amid riotous conditions, Democrats rejected, 1041 to 1568, a minority report on the Vietnam situation sponsored by backers of Senators McCarthy, McGovern, and the late Robert Kennedy.

The 1972 Democratic convention defeated two controversial proposals, a guaranteed income of $6500 for a family of four (by a vote of 999 to 1853) and a women's rights plank on abortion (by a vote of 1101 to 1583).

Comparison of Democratic and Republican platforms of 1972 and 1976 sheds further light on the policy objectives of the two parties. Democrats in 1972 referred to a guaranteed job for all as the party's "primary economic objective." The "highest national priority" was to deal effectively and immediately with the "massive, complex, and urgent needs of our cities, suburbs, and towns." The first order of business of a new Democratic administration was to be the "immediate and complete withdrawal of all US forces in Indochina." Further "a first priority" must be "eliminating the unfair, bureaucratic Nixon wage and price controls."

Republicans in 1972, on the other hand, placed "a high priority on strengthening the North Atlantic alliance." They affirmed their support for the "basic principles of capitalism" and called for reform of the welfare system and the securing of "quality health care at reasonable cost."

The 1976 platforms reflected new policy priorities. For the Democrats, control of crime was termed "an urgent national priority." "Foremost attention must be directed to the establishment of a national food and fiber policy . . ." and "a principal goal must be the continued reduction of tension with the USSR." But the "first task is to formulate a rational African policy in terms of US-African priorities, not a corollary of US-Soviet policy." From the Republican point of view, it was of "paramount importance that the American people understand that the number one destroyer of jobs is inflation." Republicans said their top commitment was "to the families of these POWs and MIAs." "The preservation of peace and stability in the Middle East is a paramount concern."

The platforms of 1980 expressed sharp differences on several national issues, such as economic policy, unemployment, abortion, the Equal Rights Amendment, social welfare, energy, nuclear power, and foreign policy.

OTHER CONVENTION BATTLES

There are other kinds of convention battles that are important, and often these are related to the outcome of the struggle for the presidential nomination.

Party Rules

Struggles over party rules are often of lasting significance. It took all of President Roosevelt's enormous stores of popularity, prestige, and guile to finally demolish, in 1936, the Democratic party's long-standing rule that the presidential nominee had to be chosen by two-thirds of the convention delegations, a rule that had long served as a major basis of southern influence in national politics. In 1972, Democratic delegates debated whether or not to accept their rules committee's recommendation of a new national Democratic charter; several party leaders, especially members of Congress, objected strenuously to the attempt to shift party control from elected politicians to the grass-roots members of the party. The same report also called for a national policy conference to meet in even-numbered years when there was no presidential election, the abolition of winner-take-all presidential primaries in 1976, and the establishment of a twenty-two-member national executive committee.

Republicans in 1976 debated creation of two new committees, one of which was to review party rules and make recommendations for structural changes. The setting up of this new rules review within the national committee was considered a defeat for party liberals, who wanted a continuation of the Rule 29 committee that had been mandated by the 1972 national convention. Liberals felt the independent committee, which had been chaired by

Table 9-3. Voting by State Delegations on Rule 16c (Curtis Motion) and the Presidential Nomination, 1976 Republican National Convention

	States with Majority for Ford	States That Split	States with Majority for Reagan
States against Curtis motion	20	3	0
States that split	1	4	1
States for Curtis motion	0	2	19

Compiled by the author from data in *Congressional Quarterly Weekly Report*, August 21, 1976, p. 2255.

Representative William Steiger of Wisconsin, had been one hopeful source of structural reform in the party.

A most dramatic example of a rules struggle occurred at the 1976 Republican national convention in Kansas City, on the motion by former Representative Thomas Curtis of Missouri to require prospective presidential nominees to name their preference for a vice-presidential running mate prior to the presidential balloting. This proposal came after Reagan had unexpectedly announced that his running mate would be Senator Richard Schweiker of Pennsylvania, and was clearly an attempt to flush out President Ford's vice-presidential choice and thus perhaps to embarrass the president. The Curtis motion failed, 1068 to 1180, the vote division being quite similar to the eventual presidential balloting (see Table 9-3). Critical to this decision was the earlier one in the Mississippi delegation to use the unit rule on this roll call vote. By this means, a 31–28 Ford majority (the voting in the Mississippi delegation included alternates) on the question of Rule 16c (the Curtis motion) became a 30–0 Mississippi division on the roll call vote. Word of the Mississippi delegation's decision to use the unit rule had evidently caused some erosion of Reagan support in a few other states.[4]

Credentials

Struggles over the acceptance of the credentials of disputed delegates have been critical features of national party conventions from the earliest days. The Democratic convention of 1848 was held up for four days over the seating of rival delegations from New York State; the convention finally seated both groups, giving each delegate half a vote. In 1860, several southerners walked out of the Democratic convention after a seating dispute, paving the way for the nomination of Stephen Douglas of Illinois and the break-up of the Demo-

4. *Congressional Quarterly Weekly Report*, August 21, 1976, p. 2255.

cratic party (not to mention the election of Abraham Lincoln, secession, and the Civil War). In the 1896 Republican convention, Mark Hanna's steamroller tactics engineered a key victory on the credentials report, after which William McKinley's first ballot nomination was in the bag. At the 1932 Democratic convention, Huey Long's dramatic speech swayed enough delegates to gain a victory for Long's pro-Roosevelt Louisiana delegation. Dwight Eisenhower's 1952 Republican nomination was immensely aided when the convention over-turned an earlier decision by the committee to seat delegates from Georgia, Louisiana, and Texas who were committed to Senator Taft. The 1972 Demo-cratic convention was torn by the credentials struggles affecting the South Carolina, Illinois, and California delegations.[5] Notable credentials disputes involving civil rights platform planks and the question of loyalty to the national ticket plagued the Democratic conventions of 1948, 1964, and 1968. In 1948, the Mississippi delegation refused to support any nominee who favored President Truman's civil rights program. In 1964, Mississippi and Alabama delegates were required, on an individual basis, to sign an oath of loyalty to the party's ticket. In 1968, underrepresentation of blacks was a factor in allegations that McCarthy forces were systematically put down in favor of Vice-President Humphrey's nomination bid.[6]

Another type of convention struggle is that over the vice-presidential nomination. Serious and open struggles over the second spot on the national ticket are rare, because most presidential nominees impose their preference on the convention, as with Roosevelt's choice of Wallace in 1940 and Truman in 1944, Eisenhower's choice of Nixon in 1952, Johnson's choice of Humphrey in 1964, Nixon's choice of Maryland Governor Spiro Agnew in 1968, and Carter's choice of Minnesota Senator Walter Mondale in 1976. George McGovern's selection of Missouri Senator Thomas Eagleton in 1972 became a critical part of the collapse of the Democratic ticket in the presidential cam-paign. A notable exception to the rule of automatic acceptance of the vice-presidential nomination was the situation that developed in the 1956 Demo-cratic convention, when Adlai Stevenson left the question open, leading to a close victory for Senator Kefauver over Senator John Kennedy of Massachusetts. Kennedy's strong showing was pointed to by observers as an indication that a Catholic politician could seriously pursue national political ambitions.

There is often a connection between the outcome of close or critical votes on credentials, rules, or platform planks and the outcome of the presidential nomination balloting, as we have already seen in the discussion of Rule 16c and the Ford-Reagan struggle at the 1976 Republican convention (Table 9-3).

5. Theodore H. White, *The Making of the President 1972* (New York: Bantam Books, 1973), pp. 217–219.
6. *Congressional Quarterly Weekly Report,* June 24, 1972, p. 1520.

Table 9-4. State Delegation Voting on Civil Rights Amendment and Presidential Nomination, 1964 Republican National Convention

	States with Majority for Goldwater	*States That Split*	*States with Majority for Another Candidate*
States against amendment	34	0	0
States that split on amendment	0	1	0
States for amendment	1	1	13

Three other important cases further illustrate this. Anti-Goldwater forces at the 1964 Republican convention in San Francisco were not successful in their efforts to use the civil rights issues as a means of stopping the Arizona senator (see Table 9-4). Oponents of the Vietnam War, who had already caused President Johnson to decide not to seek nomination for a second term, tried unsuccessfully to use the Vietnam issue to secure the nomination of Senator McCarthy or Senator McGovern in preference to Johnson's vice-president, Hubert Humphrey (see Table 9-5). At the 1980 Democratic convention, forces supporting Senator Kennedy introduced a resolution to allow delegates to "vote their consciences" regardless of the results of binding primaries in their states; voting on the resolution closely paralleled the subsequent presidential balloting among the state delegations.

State conventions can be every bit as exciting as national conventions, though seldom are matters of national import involved. These conventions have similar kinds of struggles over platforms, rules, and credentials, but in states using primary elections to nominate candidates for the major positions, the function of nomination that is so critical at national conventions is absent.

Table 9-5. State Delegation Voting on Vietnam Question and Presidential Nomination, 1968 Democratic National Convention

	States with Majority for Humphrey	*States with Majority for McCarthy or McGovern*
States against plank	37	0
States for plank	4	11

Note: There were two Georgia delegations in 1968 ("Regulars" and "Loyalists"), which accounts for the fact that the table indicates 52 states (the District of Columbia is included).

Local conventions are ordinarily much smaller and more concerned with local nominations and local party affairs than with platforms, issue statements, rules, or credentials.

PROPOSALS

The convention of the party is and should continue to be the most significant element of its organization. If the convention is to maintain its pre-eminent position, great care must be taken to ensure its legitimacy; that is, it must be based in the expressed preferences of the majority of the party members. This brings us to the problem of how to form the convention. How are convention delegates to be apportioned among the geographical units whose residents are to be represented? And, how are the individual delegates themselves to be chosen? Some aspects of these questions have already been addressed in the proposals suggested in Chapter 8 concerning the selection of delegates to national conventions; the proposals that follow here concern delegates to national, state, and local party conventions.

9-1. To apportion convention delegates among political units. Qualifying national political parties would be empowered to determine the number of delegates to their respective national conventions. If a party makes no determination as to the size of its national convention, then the number of delegates would remain the same as it was at the last previous national convention. National convention delegates would be apportioned among the states and the District of Columbia by methods described below. Seats for territories could be handled as each party might wish, except that the total number of territorial seats could not exceed one percent of the number of seats apportioned to states and the District of Columbia, no territory's delegation could be as large as half the size of the smallest state delegation, and each territory's delegation could be generally proportionate to the relative populations of the various territories represented.

Apportionment of national convention delegates among the states and the District of Columbia, of state convention delegates among the counties, and of county convention delegates among precincts would be based on the relative size of the party across the political units. In other words, a county with 5 percent of the party's total strength in the state should have 5 percent of the seats at the state convention. The determination of relative party strength could be based on any one of three kinds of official data, namely, (1) the number of party members currently registered in the political unit, (2) the number of party members who voted in the most recent primary election, or (3) the number of voters (without regard to party affiliation) who voted for the party's candidate for a particular office (such as president or governor) in the most recent general election.[7] Each of the three possible data bases have advantages and disadvantages as foundations for convention apportionment. The second alternative would produce the lowest number for a given unit, but since all units would be using the same data base, any distortion would be minimal and probably random. This method would also base apportionment on the most loyal of party members. The other two possibilities, registration lists and the poll for the party's candidate in the previous general election, would involve more persons in all units. Registration lists can be made somewhat spurious because of occasional hyped-up registration drives, often geared to single-issue campaign efforts such as abortion, gun control, busing, or tax cutting. Use of the number of voters supporting the party's candidate in the previous general election raises the anomaly of having convention apportionment based to some degree on voters who are not members of the party, since thousands of Republicans and independents would probably have voted for the Democratic candidate, and vice versa for the Republican candidate.

But, all things considered, the party's general election vote seems to be the most satisfactory basis for apportionment of convention delegates among political units, because such data is most recent, most readily available, most carefully counted, and most reflective of real party strength. The presidential vote is preferred because the apportionment base would then be the same for the party in all parts of the nation, though individual states or parties might opt for the gubernatorial base as a better reflection of idiosyncratic state interests, issues, and candidates.

The knotty question of the method of apportioning seats presents itself next. This matter of equitable apportionment can become exceedingly sticky, given the wide variety of demographic circumstances and of representational devices that have been used to meet different situations—the place system, limited voting, the Lebanese binomial system, the Bosnian mandate, etc. But there is a compelling system available that would suit the purpose at the state and national levels: the formula of equal proportions, worked out by statisticians and accepted by the Congress as the basis for congressional apportionment since 1929. It is beyond our purpose here to explain the formula in detail; briefly, it begins by giving each unit (each state for the national convention, each county for the state convention) one seat and then allocates the

---

7. Raw population would not be an appropriate basis for apportionment of seats in a party convention because Democrats, Republicans, and others are not evenly distributed among states, counties, or precincts.

remainder of seats in sequence to units which, objectively and mathematically, are most deserving of additional seats. The data base is readily available, and computers can quickly and accurately work out the rather complex calculations. The number of delegates would have to be established in advance. The larger the convention, the more precisely equitable will be the distribution. This may be illustrated by reference to the current apportionment of the US House of Representatives, which does involve some, but quite minimal, distortion. The most populous states will have the most representatives, of course, but the distribution of seats will not be exactly identical to the distribution of voters, given the inability of any system to apply numerical fractions to the inviolate human body. The data in Table 9-6 show the effects of the formula of equal proportions and the kinds of unavoidable, minimal disparities in representation it produces (again, as any system would). Since national conventions have long been more than five times the size of the House, convention apportionment under this system would be even more precisely equitable than is apportionment in the House itself.

For a national convention, the number of delegates would probably be in the range of 1,500 to 3,000, the exact number to be determined by each convention for the next convention.

For a state convention, the number of delegates ought to bear some relation to the number of counties and the number of party members. The assumption is that a state convention ought to be large enough to represent the significant interests and sections of the state and small enough to be able to work efficiently; therefore a range of 100 to 300 delegates would seem proper. The exact number, here again, would be determined by each state convention for the next one. States with a large number of counties having relatively low populations could, before working out the formula of equal proportions, combine two or more adjacent counties into a multicounty delegate district, in order to reduce overrepresentation of low-population counties.[8]

County conventions of large size would be unnecessary, unwarranted, and expensive. Therefore, one delegate would be elected by each voting unit (precinct) of the county, or combination of voting units as determined in advance by party authority. Delegates would have voting power in the

---

8. Conceivably, a state could have 50 percent of its population in one county, 15 percent in another county, 10 percent in a third, and the balance of 25 percent spread out evenly over twenty-five counties. Since each unit would receive one seat under the formula of equal proportions, the twenty-five small counties would be overrepresented inordinately in a body of reasonable size. Combining some of these counties for representational purposes before working out the apportionment formula would mitigate this problem.

Table 9-6.   Effects of the Formula of Equal Proportions on Representation of
Selected States in the US House of Representatives

State	1970 Population	Number of Seats	Population per Seat
North Dakota	617,761	1	617,761
Utah	1,059,273	2	529,636
Alabama	3,444,165	7	492,024
New Jersey	7,168,164	15	477,878
Massachusetts	5,689,170	12	474,098
Indiana	5,193,669	11	472,152
Pennsylvania	11,793,909	25	471,756
New York	18,241,266	39	467,725
Michigan	8,875,083	19	467,110
Texas	11,196,730	24	466,530
Virginia	4,648,494	10	464,849
California	19,953,134	43	464,026
Ohio	10,652,017	23	463,131
Illinois	11,113,976	24	463,082
Florida	6,789,443	15	452,629
Kansas	2,249,071	5	449,814
South Dakota	666,257	2	333,128
Alaska	302,173	1	302,173

Data based on 1970 census and congressional apportionment. States are listed in order
of population per seat.

county convention equal to the number of votes cast in their respective constituencies for the party's presidential candidate in the previous election. In
order to keep the size of the county convention within reason, it would be
provided that voting units be combined for purposes of electing county convention delegates, so that no representation unit would be smaller than 5
percent of the county's party voters. Thus the maximum size of a county
convention would be twenty delegates.

Should a particular party or state desire to make use of conventions at other levels such as municipal or multicounty legislative, judicial, or congressional districts, the same principles of apportionment and voting strength used for county conventions would be applied.

Since most states now have gubernatorial terms of four years, with the gubernatorial election generally held in even-numbered but nonpresidential years, most would probably choose to have state party conventions in the summer of each even-numbered year. However, quadrennial or annual elections would be permissible, at the discretion of the state.

9-2. To select state and county convention delegates. Now we turn to the matter of how the delegates themselves are to be chosen. (Note that the selection of national convention delegates was treated in Chapter 8 as part of the larger presidential nomination process.)

The election of party delegates to state and county conventions, and to other party conventions that might be established at municipal or multicounty levels, would take place in the state's primary. Candidates for delegate to county or state conventions would have their names placed on the primary election ballot by either one of two methods. The first would be designation by the party's county executive committee of candidates it wishes to endorse in the primary election; such endorsement must occur at least six weeks prior to the primary election, and the primary ballot will indicate the party endorsement of a candidate or candidates by appropriate language or signs, such as the use of an asterisk beside the name or names. The second method of getting on the ballot would be by filing a petition in the name of the candidate signed by a number of registered party members in the county equal to or exceeding 2 percent of the votes cast in the county for the party's presidential candidate in the most recent general election. Such petition would have to be filed at least four weeks prior to the primary election.

The result of these arrangements for the selection of state and county convention delegates would be that in the primary election each voter would be voting for one delegate from his precinct (or larger multiprecinct district) to the county convention and one delegate from his county (or larger multicounty district) to the state convention.

9-3. To evaluate public officials. A new function of conventions would be that of evaluating the performance of elected public officials and reporting the results of such evaluation to party authorities and the public in the official's constituency. Among the factors to be examined would be the official's attention to duty and contributions to the party's objectives, as outlined in the platform and established by the party's legislative caucus. This evaluation is not intended to be a means of enforcing blind obedience to stated party goals, but it would certainly be appropriate to note behavioral anomalies, such as identifying a legislator who votes more frequently in agreement with the majority of the opposition party than with his own party majority, or one who misses an excessive number of sessions or committee meetings, or one who is unethical, dishonest, bigoted, lazy, garrulous, or exhibits other habits considered unattractive or inapproporate in a representative of the people of the district. The convention could also determine the distribution of party funds to various party nominees. Such decisions, however, will ordinarily be made by the executive committee because conventions meet so seldom. Further explanations of the manifold connections between evaluative functions of party conventions and committees at various levels can be found in Chapters 6 and 7.

This function of formally evaluating public officials attempts to respond to a critical problem of America's system of representative government. William Keefe makes the point that responsible party government breaks down because the public has inadequate information on how legislatures work or on how individual legislators behave. A responsible party system, according to Keefe, requires "a strong measure of internal cohesion within the party-in-the-government in order to adopt its program . . . an electorate sufficiently sensitive to party accomplishments and failures that it can hold the parties accountable for their records, particularly in the case of the party in power."[9] Under this reform, it would become a major continuing responsibility of party organizations in each state to watch and evaluate the behavior of elected officials of their own party and of the opposition party as well.

9. Keefe, *op. cit.*, p. 186.

Chapter 10

Counting the Votes: The Electoral College

Our presidential election system, which is responsible for selecting the most important political leader in the world, consists of three basic elements.

The first, described in Chapter 8, takes place over a span of several months in the late winter and spring of the presidential election year. It is the complicated dual process of choosing delegates to the quadrennial national nominating convention of each party and at the same time expressing preferences as to the party's presidential nominee. In more than half the states, primaries accomplish this through a wide variety of state-established election systems. The chief vagary is timing. New Hampshire votes in late February, and California not until early June, so there is a gap of more than three months during which all sorts of developments may arise. This capriciously diminishes or enhances the significance of a particular state's action, out of all proportion to its size. A candidate may be made or broken as a result of his performance in the first primary; one who is strongest in states that do not hold their primaries until May or June may be out of the running long before then. Depending on the rise and fall in the fortunes of a particular candidate, the last primaries may be crucial or they may be mere frosting on the cake. We have suggested treatments for these and related problems in the proposals at the end of Chapter 8.

The second element in presidential selection, described in Chapter 9, is the nomination of each party's national ticket by the respective national conventions. The problems in this area seem to be less severe than those associated with the other two elements of the presidential election system, and thus the reform proposals at the end of Chapter 9 do not suggest drastic changes in the national conventions.

The third element, selection of the winning presidential ticket by the Electoral College, is authorized by the Constitution and operates uniformly across the nation. Whichever ticket wins the most popular votes in a state receives all of that state's electoral votes, since the effect of the state election is to choose the slate of electors associated with the party of the winning ticket. The winning electors meet in their respective state capitals to cast their votes for president and vice-president, and these electoral votes are forwarded to

Washington, where in December the president of the Senate counts them and announces the result. An absolute majority of all the electoral votes is required for election.

EVOLUTION OF THE ELECTORAL COLLEGE

The Electoral College, established in Article II of the Constitution and amended by the Twelfth and Twenty-second Amendments, is the basis of the presidential election system. Among the Founding Fathers there was a good deal of debate about the proper mechanism for selecting the chief executive, some favoring popular or direct election, others preferring selection by an intervening instituiton. It must be remembered that the political and electoral institutions of that time were still comparatively simple and untested; there were no national political parties, or even permanent state parties, and the founders, so interested in balancing the major federal elements against each other, did not in the end wish to make the chief executive dependent upon the national legislature. A particularly thorny problem was posed by the fact that about 700,000 slaves were included in the national population of 4 million; the Constitutional provision that provided for counting this population element on the basis of three-fifths for purposes of congressional representation was not satisfactory for purposes of a national presidential election, for who would cast the votes assigned on the basis of the slave population? And if slaves were not to be counted, would this not ensure permanent northern domination of presidential elections? So the slave situation made indirect election of the president the choice of the convention. As James Madison said:

> There was one difficulty however of a serious nature attending immediate choice by the people. The right of suffrage was much more diffusive in the Northern than the Southern states; and the latter could have no influence in the election on the score of Negroes. The substitution of electors obviated this difficulty.[1]

Other selection methods had been proposed at the constitutional convention—election by Congress, by the governors of the several states, by the people directly, or by national electors choosing among candidates put forth by each state as its best citizen—but they were all rejected and the system of intermediate electors was adopted in the final days of the convention. The intermediate electors were seen as free agents, as a collection of the best and

1. Senate Report No. 96-111, 96th Congress, 1st Session, "Direct Popular Election of the President and Vice-President of the United States," US Senate Committee on the Judiciary, 1979, pp. 7-8.

most patriotic minds and hearts in the United States set up to choose the president in a calm and judicious atmosphere remote from popular passions. How the nature of the electors changed very quickly was summarized by a select committee of the US Senate in 1826:

> In the first election held under the Constitution, the people looked beyond these agents, fixed upon their candidates for President and Vice-President, and took pledges from the electoral candidates to obey their will. In every subsequent election the same thing has been done. Electors, therefore, have not answered the design of their institution. They are not the independent body and superior characters which they were intended to be. They are not left to the exercise of their own judgment; on the contrary, they give their vote, or bind themselves to give it, according to the will of their constituents. They have degenerated into mere agents, in a case which requires no agency, and where the agent must be useless, if he is faithful, and dangerous if he is not.[2]

Winning the Electoral Vote

The practice is, then, for the voters in each state to vote for a slate of electors, the rival slates having been arranged by the state party conventions of the respective parties. A few weeks after the November election, when the results have been certified by the state's election officials, these electors formally cast their state's electoral votes. With rare exceptions, given the mechanics by which the electors themselves are chosen, a state's electoral votes are awarded to the presidential ticket with the most popular votes.

Today, there are 538 electoral votes, 435 representing each member of the House of Representatives, 100 representing each US senator, and 3 representing the District of Columbia as provided in the Twenty-sixth Amendment; a majority of 538 is 270 (one more than half). If no candidate receives a majority of the electoral vote, the election of the president is referred to the House of Representatives, where each state regardless of population casts one vote, and the election of the vice-president is referred to the Senate. The obvious inequality of the contingent election process remains a critical sore point in the total electoral scheme, but it is some consolation that it has needed to be used only twice, the last time in 1824 (see below).

Two things are worth noting at this point. First, a mere plurality of the popular vote in a state, rather than an absolute majority, is all that is required to win all the state's electoral votes. Theoretically, then, it makes no difference whether a candidate wins by 2 million votes or by one vote; any margin gives

2. Senate Report No. 22, 19th Congress, 1st Session, "Resolutions Proposing Amendments to the Constitution of the United States," Senate Select Committee, 1826, p. 4.

the winner all the votes. Among other things, this rule diminishes the likelihood of a third party entering the presidential contest just to keep the
strongest candidate from achieving a majority. But the candidacies of Strom
Thurmond and Henry Wallace in 1948, and of George Wallace twenty years
later, were thought to be motivated by an interest in throwing the contest
into the House. The requirement of an absolute majority applies only in the
final stage of the presidential selection process, when the electoral votes from
across the nation are counted in Washington in December.

Second, while the mechanics of the system make it quite likely that the
candidate favored by most voters will receive all of a state's electoral votes,
there is nothing in the Constitution that binds the individual elector's choice.
The occasional aberration, exemplified by the Republican elector from North
Carolina who in 1972 did not cast his vote for Richard Nixon in spite of the
fact that he (the elector) clearly had been chosen for that purpose, is an unexpected and perhaps unfortunate development, but not an unconstitutional
one. Indeed, that kind of individual discretion, a decision aloof from the
wishes of the masses, was precisely what the Founding Fathers were looking
for when they instituted the Electoral College. The American Bar Association
has identified six occasions when electors voted contrary to expectations (to
which should be added the 1972 North Carolina incident mentioned above):
(1) in 1820, a New Hampshire elector voted against his party's candidate and
for John Quincy Adams, who was not even running, (2) in 1824, the electors
of North Carolina were pledged to two presidential candidates, Andrew Jackson
and Adams, with the understanding that they would vote for the candidate
with the best chance, (3) in 1912, the Theodore Roosevelt slate of electors
in South Dakota declared before election that they would vote for William
Howard Taft if Roosevelt could not be elected and the contest was between
Taft and Woodrow Wilson, (4) in 1948, a Tennessee elector running on both
the Democratic and States' Right tickets was elected as a result of the popular
vote in Tennessee for the Democratic (Truman) ticket, yet cast his vote for
the States' Right candidate, as he had announced prior to the election that he
would do, (5) in 1956, a Democratic elector in Alabama voted for Judge
Walter B. Jones of Alabama for president instead of for Adlai E. Stevenson
and for Herman Talmadge of Georgia for vice-president instead of for Estes
Kefauver, in spite of the fact that the Stevenson-Kefauver ticket had carried
Alabama with 56.5 percent of the popular vote, and (6) in 1960, a Republican
elector in Oklahoma voted for Democratic Senator Harry F. Byrd of Virginia
for president and Republican Senator Barry H. Goldwater of Arizona for vice-
president, even though the Nixon-Lodge ticket had carried the state with 59
percent of Oklahoma's popular vote. A few states have passed laws requiring
electors to vote for their party nominees, but the constitutionality of these

laws has never been passed on by the Supreme Court.[3] It is possible for a state to elect unpledged electors. In 1960, Senator Byrd received the electoral votes of six unpledged electors from Alabama and eight from Mississippi. Four years later, the Democratic electors from Alabama were unpledged, and the names of the national Democratic ticket (Johnson and Humphrey) were not on the ballot in Alabama.[4]

There have been a number of problems connected with the operation of the Electoral College in the course of our forty-eight presidential elections. Twice, as noted earlier, the electoral vote count did not produce a majority for any candidate, and thus in 1800 and 1824 the House was called upon to make the final decision. In the 1800 election, when Thomas Jefferson and Aaron Burr tied in electoral votes because all the Jeffersonian electors voted for both Jefferson and Burr, the House required thirty-six ballots to arrive at a verdict. Through each of the first thirty-five ballots, two states had been divided; Jefferson was the choice of eight, and Burr of six (with sixteen states, nine were required for a majority).[5] On the thirty-sixth ballot, Federalist electors from Delaware, Maryland, and South Carolina voted blanks, and a Vermont Federalist absented himself. Thereby Jefferson received the votes of Vermont and Maryland since the Republicans were left to cast the votes of those states, and Delaware and South Carolina cast no votes on the deciding ballot because they had no Republican electors.[6]

The original Constitution had provided that the candidate with the most electoral votes would be president, and the candidate with the second highest total would be vice-president. This was changed after the strange 1800 experience by adoption of the Twelfth Amendment, which separated the voting for president and vice-president (and, at the same time, led to the establishment of unified national tickets, with a party's presidential and vice-presidential candidates placed side by side on the ballot). In 1824, Andrew Jackson, John Quincy Adams, Henry Clay, and William Crawford were the presidential candidates. Since no one received a majority of the electoral votes, the election went to the House, where Adams defeated Jackson, though Jackson had received more popular and electoral votes.

On four occasions, in 1860, 1912, 1948, and 1968, there were more than two major candidates in the presidential race, and the winners (Abraham

3. Commission on Electoral College Reform, *Electing the President* (Chicago: American Bar Association, 1967), pp. 25-26. Lower courts have held on both sides of the question. Cf. Ray *v.* Blair, 343 U.S. 214 (1952).
4. *Ibid.,* p. 26.
5. The congressmen from Maryland and Vermont were evenly divided, so both states had to cast blank votes.
6. Eugene Roseboom, *A History of Presidential Elections* (New York: Macmillan, 1965), pp. 44-47.

Lincoln, Woodrow Wilson, Harry Truman, and Richard Nixon respectively) received electoral vote majorities but did not have popular vote majorities.

In 1888, Benjamin Harrison received fewer popular votes than incumbent President Grover Cleveland, but did achieve an electoral vote majority.

There have been a number of presidents who did not receive popular vote majorities:

John Quincy Adams, 1824 (30.5 percent of the popular vote)
James Knox Polk, 1844 (49.6 percent)
Zachary Taylor, 1848 (47.4 percent)
James Buchanan, 1856 (45.6 percent)
Abraham Lincoln, 1860 (39.8 percent)
Rutherford Hayes, 1876 (48.0 percent)
James Garfield, 1880 (48.3 percent)
Grover Cleveland, 1884 (48.5 percent)
Benjamin Harrison, 1888 (47.9 percent)
Grover Cleveland, 1892 (46.0 percent)
Woodrow Wilson, 1912 (41.9 percent)
Woodrow Wilson, 1916 (49.3 percent)
Harry Truman, 1948 (49.5 percent)
John Kennedy, 1960 (49.7 percent)
Richard Nixon, 1968 (43.4 percent)

Of the presidents on the above list, Adams, Hayes, and Harrison all trailed an opponent in the popular vote count (the opponents, respectively, were Andrew Jackson, Samuel Tilden, and Grover Cleveland).[7]

To summarize, in the thirty-nine presidential elections from 1824, when popular votes began to be recorded, through 1976, twenty-four presidents received both electoral and popular vote majorities, twelve received an electoral majority but only a popular plurality, two received an electoral majority while trailing the opponent in the popular vote, and one was elected by the House of Representatives through the contingent election process.

The election of 1876 presented the nation with a real crisis. Republican Rutherford Hayes of Ohio and Democrat Samuel Tilden of New York ran a very close race, the outcome of which could not be finally determined because four states (Florida, Louisiana, Oregon, and South Carolina) each submitted two different certifications. Because no authority or rule was available to decide what to do with the votes from the four disputed states, Congress "invented" an extraconstitutional Electoral Commission to determine which

---

7. To the list of presidents who served without having received a majority of the popular vote may be added the vice-presidents who succeeded to the presidency on the death (John Tyler, Millard Fillmore, Andrew Johnson, Chester Alan Arthur, Theodore Roosevelt, Calvin Coolidge, Harry Truman, Lyndon Johnson) or resignation (Gerald Ford) of the president. We were without an active president during the extensive illnesses of Garfield, Wilson, and Eisenhower.

sets of contested electoral votes would be accepted. The House, the Senate, and the Supreme Court were each authorized to choose five members of the commission; with one chamber of the Congress dominated by the Republicans and the other by the Democrats, eight Republicans and seven Democrats were appointed. Not surprisingly, by a set of party-line 8-7 votes, the Electoral Commission accepted the Republican votes from each of the four disputed states, and this gave Hayes, who had trailed Tilden in the popular vote count, a one-vote electoral margin, 185-184. The decision was announced just in time for the scheduled inauguration of the new presidential term on March 4, 1877. One consequence of that hair-raising experience was that Congress passed a law that provided guidelines to reduce the possibility of future confusion or vagueness in the state-level certification of federal election returns.

Thus it might be said that the Electoral College is bloody but unbowed, remaining for this generation the rather delicate and faintly ambiguous institution by which the president is elected. It might be illuminating and thought-provoking at this point to speculate for a bit on how the Electoral College might work.

HOW THE ELECTORAL COLLEGE MIGHT WORK

When Americans cast their vote for president, they are actually choosing between rival slates of candidates for presidential electors. The presidential ballot in a state having ten electoral votes will have a place for voters to mark their choice of electors from the Democratic, Republican, or other party; to mark a party's box is to vote for all ten of its candidates. The rival slates of candidates for presidential elector have been put together by an agency of the party, usually the state convention. The winning slate is the one that receives the most votes in the state's general election. State law or party rule may specify that the slate of electors is bound to vote in accordance with the outcome of the presidential voting in the state, but as we have seen there is nothing in the Constitution or federal statutes to require that. As noted above, there have been a few occasions when a "faithless elector" has voted contrary to the popular vote in his state, but luckily these aberrations have been inconsequential. At the same time, it should be remembered that they could be very consequential indeed.

Constitutionally, there is no reason why the basis of presidential elections could not be totally reversed from present practice. That is, there is presently the legal possibility that all of the electors could be chosen with little or no reference to their presidential preferences. This would be in conformance with the original intentions of the Founding Fathers that the Electoral College be a discrete body purposely removed from mass passions or the machinations of political elites, maturely and carefully choosing the person most fit to administer the nation's public business.

The model of presidential selection described in the previous paragraph only worked in the election of the first president, George Washington, in the very brief period before permanent party movements developed among the followers of Thomas Jefferson and Alexander Hamilton. Since Jefferson defeated John Adams' bid for reelection in 1800, the main determinant of electoral voting has been the political party. Since 1828, it may further be said, the determination of who would run for president has been the result of partisan activity in state and national party conventions, rather than the result of congressional caucus maneuvering in Washington.

What if, today, we had no primaries or national conventions that concerned themselves with presidential nominations? One could visualize national conventions being concerned with platform construction and party governance, and state conventions selecting nominees for presidential elector on the basis of their personal qualifications, experience, and philosophy. Such nominees would probably have considerable experience in practical politics, but they would not necessarily be persons most known for specifically political activity. A state party convention in Colorado might choose a slate of electors that included an executive of a mining union from Pueblo, a college professor from Fort Collins, a wheat farmer from Burlington, a lawyer from Denver, a small businessman and city council member from Denver, a social worker from Grand Junction, and an insurance company executive from Littleton. The reader can build a similar list of party nominees for presidential elector from Missouri or Pennsylvania, slates whose vocational, regional, ethnic, or ideological orientations would be critical factors in the way the state would eventually play its role in the Electoral College.

In the general election, the voters in effect would be choosing among partisan slates of uncommitted electors; another possibility would be that the campaign for electors could be conducted without party slates, or even without party designation. The Electoral College, in any event, would contain members of more than one party.

Such a reversion to the intentions of the Founding Fathers would without doubt constitute a drastic change in presidential politics. The presidential electors would be, presumably (or perhaps one should say hopefully), persons who had achieved reputations for judgment, honesty, and independent thought, and their work would proceed witout the guidance of presidential primaries or state convention directives. It may be that such a college would find it difficult to decide on a candidate by a constitutional majority, and that recourse to the contingent election process might be frequent. That being the case, prompt attention to remedying the present contingent system would

Table 10-1.   Party Voting on the Direct Election Plan, US Senate, 1979

	Democrats	Republicans	Total
Favoring direct election	39	12	51
Opposing direct election	20	28	48
Total	59	40	99

The vote was on adoption of S.J. Res. 28, introduced by Senator Bayh (Democrat of Indiana), to propose an amendment to the Constitution; the motion required a two-thirds vote in favor. Generally, liberals favored the resolution, and conservatives opposed it. However, Southern Democrats voted more favorably in 1979 than they had on a cloture vote on direct election in 1970, while Northern Democrats and Republicans were less favorable in 1979 than they had been in 1970. *Congressional Quarterly* noted that senators from twenty-seven states with eight electoral votes or less split about evenly on the Bayh resolution, twenty-six for and twenty-seven against.

Congressional Quarterly Weekly Report, July 14, 1979, pp. 1407, 1408, 1421.

seem to be all the more imperative. Further it might be advisable to provide that, in the event of a tie, the candidate receiving the fewest electoral votes be dropped, beginning with, say, the fifth ballot. Without such provisions, an Electoral College in which no party had a working majority would indeed be likely to deadlock, forcing a contingent election in the House of Representatives, or making it necessary to come to a consensual decision in which the minority party could in effect determine which one of the majority party's candidates it would accept.

REFORMING THE ELECTORAL COLLEGE

There have been many proposals for reform of the presidential election system; our purpose in this section is to review the best-known.[8] The main proposal considered recently was the direct popular vote plan sponsored by Senator Birch Bayh (Democrat of Indiana), which was defeated on the Senate floor in July 1979; partisan support for the plan is summarized in Table 10-1.

8. For a review of the testimony of scores of congressional witnesses on the subject of amending the Electoral College system, see "Direct Popular Election of the President and Vice-President of the United States," Hearings before the Subcommittee on the Constitution of the Committee on the Judiciary, US Senate, 96th Congress, First Session, on S.J. Res. 28, March 27, 30, April 3, 9, 1979, pp. 598-608.

The Senate Judiciary Committee in its report to accompany S.J. Res. 28 identified four "dangerous flaws" in the present Electoral College system—the problem of the faithless elector, the inequity of the contingent election system in the House of Representatives, the possibility that a popular vote winner would lose the electoral vote, and the distortions that can accompany a winner-take-all system. Three of these problems are dealt with elsewhere in this book; the fourth requires some development. Citing the research of Steven Brams, the committee report noted that the winner-take-all rule makes it very important to carry the largest states. As a result, candidates tend to spend a disproportionate share of their time in the population centers. Table 10-2 demonstrates this in

Table 10-2. Electoral Votes and Campaign Stops, by State, 1976 Presidential Campaign

State(s)	Electoral Votes	Number of Campaign Stops by Carter, Mondale, Ford, and Dole, Fall 1976
California	45	43
New York	41	41
Pennsylvania	27	27
Texas	26	19
Illinois	26	37
Ohio	25	38
Michigan	21	13
9 states with 11-19 electoral votes	13.4 (average)	12.2 (average)
4 states with 10-14 electoral votes	10.0 (average)	6.5 (average)
15 states with 5-9 electoral votes	7.3 (average)	4.9 (average)
15 states with 3-4 electoral votes	3.6 (average)	1.7 (average)

It may be that the relatively large number of stops in states such as Ohio, Illinois, and Missouri was due in part to their geographical location, and that states like New Jersey and Michigan were visited less because of their closeness to other large states where there would be considerable media overlap.

Source: Adapted from table headed "Candidate Stops Along Campaign Trail–1976" in Report No. 96-111, 96th Congress, 1st session, *Direct Popular Election of the President and Vice-President of the United States,* US Senate Committee on the Judiciary, 1979, p. 26.

terms of the campaign appearances of Jimmy Carter, Walter Mondale, Gerald Ford, and Robert Dole in the general election campaign of 1976. Brams also developed a "3/2s rule" in presidential campaigning, finding that the relative attention given to the larger states is even greater than their proportion of the electoral vote total would indicate.

> We think that probably the most compelling conclusion that emerges from our analysis . . . does not concern campaign strategy but rather concerns the severely unrepresentative character of presidential campaigns under the Electoral College. By forcing candidates—and, after the election, incumbent presidents with an eye on the next election—to pay much greater attention in terms of their allocations of time, money, and other resources to the largest states, the Electoral College gives disproportionate weight to attitudes and opinions of voters in these states. On a per capita basis, voters in California are 2.92 times as attractive campaign targets as voters in Washington, D.C.; even greater than this ratio of the most extreme individual biases is the most extreme electoral-bias ratio that makes California 8.13 times as attractive per electoral vote as Alaska. . . .
>
> [A candidate's search for broad-based nationwide support] is the goal that we believe the electoral system should promote. The Electoral College subverts this goal by giving special dispensation to particular states and, additionally, fostering manipulative strategies in them. As an alternative, we think that direct popular-vote election of the president, which would render state boundaries irrelevant, would encourage candidates to maximize their nationwide appeal by tying their support directly to potential votes everywhere on a proportionate basis.[9]

The following paragraphs summarize the proposals that have been put forth in the past generation to reform or eliminate the Electoral College.

The contingent election process. The Constitution specifies that if the electoral vote is inconclusive, the House of Representatives shall make the decision, with each state having just one vote irrespective of population. The inequity of giving each state one vote in the House—where California has forty-three members and Alaska only one—is obvious. One way to reform the contingent election process would be to give each member of the House one vote. Another way would be to provide for a joint session of Congress to settle inconclusive elections, with each member casting one vote; this is the same distribution of power that exists in the Electoral College itself, except for the three electors representing the District of Columbia. Another way around the difficulty posed by the inequitable contingent election process

9. Steven J. Brams and Morton D. Davis, "The 3/2's Rule in Presidential Campaigning," *American Political Science Review,* LXVIII, March 1974, pp. 133-134.

would be to change the presidential election system so that there would be no
necessity for a contingent election at all.

The discretion of electors. Several proposed amendments have centered their
attention on the simple matter of eliminating the office of presidential elector
and providing that a state's electoral votes be automatically cast for the candidate certified as having received a plurality of the popular vote in the state.

Direct popular election. This proposal has received the most attention and
support over the years. The system would provide for a tabulation of all
the popular votes cast in the fifty states and the District of Columbia, stipu-
lating a minimum plurality. There have been a number of variations in the
direct popular election system. The current and best-known version, that
sponsored by Senator Bayh and more than forty other senators in 1977,
would require that a condidate have at least 40 percent of the nationwide
vote to be elected. Failing that quota, there would be a second national
popular vote, limiting the candidates to the two who received the most
votes in the original balloting.[10] Of course, the popular vote approach
could incorporate the present, or a reformed, contingent vote in the Congress
to declare the winner. Objections to the direct popular vote system have
focused on two problems: first, the reduced significance of majorities within
the separate states, with a resulting tendency on the part of candidates to
downplay the importance of the states as states; and second, inaccuracy
(honest or otherwise) in the tabulation of the popular vote.

The problem of an inaccurate count of voting returns and its special
danger in a direct popular election was discussed by V. Lance Tarrance, a
political consultant, and Richard M. Scammon, perhaps the nation's foremost
elections analyst, during the course of Senate Judiciary Committee hearings
in 1977. Tarrance was concerned that an inaccurate count in, say, Texas or
Illinois, would affect the national outcome directly, whereas under the present
electoral system the erroneous data would affect only the vote in the specific
state. As Tarrance said:

> The Electoral College provides perhaps a unique statistical service—a
> service never foreseen by the constitutional writers. The Electoral College

10. Political journalist Neal Peirce has stated his opposition to presidential runoff elec-
    tions. Responding to a question from Senator John Chafee (Republican of Rhode
    Island) as to whether he thought the 40 percent quota should be higher, Peirce re-
    plied: "Frankly, I think there should be no provision at all for runoff. I would
    prefer to see the victory awarded to the candidate who receives the most votes,
    without having a minimum percentage figure." "The Electoral College and Direct
    Election," Hearings before the Committee on the Judiciary, US Senate, January 27,
    February 1, 2, 7, and 10, 1977, p. 250.

"cleans out" much of the error debris in our election tabulation system by concentrating on state outcomes rather than a national outcome.

However, a direct popular election, if a close one, could be challenged by many diffuse errors in the election return tabulation, enough to cause doubt as to the election outcome itself. The last thing this already alienated electorate needs is a perceived, if not real, systemic dysfunction.

My election tabulation research experience in the state of Texas . . . revealed serious errors as to the accountability of certified county totals. . . .

If the administrative errors in ascertaining a close vote among the fifty states is roughly the same as in Texas, then it would be computationally impossible to certify—factually as well as in a perceived sense—the election outcome for weeks or months. The structural stress placed on the political system by such a potential tabulation nightmare—as I would envision in a close direct election—may be more than the system or the political order can absorb.

The Electoral College system, for all its peculiar features, works very well in an election outcome sense—and does not highlight the structural cracks in a diffused election tabulation system in this country. The direct popular election concept is simply a genuflection without knowledge of what administrative stresses it would create.

In essence, we do not know in this country what our known error structure would be in a direct popular election. . . . if you do not know or understand how to apply your error tolerance, then you cannot, in my opinion, with confidence restructure the future.[11]

Scammon agreed with Tarrance about the problem of errors but did not feel that the direct election system would make the situation significantly worse:

The point that Mr. Tarrance makes about errors is perfectly valid. Just last week we found a mistake on the presidential vote in the state of Vermont in which one city in that state had listed all of its wards, but totaled only the first three. There were thousands of votes of adjustment between Mr. Ford and Mr. Carter there. There are some in this country who even today maintain that Mr. Kennedy was never really elected and that if you were to ever recount the state of Illinois in 1960 you might get a different result.

. . . I would see no administrative problem with respect to a national presidential election that does not already exist with respect to the election of electors in each of the fifty-one jurisdictions with which we are concerned.

11. Testimony of V. Lance Tarrance, *The Electoral College and Direct Election,* Hearings before the Subcommittee on the Constitution of the Committee on the Judiciary, US Senate, 95th Congress, First Session, July 28, 1977, pp. 201-202.

... The only possibility that I could see for any difficulty in presidential elections on a popular basis would be the kind that faced this body in the election in New Hampshire. When you get in an election that is desperately close and by "desperately" I mean ten votes, two votes, fifteen votes, then honest men could contest ad infinitum over the reality in any election.

This we have, of course, had in this country in 1876. You can still have an argument more than a century later as to who stole what from whom in the presidential election of that year and whether or not the contested election votes in those states, which were contested, were, in fact, cast for the one candidate or the other.[12]

The district system. Under this proposal, associated with the names of former US Representative Frederick Coudert (Republican of New York) and Senator Karl Mundt (Republican of South Dakota), states would be divided into a number of presidential elector districts corresponding to the number of seats held by the state in the House of Representatives (the electoral districts could be the same as the congressional districts, but the proposal when made in the 1950s seemed to envision districts of equal population, which was not always the case in the years prior to the congressional reapportionment decision). Votes would be tabulated by district, and a candidate would receive one electoral vote for each district in which he received a plurality of the votes cast. The state's final two electoral votes, those based on its two United States senators, would be awarded to the candidate receiving the statewide plurality. Thus if, in Maryland, the Republican candidate carried five districts and the Democratic candidate three, while the Democrat carried the state as a whole, the Republican candidate would receive five electoral votes from Maryland and the Democrat five as well. As is presently the case, a majority of the national electoral vote would be needed to win.

The proportional system. This plan is associated with the names of former Representative Ed Lee Gossett (Democrat of Texas) and former Senator Henry Cabot Lodge, Jr., (Republican of Massachusetts). It would apportion the state's electoral votes according to the distribution of the popular vote in the state, carrying the mathematical calculation to three places beyond the decimal. If the popular vote in Arizona were divided 55 percent to the Republican and 45 percent to the Democrat, the Republican candidate would receive 3.300 of Arizona's six electoral votes and the Democrat would receive 2.700. Again, a majority of the national electoral vote would be required.

12. Testimony of Richard M. Scammon, *op. cit.,* pp. 210-211. The New Hampshire election referred to was the Senate race of 1974 between John Durkin and Louis Wyman. The results were so close that the Senate declared a vacancy and called for a special election to be held on September 16, 1975, which Durkin won.

The federal plan. In the 1970s, Senators Thomas Eagleton (Democrat of Missouri) and Robert Dole (Republican of Kansas) proposed a rather complicated election plan. A candidate would be elected if he received a plurality of the national popular vote and at the same time carried either one more than half of the states (twenty-six) or carried states that together contained more than half of the nation's population. If no one met these requirements, any votes going to candidates other than the two receiving the most electoral votes would be redistributed to the candidate who won the most votes in the state involved. The Eagleton-Dole plan does address some of the critical problems of the present system, but its complexity may have reduced levels of support for its adoption.

The bonus plan. In 1978, the Twentieth Century Fund summarized its study of the mechanics of the Electoral College system by recommending that in addition to electoral votes received under the present system, the candidate who won a plurality of the national popular vote would receive a bonus of 102 votes (in effect, two from each state and the District of Columbia). This would almost certainly mean that the national popular leader would receive the required majority in electoral votes (which would then be 321 out of a total of 640).

The multiplicity of reform proposals has been a barrier to Electoral College reform. While most citizens and many experts seem to agree that change is needed, there has not been sufficient consensus on which plan ought to be adopted.

IN DEFENSE OF THE ELECTORAL COLLEGE

Two scholars and one journalist, in testifying before the Senate Judiciary Committee concerning Electoral College reform, have summarized dramatically the views of those who feel it would be both dangerous and unnecessary to tamper with our present system of electing the president.

According to Jeane Kirkpatrick, professor of political science at Georgetown University:

... the constitutional system is complex, as the Electoral College is complex, because it seeks complex goals—democracy and liberty, responsiveness to majorities and to minorities, national government and federal government.

... political reforms, based on the very best motives and intentions, frequently produce unintended consequences which are remote from the desires or expectations of their authors.

As a ... student, I read about unanticipated consequences in Artistotle, Burke, and elsewhere, but I did not think much about the whole subject until I began the study . . . [of] the Democratic party's reforms beginning in 1968. I then spent several years studying the whole process of party reform, and the more I studied it, the more I became impressed by the gap that there often is between the motives and intentions of reforms and their consequences.

. . . the debate is not over whether we should elect a president by popular vote but about how we aggregate the votes. . . . the lower the level of aggregation the more important are the votes of small groups . . . it is clear that the Polish vote is more important in Milwaukee than it is in Wisconsin, and more important in Wisconsin than it is in the nation. . . .

I believe that if we made the nation a single constituency that this would very dramatically alter the basis of group politics. . . . Direct election would increase the likelihood that candidates would seek to construct that majority which is most homogeneous. That most homogeneous majority is variously termed the "real majority," "the silent majority," "middle America," "forgotten America." It has a number of readily identifiable characteristics. It is white, Christian, middle class, relatively conservative in its views. A rational campaign strategy under conditions of a national electorate—with votes aggregated at the national level—would probably forego the support of controversial minorities. . . .

I also think direct election would probably have an adverse effect on the federal system, because states would no longer be the action units of presidential politics. The presidency is, after all, our most important office, and if states and state parties are not relevant to it, then significant political processes are less likely to be organized around them.[13]

Walter Berns, resident scholar at the American Enterprise Institute, focused on the danger that abandonment of the Electoral College might undermine the two-party system and the "moderate character" of politics that is promoted by it:

I favor retention of the Electoral College. I favor it because it has served us well over the years. I favor it because I am persuaded that the proposed alternative, direct popular election, would or is likely to have consequences that we should all regret.

. . . it is the Electoral College that discourages the losers in a party convention from running on a separate ticket, or, stated otherwise, it is the Electoral College that leads losing candidates to accept the party convention's choice of a candidate. Under a system of direct election, the man who loses in the convention—say, Governor Rockefeller in 1964—would be more inclined to run on a separate ticket. . . .

The men who founded this country surely recognized the entitlements of a popular majority, but, with an eye to the qualifications or qualities

13. Hearings on direct popular election, 1979, *op. cit.,* pp. 99-101.

required of an office, they devised institutions—the Electoral College being one of them—that modify or qualify the majority principle. Nothing could be clearer than that the Founders sought free institutions that would, nevertheless, protect the country from what we today call populism.

The organizing principle of this body—the Senate of the United States —is surely not majority rule, and its procedures are not simply democratic. Federal judges are not elected at all. If legitimacy springs only from the principle of one man, one equally weighted vote, upon what meat do these our judicial Caesars feed that they have grown so great? Indeed, if only this populist principle, why vote at all? Why not select officers by lot? That is truly democratic, for that, and that only, is a system that pays no attention to qualifications, or insists that all men are equally qualified.

Why, indeed, representative government if we are not permitted institutions intended to produce competent representatives? In short, what we should be disputing . . . is the issue that the Founders disputed; namely, what system is more likely to produce a president possessing the qualities required of the person who holds this office. I, too, may be blind, but I have yet to encounter a proponent of this so-called electoral reform who argues that a president directly elected by the people will be a better president.

Indeed, we are warned of the possibility of a president who lacks a majority or a plurality of the popular vote, as if that alone matters, as if legitimacy springs only from numerical preponderance or popularity . . . as if the American people have lost their attachment to . . . constitutionalism. What is constitutionalism if not a qualification on majoritarianism?[14]

Washington Post Columnist George Will opposed tinkering with the Electoral College machinery:

. . . The Electoral College does not function as the Founding Fathers originally thought it would but, of course, neither does the Senate. It would be a melancholy development if we were to do away with either for so flimsy a reason.

The fact is that the Electoral College works well—and I shall at this point not insist on a parallel with the Senate. The Electoral College is, in fact, the world's most tested and vindicated mechanism for choosing a chief executive. That is a large claim, but I think a true one. . . .

I think it is making democracy too simple to say that any system that could produce a president who received much less than a majority of the popular vote is undemocratic. Actually . . . an electoral-vote victory by a candidate who loses the popular vote by a substantial margin is improbable and has never happened. And only extremely dogmatic majoritarians think democracy would be "subverted"—to use Senator Bayh's

14. Hearings on direct popular election, 1979, *op. cit.*, pp. 131, 133-134.

words—if the Electoral College gave the presidency to a candidate who lost the popular vote by a wafer-thin margin. It is odd to say that the "nation's will" could be "frustrated" in a standoff.

Bayh is fond of the somewhat feverish thought that under the Electoral College a candidate "could" win with just 25 percent of the vote by narrowly winning in the eleven largest states, even if he did not get a single vote in any other state.

But under direct election, a candidate "could" sweep Alaska's 231,000 eligible voters, lose forty-nine states by an average of 4,700 votes, and win. This "possibility" is about as probable as the one that Senator Bayh is fond of imagining. . . .

I believe that Irvin Kristol and Paul Weaver expressed the point well when they said:

In recent decades, the democratic idea has been vulgarized and trivialized. From being a complex idea, implying a complex mode of government, appropriate to a large and complex society, the idea of democracy has been debased into a simple-minded arithmetical majoritarianism—government by adding machine.[15]

PROPOSALS

Each election year has brought with it several proposals for revision of our presidential election system, but there has been no consensus on which of several possible reform routes should be taken. The nation should be able to construct a coherent and consistent set of changes that would improve the nomination and election processes without damaging or disrupting the continuity of the election system we have or infringing on valid local interests and traditions. Where there has been needless waste of effort, confusion, dysfunction, duplication, or irresponsibility, we need to establish simplicity, uniformity, and clarity.

The proposals suggested in Chapter 8 concerning presidential primaries and the selection of delegates to the national conventions could be effected by federal statute or by rules changes on the part of the political parties. But to change the Electoral College would require amending the US Constitution, a process that would involve much effort over a period of several years. The changes envisioned here may be broken down into three individual proposals.

10-1. To elect the president by popular majority. A presidential ticket would be elected if it receives an absolute majority of the total number of popular votes cast across the nation. In the event that no ticket receives an absolute

15. Hearings on direct popular election, 1979, *op. cit.*, pp. 221-222.

popular majority, then the electoral vote would come into play. With the current 538 electoral votes, it would require, as at present, 270 to be elected.

10-2. To remove the discretion of electors. In the event that electoral votes are required to be counted, they would be cast automatically for the ticket certified by state election authorities as having received the most votes in the state.

10-3. To change the contingent election system. In the event that no ticket wins a popular majority and the electoral vote count is not determinant, then a contingent election would be held in a joint session of the new Congress convening in the January following the November election. Only the two tickets receiving the largest number of electoral votes would be involved in the contingent election. An absolute majority of voting senators and representatives would be required; given the current membership, if all vote, it would take 268 votes to be elected in the joint session. Each senator and representative would be eligible to cast one vote on each ballot. This contingent presidential election would be the first order of business for the new Congress. The presiding officer of the joint session would be the incumbent vice-president or, in the event of vacancy in that office, the Speaker of the House. The presiding officer would not vote, except in case of a tie.

Every victorious presidential candidate of this century, and the great preponderance of earlier presidents, would have been elected under these provisions. Tilden in 1876 had a popular vote majority (50.97 percent), so he, rather than Hayes, would have won under this proposed system. It is interesting to note that the next three presidential elections (1880, 1884, and 1888) all produced popular margins closer than the margin in the Hayes-Tilden race. In only one, that of 1888 when Harrison defeated Cleveland, did the electoral vote winner trail his rival in the popular vote. In this century, Woodrow Wilson in 1912 and 1916, Harry Truman in 1948, John Kennedy in 1960, and Richard Nixon in 1968 each failed to achieve a majority of the popular vote, but would have won under this new proposal because of their majorities in the Electoral College. Table 10-3 summarizes information on the popular and electoral votes in every presidential election.

These proposals do three fundamental things. They provide that the winner of the national popular majority shall be elected. They keep the Electoral College as a potentially significant element, ensuring that candidates will consider the importance of winning internal state pluralities. And they make more equitable the provisions of the contingent election process. None of these changes is really of crucial importance *unless* we have one of those occurrences that has been dreaded for so long—an electoral vote winner who

Table 10-3. Popular and Electoral Voting for President, 1789-1976

Year	Major Candidates*	Winner's Percentage of National Popular Vote	Electoral Vote Distribution
1789	Washington	unknown	69-0
1792	Washington	unknown	132-0
1796	Adams-Jefferson	unknown	71-68
1800	Jefferson-Burr	unknown	73-73**
1804	Jefferson-Pinckney	unknown	162-14
1808	Madison-Pinckney	unknown	122-47
1812	Madison-Clinton	unknown	128-89
1816	Monroe-King	unknown	183-34
1820	Monroe-Adams	unknown	231-1
1824	Adams-Jackson-Clay-Crawford	30.9	84-99-37-41**
1828	Jackson-Adams	56.0	178-83
1832	Jackson-Clay	54.2	219-49
1836	Van Buren-Harrison	50.8	170-73
1840	Harrison-Van Buren	52.9	234-60
1844	Polk-Clay	49.5	170-105
1848	Taylor-Cass	47.3	163-127
1852	Pierce-Scott	50.8	254-42
1856	Buchanan-Fremont	45.3	174-114
1860	Lincoln-Douglas-Breckenridge-Bell	39.8	180-12-72-39
1864	Lincoln-McClellan	55.0	212-21
1868	Grant-Seymour	52.7	214-80
1872	Grant-Greeley	55.6	286-80***
1876	Hayes-Tilden	48.0	185-184
1880	Garfield-Hancock	48.3	214-155
1884	Cleveland-Blaine	48.5	219-182
1888	Harrison-Cleveland	47.8	233-168
1892	Cleveland-Harrison-Weaver	46.0	277-145-22

Table 10-3. Popular and Electoral Voting for President, 1789-1976 (continued)

Year	Major Candidates*	Winner's Percentage of National Popular Vote	Electoral Vote Distribution
1896	McKinley-Bryan	51.0	271-176
1900	McKinley-Bryan	51.7	292-155
1904	Roosevelt-Parker	56.4	336-140
1908	Taft-Bryan	51.6	321-162
1912	Wilson-Roosevelt-Taft	41.8	435-88-8
1916	Wilson-Hughes	49.2	277-254
1920	Harding-Cox	60.3	404-127
1924	Coolidge-Davis-LaFollette	54.1	382-136-13
1928	Hoover-Smith	58.2	444-87
1932	Roosevelt-Hoover	57.4	472-59
1936	Roosevelt-Landon	60.8	523-8
1940	Roosevelt-Willkie	54.7	449-82
1944	Roosevelt-Dewey	53.3	433-99
1948	Truman-Dewey-Thurmond-Wallace	49.5	303-189-39-0
1952	Eisenhower-Stevenson	55.1	442-89
1956	Eisenhower-Stevenson	57.4	457-73-(1)
1960	Kennedy-Nixon-Byrd	49.7	303-219-15
1964	Johnson-Goldwater	61.1	486-52
1968	Nixon-Humphrey-Wallace	43.4	301-191-46
1972	Nixon-McGovern	60.7	520-17-(1)
1976	Carter-Ford	50.1	297-241

*The winner is listed first, followed by losing candidates in order of their popular vote. The electoral vote column follows the same order.

**Election outcome decided in House of Representatives because of inconclusive electoral vote.

***The defeated Democratic candidate, Horace Greeley, died November 29, 1872, several weeks after the general election but before the casting of the electoral votes. Sixty Democratic votes were scattered among various candidates; seventeen were not cast.

Source: For 1789-1972, Congressional Quarterly's *Guide to U.S. Elections,* 1975, pp. 242-299; for 1976, *Congressional Quarterly Weekly Report,* December 18, 1976, pp. 3330, 3334.

defeats the popular vote favorite, an election that turns on an individual elector voting contrary to "instructions" from the voters of the state, or an election that must be resolved in Congress. The compromise solutions suggested in these proposals remove these possibilities and, it is hoped, will gain sufficient public support to take their place in the US Constitution.

The general reform of the presidential selection process suggested in Chapter 8 and in this chapter will seem unduly complicated only to those who have not observed and reflected seriously upon the immense difficulties involved in perfecting a national election system in which 80 million or more citizens habitually participate.

The proposed reforms (1) acknowledge the importance of party members and conventions in selecting a presidential ticket, (2) emphasize and protect the role of the individual citizen in determining national political leadership, (3) provide federal protection for the sanctity of the vote and for the effective measuring of popular preferences, (4) establish a workable, understandable, visible, democratic, and equitable system in each state, and (5) produce a president and vice-president who have clearly established themselves as the preference of the voters.

Chapter 11
Concluding Reflections

The topic of political change is controversial for several reasons. Some people want considerable change, some want minor tinkering with the system, and others want no change at all. Those who are in favor of change often disagree on two basic considerations—the things that ought to be changed, and the way they should be changed.

For example, Arthur Schlesinger, Jr., regards party reform as an objective that is less important than sharpening the working of constitutional institutions such as the presidency. In his view, the only serious remaining function of American parties is to be "an instrument of presidential leadership." To Schlesinger, "the problem is not imperfect structure: it is vanishing function." The task, therefore, is "not to engage in artificial resuscitation of a system that has served its time but to invent the morals and machinery appropriate to the electronic age."[1]

Agreeing with the need for parties to adjust to modern technology, Theodore Becker wrote that citizens feel frustrated with their electoral machinery. ". . . citizens continue to rally in large numbers around such issues as abortion, laetrile, nuclear energy, environmental protection, the Panama Canal treaty. . . . Nonetheless, these citizen activists find themselves using ancient tools in an antiquated political system. . . . Lots of effort reaps scant rewards."[2]

1. Arthur Schlesinger, Jr., "Can the Party System Be Saved?" a paper prepared for the Project '87 Conference on the American Constitutional System Under Strong and Weak Parties, Williamsburg, April 27-28, 1979, pp. 10-11.
2. Ted Becker, "The Constitutional Network: An Evolution in American Democracy." Chapter 17 in Clement Bezold (editor), *Anticipatory Democracy: People in the Politics of the Future* (New York: Vintage Books, 1978), p. 290. Becker goes on to encourage the use of new communications technologies by citizens who wish to share and dramatize their policy concerns and thereby to make an impact on the policy decisions and institutions. Particularly intriguing is his notion of a "constitutional network," as was used in the effort to change Hawaii's state constitution.

After reviewing abuses practiced by parties as recently as the 1960s, the Washington *Post* editorialized on the need for careful reform:

... Only the blindest of nostalgia buffs could weep for the elimination of such methods from our politics. And now twelve years later, the system, which had been rightly branded unresponsive and rigid, has been thoroughly overhauled. The problem, which we will come back to, is finding those elements of the present "reformed" system that are true reforms and worth saving—as distinct from some that have just preserved old trouble or created new.[3]

Everett Carll Ladd, Jr., calling for the development of concrete proposals to help rebuild the parties, has said that "solutions will come if, and only if, an intellectual corrective occurs." He concluded with this thought:

... American democracy simply cannot function effectively in the latter quarter of the twentieth century unless its core representative institutions —and specifically here, the political parties—are revivified organizationally. If recognition of this fact is achieved, it will not be hard to find a variety of modest means which, without flying in the face of the American political tradition and experience, will rebuild the parties a bit and equip them better to perform their central tasks.[4]

The lack of consensus about the need for political change in America results in part from disagreements about which elements we are trying to improve and whether a particular change is likely to have that effect. The situation is like that faced by economists. A proposed cure for one specific economic problem, such as inflation, may have a negative effect on another factor, such as unemployment or productivity. Our political problems, as noted in Chapter 1, include low voter turnout, low interest in party affairs, powerlessness on the part of party officials, and lack of clear party responsibility in policy-making. All are complex phenomena, and while it might be

---

3. "Post-Reform Politics: Remembering the Bad Old Days," Washington *Post,* January 17, 1980, p. A 26. The editorial had earlier referred to three previous abuses. First, Democratic national convention delegates from eight states in 1968 were chosen through a process established prior to 1968, "long before the issues or the candidates of that election year had even emerged." Second, proxy votes from "phantom addresses" had been cast in the Hawaii state Democratic convention. Third, Democratic party officers in Missouri had refused to reveal the time or place of critical party meetings, thus making legendary operators Boss Tweed and Mark Hanna "look like St. Francis of Assisi" by comparison. Copyright © 1980, *The Washington Post.*
4. Everett Carll Ladd, Jr., "Party Reform since 1968—A Case Study in Intellectual Failure," a paper prepared for the Project '87 Conference on the American Constitutional System Under Strong and Weak Parties, Williamsburg, Va., April 27–28, 1979, pp. 31–32.

possible to reach consensus on how to approach one specific problem, it is difficult to predict the impact of that solution on the other problems. In economics and politics, it takes wisdom, luck, and patience to find solutions that are acceptable to decision-makers, do not trespass any constitutional or philosophical barriers, and have more good than bad effects.

This book has proposed reforms designed to simplify and make more uniform our political life, so that our leaders can be selected in a more rational, clear, orderly, and popular manner. If lesser purposes or positions were at stake, it would be very difficult to convince millions of minds that the changes are worth the massive effort required.

The proposals at the end of Chapters 4 through 10, considered together, constitute a coherent national reform program. They would make party organs and nominations more open and democratic, eliminate governmental financial support for parties and candidates, provide for popular election of the president while keeping the electoral vote as a significant element in presidential selection, standardize and simplify the entire presidential nomination process, and uphold the primacy of national and state conventions in party affairs. The proposals can be topically summarized by grouping them in terms of five basic objectives. The first objective, to raise levels of popular interest and participation in politics, especially party affairs, is approached through Proposals 5-1 (to choose party directors) and 6-3 (to establish regular county caucuses). The second objective, to make party officials more visible, independent, permanent, powerful, and responsible, is approached in Proposals 4-5 (to enhance the party role in campaign finance), 7-2 (to approve candidates), 8-3 (to provide for delegate selection in nonprimary states), 8-4 (to bind the convention voting of committed delegates), and 9-3 (to evaluate public officials). The third objective, to simplify, standardize, and make more equitable the electoral process, is approached in Proposals 4-1 (to recognize national parties), 4-2 (to define national voting eligibility), 7-1 (to nominate candidates for federal office in a party primary), 7-3 (to fill vacant offices), 8-1 (to establish a national presidential primary system), 8-2 (to establish a delegate selection mechanism), 10-1 (to elect the president by popular majority), 10-2 (to remove the discretion of presidential electors), and 10-3 (to change the contingent election system). The fourth objective, to simplify, standardize, and make more efficient our party processes, is approached through Proposals 6-1 (to establish party committees), 6-2 (to define the powers of party committees), 7-4 (to fill nomination vacancies), 7-5 (to provide for nominations by convention, in certain cases), 9-1 (to apportion convention delegates among political units), and 9-2 (to select state and county convention delegates). The fifth objective, to regulate campaign resources, is approached in Proposals 4-3 (to withdraw federal campaign subsidies) and 4-4 (to maintain federal regulatory activities).

Our changes would enhance the importance of the parties—they would be much more than the mere "gatekeepers" to the ballot that Walter Dean Burnham says they have become. There is good reason to hope that American political parties will become more significant and beneficent as they become more visible and democratic.

By "democratic" I do not mean a phony democracy, such as the no-choice referenda common to totalitarian systems that seek a popular veneer ("Shall Ogan Mefta assume complete powers as national leader—Yes or No?"), or the ill-conceived, riggable balloting for starting lineups in baseball's annual All-Star game. Democracy as used here means a system in which citizens have an equal, secret, and effective vote. Democracy is, in some ways, a fragile and unpredictable way to govern a society, but it is at the same time the process most likely to nurture the kind of balance between popularity and responsibility that produces stability.

Our proposals would require various kinds of rules changes—several could be made by the parties at the national or state level, some could best be handled through state legislation, a number would need federal legislation, and a couple would require an amendment to the US Constitution. The reforms could be adopted comprehensively or piecemeal. It may be that state legislatures, because they are more volatile bodies with higher rates of turnover, would be a more likely source of political reform than the Congress.

Significant political change might take us in any direction, and the prudent reformer will want to have some idea of where changes are likely to lead us in ten or twenty years' time. The American political system at the turn of the twenty-first century may be very similar to what it is today, with two consensual, amorphous parties battling every four years to see which will gain occupancy of the White House, and every two years to see if at the other end of Pennsylvania Avenue the Republicans can muster enough votes in Congress to sustain a presidential veto. On the other hand, some sort of polarizing change may occur, with the Democratic party becoming distinctly and exclusively liberal across the land and the Republican party becoming more conservative. We may move to a more region-oriented system, with the two major parties becoming even less centralized and cohesive than they are presently, in response to local issues, pressures, and candidates. By the year 2000, one or both of the present major parties may decline and die, to be replaced by new parties based on new problems, groups, ideas, and interests. Or, they may face permanent national competition from third or fourth parties. Finally, the turn of the next century could find us with a nondemocratic system, or subservient to a foreign authority.

It is no doubt presumptuous to offer such major and gratuitous suggestions for changing political systems that have, after all, survived in a reasonably successful democracy. The odds against achieving piecemeal reform of any aspect of the national political system, or against substantial reform in any particular state, are immense enough; the odds against adoption of sweeping national reforms are virtually incalculable. A great expenditure of intellectual and political capital would be required. But to identify problems and to suggest solutions is surely of some service to the state. Readers are urged to think about these ideas critically, and to try to invent better ones; part of this intellectual process should be to imagine what will evolve in this country if changes are adopted. If this book does no more than to encourage a few thousand college students to ponder more deeply the costs and benefits of political participation and the positive and negative sides of specific reform proposals, the effort of developing these proposals will have been well repaid. If policy-makers are moved to think seriously about these proposals, all that one could reasonable hope for will have been accomplished. To raise the level of political dialogue and thereby to organize our manifold options into more coherent and efficient packages is something the nation badly needs. While recognizing the difficulties involved in attaining these reforms, this conviction remains: the reforms *would* strengthen the political system.

Talk of political reform seems naturally to center on curing certain perceived dysfunctions. While attempting to identify and rectify what is thought to be bad about the system, we must be sensitive enough to recognize and safeguard the things that are good. Our political-electoral system, obviously, has important strengths—its capacity for building consensus, for finding solutions to political problems that are acceptable to the bulk of persons involved; its talent for communicating, for exchanging ideas and perspectives from region to region, from state to nation, from executive branch to legislative branch; its ability to choose leaders, elect presidents, governors, senators, congressmen, and legislators without serious signs of rancor, corruption, vengeance, or convulsion; its faculty for receptivity, for adapting and channeling the enthusiasm of individuals and groups in behalf of a candidate and for giving sympathetic ear to all kinds of appeals from all kinds of sources—and we should strive to be wise enough in our efforts to reform the system that we do not weaken or destroy it.

Without doubt, some will oppose political change simply because it would upset the status quo, the situation with which they are familiar. Change is threatening. It is entirely possible that many party officials whose positions would be strengthened by these proposals will be among the most vociferous opponents of those changes. Such opposition says something about the deplorable condition we find our parties to be in.

The charge may be raised that these proposals are only cosmetic changes, that they do not get at deeper systemic or societal problems. Whether such deeper problems exist, and what they may consist of, and how they might best be attacked, are important questions, but they are outside our purview. And in any event, the reforms suggested here will almost certainly bring indirect benefits to the system, such as higher levels of participation, greater visibility of political decision-making, and more real democracy.

Finally, policy-makers and citizens alike need to be reminded that they must, for today, work with the system as it is, not as it ought to be. This means working with party officials, interest-group leaders, and other influential persons to encourage continuous and systematic attention to improving the structure and style of American politics. The constant effort of good citizens should be to work for reasonable, democratic, and efficient institutions and processes. The inevitable results will be broader involvement, wiser decisions, and deeper patriotism.

Research Exercises

The following research exercises correspond to the first ten chapters of the book. Students are encouraged to find and use the maximum number of relevant sources in working on the research exercises. Among the more likely general sources are: Barone, Ujifusa, and Mathews' *Almanac of American Politics* (biennial editions); Scammon's *America Votes* (biennial editions); *The Book of the States* (biennial editions); the *Municipal Yearbook* (annual editions); weekly news periodicals such as *Time, Newsweek, U. S. News & World Report, Congressional Quarterly Weekly Report,* and *National Journal;* and daily newspapers such as the *New York Times, Washington Post, Chicago Tribune, Los Angeles Times, Christian Science Monitor,* and *Wall Street Journal.* Additional special sources are listed with the individual exercises.

Chapter 1: Foreign Elections

Describe a national parliamentary election in any foreign nation held in the past five years. Summarize and discuss the policy issues debated; the major political leaders involved; the positions taken by regional, factional, ideological, economic, or ethnic groups in the nation; changes in the number of seats held by each parliamentary party; changes in national political leadership; and likely changes in domestic and foreign policy directions resulting from the election.

Special sources: *Keesing's Contemporary Archives, Facts on File,* the U. S. Department of State's *Background Notes, New York Times, Manchester Guardian.*

Chapter 2: Citizen Attitudes

Conduct your own poll to assess respondents' attitudes about democracy in general, political parties, major political leaders, and sense of political efficacy. You can also ask your respondents factual questions, in order to get a sense of their political knowledge. Finally, you can ask them about how often they participate in politics, by voting, by contributing time or money to campaigns, by discussing and reading about politics, etc. It would be interesting to see what you can learn about interconnections among these political attitudes, knowledge, and participation levels. A battery of fifteen or so simple questions is recommended. You should talk to at least twenty persons of voting age, randomly chosen in your area, preferably persons with whom you are not acquainted. The suggested sample size of twenty will not make your findings valid in any general way, but the experience will teach you a good deal about human nature, political beliefs, and polling methods.

Special sources: the Urban Institute's *Obtaining Citizen Feedback;* Terrence Jones's *Conducting Political Research* (New York: Harper and Row, 1971); and Norman Nie, Sidney Verba, and John R. Petrocik's *The Changing American Voter* (Cambridge: Harvard University Press, 1976).

Chapter 3: Legislative Roll-Call Voting

Analyze the outcome of any congressional or state legislative roll-call vote in the past three years. Select an issue that is important, manageable, interesting to you, and divisive (that is, a roll-call vote in which at least twenty percent of the members voting are on the losing side). Note the impact of the legislators' party affiliation on the outcome; if all Democrats vote "yes" and all Republicans vote "no," then party has determined the outcome completely, but if Democrats and Republicans both divide equally in support and opposition, then party has had an insignificant effect. Speculate about other factors such as ideology, region, age, vocation, or church affiliation, that might have been as influential as party affiliation in determining the outcome of the roll call. Did the president (or, at the state level, the governor) take a position on the measure and, if so, how did Democratic and Republican members react to the executive's attempts to persuade them?

Special sources: For congressional roll calls, see the vote charts published in almost every issue of the *Congressional Quarterly Weekly Report,* as well as the articles about the policy questions that may have been published in earlier or subsequent issues. For state legislative roll calls, you will have to obtain access to the daily journals of the legislature to find the votes, and you will probably need to rely on daily newspapers for accounts of the background to the vote. If you have a statistical turn of mind, you will find it very educational to develop a two-by-two table from your roll call, placing the names of Democrats and Republicans in the proper cell depending on whether they voted "yes" or "no." Then you can calculate the phi coefficient or Yule's Q, as done in Table 3-6. A statistics book will give you the formulas.

Chapter 4: Campaign Analysis

Describe the activities, functions, and hierarchical relationships of the members of the campaign staff in a race for governor, U. S. senator, or U. S. representative in the past five years. Describe what each staff member did for a living (if anything) before and after the campaign.

An alternative project related to a campaign would be to speculate about the relative impact on the vote (for governor, senator, or representative) of the voters' party affiliation, ideological orientation, issue position, and orientation toward the personalities of the two candidates involved (as done in Chapter 2 with the 1978 Clark–Jepsen race in Iowa).

Special sources: daily newspaper articles, interviews with campaign staffers, reporters, and other observers.

Chapter 5: Party Leader Biography

Write a biographical sketch of a state or county party chairman, describing his or her personal and vocational background, social affiliations, political experience and qualifications, political attitudes and values, and orientation with respect to current issues and political personalities at the national and state levels.

Special sources: daily newspaper articles and personal interviews with the subject and those familiar with various facets of his or her career.

Chapter 6: Party Organization Analysis

Construct an organizational chart of a major political party at the state, district, county, or municipal level (see the examples in the book). Consult party influentials, news reporters, and other available sources to get the necessary background data. Show how long each person involved has served in their present capacity, and see if you can account for the reasons why each was originally chosen. Identify important "outside" individuals or groups who seem or are thought to have considerable influence on this party unit. Comment on the specific duties and general powers assigned to the unit you are studying.

Special sources: newspaper articles and personal interviews with organizational members and others familiar with the party at that level of activity.

Chapter 7: Party Nominations and Factions

Analyze one state party's major nominations for statewide office over at least the past six years, including a description of the system employed (primary, convention, caucus?). Be sure to include at least the candidates for U. S. senator, governor, lieutenant governor, and attorney general (if elective). You may also include the candidates for U. S. representative, depending on the number apportioned to the state you are studying. Look for and comment on evidences of personal, ideological, economic, or regional factionalism in the nomination decisions.

Special sources: daily newspapers in the state, special election publications issued by or special election articles published in the *Congressional Quarterly Weekly Report* or the *National Journal,* various editions of the *Almanac of American Politics, America Votes,* or official state tabulations (for county-level voting returns if applicable), and personal interviews with journalists, local party leaders, and other observers.

Chapter 8: Presidential Nominations

Describe as completely as you can, in a particular state, a recent presidential primary or state party convention to choose delegates to attend the national convention of the party. Using all available evidence, make conclusions about the role of that selection process in terms of (1) its effect on the ultimate presidential nomination and election, and (2) its effect on the future political direction of that particular state and its major political figures.

Special sources: daily newspaper accounts and personal interviews with party leaders, journalists, and other observers.

Chapter 9: Convention Decisions

Describe and analyze any roll call vote in a recent national, state, district, or county party convention having to do with the party's platform, credentials, or rules. Look for connections between that roll call and a convention nomination (such as the presidential nomination at the national convention) or some other convention roll call. This analysis will involve the construction of a two-by-two matrix, as with the legislative roll calls in the exercise for Chapter 3.

Special sources: Bain and Parris, *Convention Decisions and Voting Records* (Washington: Brookings Institution, 1973); daily newspaper or weekly newsmagazine accounts, and interviews with convention participants or observers.

Chapter 10: Presidential Election Reconstruction

Reconstruct any recent presidential campaign (including party primaries and convention nominations as well as the general election) as if the reforms proposed in Chapter 8 had been established and as if one of the alternatives to the present Electoral College system described in Chapter 10 had been put into effect. This will require some imagination, but be as empirical as you can. The question to which you should address yourself is what effect such changes would have had on the identity of the major party tickets and on the outcome of the general election vote. The instructor may divide the country into regions, each region containing from four to twelve states depending on the number of individuals or teams involved in this exercise.

Special sources: *Congressional Quarterly* or *National Journal* descriptions for highlights and personalities of past election campaigns, *America Votes* for vote returns.

Bibliography

Abbott, David W., and Edward T. Rogowsky. *Political Parties*. Chicago: Rand McNally, 1978.

Adamany, David. *Campaign Financing in America*. North Scituate, Mass. Duxbury Press, 1972.

_____, and George E. Agree. *Political Money: A Strategy for Campaign Financing in America*. Baltimore: John Hopkins University Press, 1975.

Agranoff, Robert. *The Management of Election Campaigns*. Boston: Holbrook Press, 1976.

Alexander, Herbert E. *Money in Politics*. Washington, D.C.: Public Affairs Press, 1972.

_____. *Financing Politics: Money, Elections and Political Reform*. Washington, D.C.: Congressional Quarterly Press, 1976.

Almond, Gabriel, and Sidney Verba. *The Civic Culture*. Boston: Little, Brown, 1965.

American Political Science Association. *Toward a More Responsible Two-Party System*. New York: Rinehart, 1950.

Bain, Richard, and Judith Parris. *Convention Decisions and Voting Records*. 2nd ed. Washington, D.C.: Brookings Institution, 1973.

Barber, James. *Choosing the President*. Englewood Cliffs, N.J.: Prentice-Hall, 1974.

Baus, Herbert M., and William B. Ross. *Politics Battle Plan*. New York: Macmillan, 1968.

Bickel, Alexander M. *Reform and Continuity: The Electoral College, the Conventions, and the Party System*. New York: Harper & Row, 1971.

Brams, Steven J. *The Presidential Election Game*. New Haven, Conn.: Yale University Press, 1978.

Broder, David. *The Party's Over*. New York: Harper & Row, 1971.

Burnham, Walter Dean. *Critical Elections and the Mainsprings of American Politics*. New York: W.W. Norton, 1970.

235

Burns, James MacGregor. *The Deadlock of Democracy.* Englewood Cliffs, N.J.: Prentice-Hall, 1963.

Campbell, Angus; Phillip E. Converse; Warren E. Miller; and Donald E. Stokes. *The American Voter.* New York: John Wiley & Sons, 1960.

Carter, Carrol Joseph. *The Colonels of Politics: The Local Political Leadership of Colorado County Chairmen.* Boulder: University of Colorado, Governmental Research Bureau, 1971.

Chambers, William N., and Walter Dean Burnham. *The American Party System.* 2nd ed. New York: Oxford University Press, 1967.

Clem, Alan L. *The Nomination of Joe Bottum.* Vermillion, S.D.: University of South Dakota, Governmental Research Bureau, 1963.

Cotter, Cornelius, and Bernard Hennesey. *Politics Without Power: The National Party Committee.* New York: Atherton, 1964.

Crotty, William J. *Political Reform and the American Experiment.* New York: Thomas Y. Crowell, 1977.

_____, ed. *Approaches to the Study of Party Organization.* Boston: Allyn & Bacon, 1968.

David, Paul T.; Ralph M. Goldman; and Richard C. Bain. *The Politics of National Party Conventions.* Washington, D.C.: Brookings Institution, 1960.

Davis, James W. *Presidential Primaries: Road to the White House.* New York: Thomas Y. Crowell, 1967.

DeVries, Walter, and Lance Tarrance. *The Ticket Splitter.* Grand Rapids, Mich.: Eerdmans, 1972.

Diamond, Martin. *Testimony in Support of the Electoral College.* Washington, D.C.: American Enterprise Institute, 1977.

Domhoff, G. William. *Who Rules America?* Englewood Cliffs, N.J.: Prentice-Hall, 1967.

Downs, Anthony. *An Economic Theory of Democracy.* New York: Harper & Row, 1957.

Dunn, Delmar D. *Financing Presidential Campaigns.* Washington, D.C.: Brookings Institution, 1972.

Duverger, Maurice. *Political Parties.* New York: John Wiley & Sons, 1954.

Eldersveld, Samuel J. *Political Parties: A Behavioral Analysis.* Chicago: Rand McNally, 1964.

Epstein, Leon. *Political Parties in Western Democracies.* New York: Praeger, 1967.

Fenton, John. *Midwest Politics.* New York: Holt, Rinehart & Winston, 1966.

_____. *People and Parties in Politics.* Glenview, Ill.: Scott, Foresman, 1966.

Fishel, Jeff. *Party and Opposition: Congressional Challengers in American Politics.* New York: David McKay, 1973.

_____. *Parties and Elections in an Anti-Party Age.* Bloomington, Ind.: Indiana University Press, 1978.

Gelb, Joyce, and Marian Leif Palley. *Tradition and Change in American Party Politics.* New York: Thomas Y. Crowell, 1975.

Goldbach, John, and Michael Ross. *Politics, Parties, and Power.* Pacific Palisades, Cal.: Palisades Publishers, 1980.

Greenstein, Fred. *The American Party System and the American People.* 2nd ed. Englewood Cliffs, N.J.: Prentice-Hall, 1970.

Hackett, Clifford P. "Learning From the U.S. Congress: Are There Any Lessons for the New European Parliament?" *European Community,* November–December, 1978.

Hershey, Marjorie Randon. *The Making of Campaign Strategy.* Boston: D.C. Heath, 1974.

Hess, Stephen. *The Presidential Campaign: The Leadership Selection Process After Watergate.* Washington, D.C.: Brookings Institution, 1974.

Huckshorn, Robert J. *Party Leadership in the States.* Amherst, Mass.: University of Massachusetts Press, 1976.

_____. *Political Parties in America.* North Scituate, Mass.: Duxbury Press, 1980.

_____, and Robert C. Spencer. *The Politics of Defeat.* Amherst, Mass.: University of Massachusetts Press, 1971.

Keech, William, and Donald Matthews. *The Party's Choice.* Washington, D.C.: Brookings Institution, 1977.

Keefe, William. *Parties, Politics, and Public Policy in America.* 3rd ed. New York: Holt, Rinehart, & Winston, 1980.

Kessel, John. *Presidential Campaign Politics.* Homewood, Ill.: Dorsey Press, 1980.

Key, V.O. *Southern Politics in State and Nation.* New York: Alfred Knopf, 1949.

_____. *The Responsible Electorate.* Cambridge: Harvard University Press, 1966.

Kingdon, John. *Candidates for Office: Beliefs and Strategies.* New York: Random House, 1968.

Kirkpatrick, Jeane Jordan. *Dismantling the Parties: Reflections on Party Reform and Party Decomposition.* Washington, D.C.: American Enterprise Institute, 1978.

Knoke, David. *Change and Continuity in American Politics: The Social Basis of Political Parties.* Baltimore: John Hopkins University Press, 1976.

Ladd, Everett Carll, Jr. *Where Have All the Voters Gone?* New York: W.W. Norton, 1978.

_____, and Charles D. Hadley. *Transformations of the American Party System: Political Coalitions from the New Deal to the 1970s.* New York: W.W. Norton, 1975.

Lamb, Karl. *As Orange Goes: Twelve California Families and the Future of American Politics.* New York: W.W. Norton, 1974.

_____, and Paul Smith. *Campaign Decision Making: The Presidential Campaign of 1964.* Belmont, Cal.: Wadsworth, 1968.

Lengle, James I., and Bryan Shafer. *Presidential Politics: Readings on Nominations and Elections.* New York: St. Martin's Press, 1980.

Leuthold, David A. *Electioneering in a Democracy.* New York: John Wiley & Sons, 1968.

Lipset, Martin Seymour. *Political Man.* New York: Doubleday, 1960.

_____, ed. *Emerging Coalitions in American Politics.* San Francisco: Institute for Contemporary Studies, 1978.

Lockard, Duane. *New England State Politics.* Princeton, N.J.: Princeton University Press, 1959.

McGinnis, Joe. *The Selling of the President, 1968.* Los Angeles: Trident Press, 1969.

Maisel, Louis, and Joseph Cooper. *The Impact of the Electoral Process.* Beverly Hills, Cal.: Sage Publications, 1977.

Mann, Thomas. *Unsafe at Any Margin: Interpreting Congressional Elections.* Washington, D.C.: American Enterprise Institute, 1978.

Matthews, Donald R., ed. *Perspectives on Presidential Selection.* Washington, D.C.: Brookings Institution, 1973.

Mazmanian, Daniel E. *Third Parties in Presidential Elections.* Washington, D.C.: Brookings Institution, 1974.

Michels, Robert. *Political Parties.* New York: Free Press, 1949.

Milbrath, Lester W., and M.L. Goel. *Political Participation: How and Why Do People Get Involved in Politics?* 2nd ed. Chicago: Rand McNally, 1977.

Miller, Warren E., and Teresa E. Levitin. *Leadership and Change: Presidential Elections from 1952 to 1976.* Englewood, N.J.: Winthrop Publishing, 1976.

Morrow, Lance. "The Decline of the Parties." *Time,* November 20, 1978.

Nie, Norman; Sidney Verba; and John Petrocik. *The Changing American Voter.* Cambridge: Harvard University Press, 1976.

Parris, Judith. *The Convention Problem.* Washington, D.C.: Brookings Institution, 1972.

Peirce, Neal. *The Megastates of America.* New York: W.W. Norton, 1972.

_____. *The People's President.* New York: Simon & Schuster, 1968.

Perry, James M. *The New Politics: The Expanding Technology of Political Manipulation.* New York: Clarkson N. Potter, 1968.

Phillips, Kevin. *The Emerging Republican Majority.* Garden City, N.Y.: Doubleday, 1969.

Polsby, Nelson, and Aaron Wildavsky. *Presidential Elections.* 5th ed. New York: Scribner's, 1980.

Pomper, Gerald M. *Elections in America.* New York: Dodd, Mead, 1971.

_____. *Electoral Behavior.* New York: Dodd, Mead, 1975.

_____. *The Election of 1976.* New York: David McKay, 1977.

Ranney, Austin. *Curing the Mischiefs of Faction: Party Reform in America.* Berkeley: University of California Press, 1975.

_____. *The Federalization of Presidential Primaries.* Washington, D.C.: American Enterprise Institute, 1978.

Royko, Mike. *Boss.* New York: E.P. Dutton, 1971.

Rusher, William. *The Making of the New Majority Party.* Ottawa, Ill.: Green Hill Publishers, 1975.

Sale, Kirkpatrick. *Power Shift: The Rise of the Southern Rim and Its Challenge to the Eastern Establishment.* New York: Random House, 1975.

Saloma, John S., III, and Frederick H. Sontag. *Parties: The Real Opportunity for Effective Citizen Politics.* New York: Alfred Knopf, 1972.

Sartori, Giovanni. *Parties and Party Systems: A Framework for Analysis.* New York: Cambridge University Press, 1976.

Sayre, Wallace S., and Judith H. Parris. *Voting for President: The Electoral College and the American Party System.* Washington, D.C.: Brookings Institution, 1970.

Scammon, Richard, and Ben Wattenberg. *The Real Majority.* New York: Putnam's, 1970.

Schlesinger, Arthur, Jr. "The Crisis of the Party System: What Has Gone Wrong?" *Current.* July/August, 1979.

Scott, Ruth, and Ronald Hrebenar. *Parties in Crisis.* New York: John Wiley & Sons, 1979.

Sorauf, Frank. *Party Politics in America.* 4th ed. Boston: Little, Brown, 1980.

Steinberg, Alfred. *The Bosses.* New York: Mentor Publishers, 1972.

Sundquist, James L. *Dynamics of the Party System.* Washington, D.C.: Brookings Institution, 1973.

Van Doren, Ronald. *Charting the Candidates '72.* New York: Pinnacle Books, 1972.

Watson, Richard A. *The Presidential Contest.* New York: John Wiley & Sons, 1980.

Wayne, Stephen. *The Road to the White House.* New York: St. Martin's Press, 1980.

White, Theodore. *The Making of the President, 1972.* New York: Bantam Books, 1973.

Witcover, Jules. *Marathon: The Pursuit of the Presidency, 1972-1976.* New York: Signet Books, 1977.

Index